‖‖‖ ‖‖‖‖ ‖ ‖‖‖‖ ‖ ‖‖‖ ‖‖‖‖‖‖‖‖‖‖ ‖‖ ‖ ‖‖‖
W9-COZ-978

For All the <u>Write</u> Reasons

Forty Successful Authors, Publishers,
Agents, and Writers
Tell You How to Get Your Book Published

For All the <u>Write</u> Reasons

Forty Successful Authors, Publishers, Agents and Writers Tell You How to Get Your Book Published

Patricia C. Gallagher

Young Sparrow Press
P.O. Box 265 PG
Worcester, PA 19490
(215) 364-1945

This book is not a substitute for sound publishing or legal advice. All information presented in this book is presented in good faith, thus no liability is assumed with respect to the use of information within. The author, publisher, and contributors assume no responsibility for errors, inaccuracies, omissions, or any other inconsistency herein. In all matters related to contracts, negotiations, printing, specific application, and publishing, professionals, accountants, and attorneys in the field should be consulted. This book does not imply endorsement of any of the products or services mentioned by the contributors. Individuals should proceed accordingly and research all matters related to their particular project.

iv

For All the Write Reasons. Copyright 1992 by Patricia C. Gallagher.
Printed and bound in the United States of America. All rights reserved. No
part of this book may be reproduced in any form or by any electronic or
mechanical means, including information and retrieval systems without
permission in writing from the publisher, except by a reviewer who may
quote brief passages for a review. Published by Young Sparrow Press, P.O.
Box 265 PG, Worcester, PA 19490. (215) 364-1945 First paperback
printing, 1992.

Library of Congress Cataloging in Publication Data   Dewey Decimal 808.02
1.   Self-Publishing
2.   Desktop Publishing   Personal narratives
3.   Publishers and Publishing
4.   Authorship   Personal narratives
5.   Books – Marketing
6.   Editors – Editing
7.   Writing

Library of Congress Catalog Card Number: 91-066100

Gallagher, Patricia C. — First Edition
          For All the Write Reasons
          Bibliography: p.
ISBN 0-943 135 19 2 $24.95

What Others Are Saying About This Book

"From now on when correspondents ask me 'How can I do my own publishing?', I shall refer them to the many fine chapters in your explanatory book. And congratulations."

James A. Michener

"An unpretentious guide for potential writers. Patricia Gallagher has clearly blended a mixture of authors who share their experiences in the publishing maze."

— Parent/Professional Publication

"What a great way to share information. The book is a gold mine of ideas."

— Blue Penguin Publications

"This book shares insight that could otherwise be learned from experience, trial and error, and mistakes."

— Barbara Brabec Productions

"Lively, informal first hand accounts detailing the hazards and triumphs on the road to successful authorship. Both inspiration and information beginning writers will find invaluable. Highly recommended!"

Nancy Dibble, senior Editor, Writer's Digest Book Club

"This book radiates with a go-ahead spirit which most of us need and appreciate."

— Midlife Musings

"An outstanding blend of reality and inspiration. A must-have for any aspiring writer."

— I.S.S. Publications

"Packed with nitty gritty details that can only be learned by reading first-person accounts of other's publishing successes and failures."
> *— Bluestocking Press*

"Anyone planning on writing a book would gain valuable insight by reading this book."
> *— Lawrence and Co. Publishing*

"Writing's hard. Making money from writing is even harder. Use this book and make more sooner."
> *— JLA Publications*

"Inspirational! The diversity and creativity of the contributors speak to every would-be writer. You can do it too, says FOR ALL THE WRITE REASONS."
> *— Canticle Publishing*

"Who needs seminars? *FOR ALL THE WRITE REASONS* is like 'doing lunch' with the experts."
> *— Strawberry Patch Publications*

"Trisha Gallagher's book is more than a how-to of publishing. Start this book today and you will be equipped to start your book tomorrow."
> *— Para Publishing*

"Patricia Gallagher's book is the perfect resource to help you discover the keys to publishing success. It will help you achieve your publishing goals."
> *— Organization Unlimited*

"This book should save time, energy, and money for countless authors. Learning by trial and error is not the best way."
> *— Career Women Unlimited*

"It's as if the different writers were sitting at your kitchen table, sharing their personal thoughts and tips."
> *— Doris Patterson*

"My self-publishing adventure would have been more realistic and less stressful if I had read other self-publishers' stories in FOR ALL THE WRITE REASONS. Being forewarned would have been to be forearmed."

— *April Hubbard*

"FOR ALL THE WRITE REASONS does away with all the excuses would-be writers have for not writing as they read the first-hand experiences of authors who have had their books published, no matter what the obstacles."

— *Priscilla Huff*

"Trisha Gallagher and the 39 other experts in their fields provide a wealth of information to make publishing and writing endeavors more successful."

— *Catharine Thomas Skwara, editor of News & Views*

"An exciting collection of facts, thoughts and ideas on every aspect of writing— from beginning to end."

— *Rita Tarmin, newspaper reporter*

"The personal stories and advice from writers who have learned the hard way are indispensable."

— *Evelyn Clarke Mott*

"I wish this book had been available when I published my first book! It will guide you through the complicated maze of publishing."

Terry Rafferty

To my wonderful husband John

To my beautiful children:

Robin, Katelyn, Kristen and Ryan

To my loving parents, Bob and Claire Mohan

and my family for their enthusiastic support

Acknowledgments

This book and the others that I have written have come about because many people reached out and helped a fledgling author. Mr. Peter Manakos of the Lansdale Public Library went out of his way to assist me with the technicalities of publishing. Marion Peck, of the Montgomery County Library read my first manuscript and offered many helpful suggestions. I am grateful to Paula Du Pont-Kidd who has been a great friend as well as interested editor. I hope that every writer has the opportunity to work with someone who is so competent and easygoing. My parents have been great and just seem to know when to volunteer to watch my children when a critical project is due. My husband, John, people say is a "saint" because, although he is not at all interested in writing a book, he does a good job of faking genuine interest! To Peter, Marion, Paula, Bob and Claire Mohan and John Gallagher, I offer a great big thank-you.

About the Contributors

My appreciation and lasting gratitude to all of the contributors of this book, who are named alphabetically. Their generous sharing of their experiences will help others avoid costly mistakes and enjoy the process of writing a book. My sincere thanks to Lou Alpert, Joan Wester Anderson, Becky Barker, Jean Horton Berg, Jane Bluestein, Barbara Brabec, Julie Adams Church, Gloria T. Delamar, Mary Flower, Peggy Glenn, Michelle S. Gluckow, Teresa Griffin, Jane Dewey Heald, Jeff Herman, Michael Hoehne, April Hubbard, Priscilla Huff, Evelyn Kaye, Kate Kelly, John Kremer, Vicki Lansky, Jeffrey Lant, Judy Lawrence, Dorie Lenz, Carol J. Manna, Claire Mohan, Evelyn Clarke Mott, Doris Patterson, Jean Ross Peterson, Diane Pfeifer, Dan Poynter, Tom & Marilyn Ross, Marcia Routburg, Catherine Thomas Skwara, Rita Tarmin, Charlotte E. Thompson, Frances Weaver, James Lee Young, and Jane Williams.

Preface

The idea for this book came about when my mother, also a writer, and I were musing that our dear husbands seem to tire when we begin talking about our favorite topic—book publishing. All of a sudden, normally energetic and talkative spouses remember an urgent chore they must do, such as replacing a lightbulb or gluing a loose piece of wallpaper. They dash from the room as quickly as possible when they sense that our conversation is about to turn to discussing how we might have discovered a less expensive printer or a new contact person for a TV show.

A few years ago, we thought we needed to meet others of "our own kind," thus we began a local writers group. We kiddingly called ourselves "The Future Famous Writers of America." We legitimized our group name for press releases in the local papers, and were known as the Bucks-Mont Writers Network.

I was intrigued by the many ways that authors entered into the publishing world and my natural curiosity of asking why, how and when each writer began, crystallized into a thought. If I thought that their information was so interesting, probably lots of new and experienced writers would feel the same way. Over the years, I kept a file of people who had been written about in the newspapers or magazines. Using the philosophy of "nothing ventured, nothing gained," I found each author's telephone number and gave a call. My proposal was simple. "Would you like to share your publishing experiences with thousands of people via my new book?" If the answer was "yes," I sent them a list of interview questions and asked them to simply tell their stories.

Thus, in the pages that follow you will find out how forty successful authors got their start in writing and how they got their materials published. This book is unique because you will learn through the experiences of others. Just pretend that all of these authors are your friends and they are all gathered around you to help you write, publish and market your book FOR ALL THE WRITE REASONS!

Foreword

I became an author by watching authors. I am as interested in the dynamics of a long-forgotten book on how to train a puppy as the creative flow of a great literary talent. It is an interest that has served me through fifteen years of working with authors. When I got my first job in book publishing, as a publicist at Simon & Schuster in the mid 1970's, I brought a sense of wonder and awe to my work. Who were these anointed creatures who got their books published? How did they pull it off?

I soon discovered that most authors are working people who make their livings independently of the publishing industry. They couldn't care less about climbing into a tower to become artistes. They have something they think is important, they express themselves in plain English, and they make the time to write their books. Most of them don't become rich or famous, but they make a few bucks and have the enormous satisfaction of seeing their work in print.

At Simon & Schuster, I sometimes snuck away from the publicity department to spend an hour or two poking through old author correspondence files. It would be too elegant to call them archives. The files were closer to archaeological sediment, yesterday's dramas that some "corporocrat" shoved into a room full of scraped and dented gray cabinets that looked like props from the set of "Barney Miller".

My illicit prying fortified what I was learning in my work: that becoming published was a hit-or-miss proposition. Getting published successfully was even more so. A children's book author was turned down after several months of suggested revisions. The manuscript, she was told, just didn't have that *je ne sais quoi,* but thank you for thinking of us. I could feel the pain arc out of the manila folder, across a quarter of a century and into my consciousness for weeks.

There were lovely stories, too. A novelist toiling away at a menial job hit the bestseller list and got rich. Just like that. It was the kind of fantasy I'd come to New York to see up close, and there it was right in the file. Don't be too quick to buy all that slop about money not buying happiness. If you're not self-destructive, publishing a book that becomes a success may bring happiness.

I felt I made friends with some of these authors, the successful and the not-so-successful. If I learned anything from those files, it was the incredibly passive lot of yesterday's writer. Well into the Sixties, they mailed their manuscripts and waited for news. Agents, alumni of the same fine schools and clubs as the editors, had yet to emerge as quasars in the industry. Their genteel dealmaking wouldn't inspire your average janitor to give up a day job.

I knew from my first visit that the file room was doomed. The company was marked for takeover by a conglomerate whose executives, in their well-creased, decidedly non-publishing suits, would blanch at such wasteful use of Rockefeller Center real estate. The bashed-in files and, I fear, four decades of correspondence between authors and their publisher went to the dump when we moved. But by then, I'd developed a feel for the joy and angst of the published author, then and now. Trust me. Now is much better.

Today, we take charge of our careers. We have hundreds of options for every idea, thousands of faces, and billions of dollars in our industry. We have audio, video, movie, and television opportunities when we write. There are more than twenty-five hundred talk shows to plug our books. We can publish and distribute our own work, sell our wares in the booming international market. Publishing today is only as limited as our vision.

As always, there's a drawback. The very magnitude of these opportunities is daunting to the everyday person with a good book idea. It's hard to know where to start.

For All The Write Reasons takes the guesswork out of getting published in today's market. In the following pages, you'll meet forty new friends—authors, publishers, and agents who will share their experiences, and their mistakes, with you. Think of it as a much more exciting, current, version of my lost file room.

The authors are working people—a teacher turned children's storyteller, a television personality, a newspaper reporter, a physician, a mother who wrote her story after unspeakable personal tragedy. You will be free of the shackles of mystique. Getting a book published is a job, not a lifelong mission, not a Holy Grail.

The stories will guide you through your own decisions, to your own published book. You may decide to get a literary agent and enter the lottery of the major trade publishers, or become one of those clever reference authors who bag money year in, year out, edition after edition. You may choose to start your own publishing house and keep all the profits. Technology gives us unprecedented options to do so.

Whatever your path, get ready to become a published author. Your forty new friends are about to show you how.

William Parkhurst is a media consultant to book publishers as well as the author of three books: How To Get Publicity (Times Books), The Eloquent Executive (Avon), and True Detectives (Crown).

Contents

Introduction

" "For All the Write Reasons: Forty Successful Authors, Publishers, Agents, and Writers Tell You How to Get Your Book Published" is an invaluable guide for writers and "want-to-be-writers." Anyone who is writing a book, has already been published, or is a future famous writer who says "I ought to write a book, but I don't know where to begin," will be inspired by these stories. In 1984, I began clipping, filing, and writing notes about operating a home-based child care business. My initial intent was to prepare hand-out materials for the day-care workshops I taught at the community college. I quickly realized that there was a great deal of interest in the subject and eventually the little spiral-bound, home-made version of my class notes became my first published book, "Start Your Own At Home Child Care Business," which was released by Doubleday in both a hardcover and paperback edition in June 1989.

How did all this begin for me?

Six years ago, I resigned from my position as an account executive-industry consultant for AT&T to become a full-time mom to my two daughters, three-month-old, Katelyn, and eighteen-month-old, Robin. My vision of my life at home was idyllic. There would be no boss, no performance evaluations, no rushing to get out the door in the morning, no stress. I pictured my days to be at a leisurely pace going to aerobics classes, getting a great tan, wearing fashionable sport clothes and going to lunch with friends. But there was one major shortcoming to be reckoned with: if there isn't a corporate workplace, there isn't a paycheck. I found that I needed to supplement my family's income so I decided to offer a child-care program in my home for eleven kids. I traded in notions of fashionable clothes for jogging suits and jeans and the elegant lunches with neighbors became left-over peanut butter and jelly sandwiches with Robin and Katelyn. But my life certainly didn't slow down or become dull! I have written six books; appeared on most of the major TV shows; toured the country with my books (and my kids!); and spent a lot of time, money and energy on promotion. I also learned a whole new business and added two more babies to our family, Kristen and

Ryan. I have made many mistakes—and many friends along the publishing way. This new-found interest has been very exciting, challenging, and lots of fun.

Why did I write this book?

During the years that I tried to find my way through the self-publishing and New York publishing maze, I talked to many other authors and became very good friends with several. (Although some of us have never met in person.) Our "telephone networking" has helped all of us, (and Ma Bell too, since my monthly phone bill runs about $150). This book is my attempt to "introduce" you to my circle of publishing friends and to share our collective wisdom with you. The idea for this book came about when I was asked to offer seminars on the "how-to's" of publishing.

At the seminars, I found it encouraging that there were so many writers in the tri-state area. I teach about seventeen, one-evening seminars a semester and observe an average of thirty students per class. Their "write reasons" for writing are varied and each person is sincere about the merits of their work.

Some of the reasons the aspiring authors want to publish are:

1) "I want to share what happened with my family to help others."
2) "I wrote this book for my students and they enjoyed it so much, I wanted it to get wider exposure."
3) "I invented the best diet: quick, easy and safe."
4) "I have a great way for people to earn money from home."
5) "My recipes are unique and fun to make."
6) "There are just so many humorous things that happen when raising a family, maybe I'll be the next Erma Bombeck."
7) "We learned so much about the adoption process and want to ease the way for others."

There was also a gamut of experience levels in the classes. The novices had questions about margins, copyrights and query letters, while the previously published authors had more sophisticated interests such as literary awards and national writers' conferences. I found meeting all the needs of the students to be a bit of a challenge until I recognized the approach that appealed to most of the authors. The participants were really excited when I taught with samples, using press kits and finished books by people "just like you" who had successfully published books.

As for my approach to this book, I knew the mechanics of publishing were important. However, there are several books that discuss ISBN numbers (International Standard Book Numbers), bar codes, query letters, and production which are widely available in bookstores and library collections. My book publishing niche would be a book of "success stories." And who could better tell their stories but my network of long-distance colleagues, my "telephone friends" from all over the country! I contacted thirty-nine published authors and asked them if they would like to tell their "rags to riches stories" in a chapter in my book, "For All the Write Reasons." I explained to the writers that my aim was to make the book helpful to both new and experienced writers. They enthusiastically responded with their tricks of the publishing trade which await you on the following pages.

Using this book

My fellow writers are an honest group and for that reason, you will read that the life of a writer has its ups and downs. Publishing and writing is hard work and everyone tells you so. But I think you will feel the excitement in each author's style and you will be inspired and encouraged by what they have to say. Being an author or publisher is now in their blood and they are always thinking of the next project. It doesn't matter whether you are writing for fun or profit, there is a certain thrill that comes with seeing your own words in print. Read the other writing books on the market, attend publishing trade shows, subscribe to writers' magazines and join a writers' group in your area. My hope is that as you are reading this book, you will feel as if you are sitting in my living room, sipping a cup of hot tea, with a group of your newly found writing friends, and that in the pages of this book we have formed a great "writers-helping-writers" spirit!

Patricia C. Gallagher

The secret, I discovered, to lifting my severe case of "writer's block" was writing about topics I could get excited about and with which I had some firsthand knowledge.

chapter 1

MBA, Motherhood, and Marketing— The Unlikely Ingredients of My Publishing Career

by Patricia C. Gallagher

N ow, finally I can reveal what I couldn't tell Sally, Geraldo, or Oprah and the dozens of radio and TV talk show hosts across the country: I've always hated writing. They probably still would have me on their shows anyway because as an author of six books, one published by Doubleday, I've carved a niche for myself as a quality child-care advocate and a magna cum laude graduate of the school of publishing triumphs and frustrations.

All through college, I paid someone to proofread my term papers because I cringed at the thought of having to read my writing a second time. When I left to spend my junior year in Mexico, I told everyone not to expect any letters or postcards. I relied on the great technology of Ma Bell to communicate. The secret, I discovered, to lifting my severe case of "writer's block" was writing about topics I could get excited about and with which I had some firsthand knowledge. Not only have topics such as day-care, children, and publishing sparked a creative energy in me, they have proven profitable as well.

Business suit and heels to jeans and sneakers

In 1984, after the birth of my second daughter, I resigned from my position as an account executive/industry consultant for AT&T. In order to replace that income, I researched home-based business ideas I could pursue while caring for a new baby, Katelyn, and an active toddler, Robin. I narrowed my choices by evaluating my strengths and weaknesses and finally opted for starting a child-care program in my own home. Since it seemed like a great way to be home with the kids while at the same time earn a supplemental income, I thought that maybe other mothers at home would be interested in a little "how-to-start-a-child-care-business" booklet.

As I learned about licensing, zoning, and insurance, I jotted down notes on a yellow pad. When I discovered a recipe for homemade modeling clay, I wrote down the ingredients. As the weeks went on, the pad filled with rainy day activities, outdoor games, and the day-to-day happenings in caring for a house full of children.

I called a local community college and proposed a one-night seminar on the topic of starting a child-care business. They asked for a course description for the catalog, an outline, and handouts for the class. I had a friend type my scribbled notes in order to make a fifty-page, eight-and-a-half by eleven inch booklet. Bridget, my eight-year-old niece, designed the cover with her stick drawing of a house with a little bear with the words, "Home Sweet Home." To clarify what the book was about, I subtitled it, "A Comprehensive Guide to Organizing a Profitable Home-Based Child Care Business." I printed about twenty-five copies of the book with a cardboard stock cover and had it spiral bound at the local quick-print.

The demand for the books grew as I offered the same course at five different schools. I added new information based on the questions people asked during the seminars. The original fifty pages expanded to more than 200 and I discovered the miracle of clip art illustrations to fill in some spaces. The title changed several times and the cover and content improved with each printing. But, despite the many enhancements, it still wasn't bookstore quality. A few bookstores offered to take the books on a consignment basis. However, I learned that without aggressive promoting, books sold on consignment in bookstores end up gathering dust and unsold copies eventually have to be picked up. I had a little luck when a local children's clothing store displayed my book but since they required a fifty percent discount, this was certainly not going to make me a millionaire overnight.

Sparking Doubleday's interest

The title changed to "How to Put Pizzazz Into Your Child Care Program," and in a subsequent printing, it was renamed "Child Care and You." After several years of printing and marketing my own book through speaking engagements and seminars, I had the good fortune of meeting an editor from Doubleday who was interested in publishing my book. Six months after our initial meeting at the American Booksellers Association convention, I signed a contract. One year after the agreement was signed, the editor's suggestions for improvements arrived at my doorstep via Federal Express. During the next three months, I wrote and rewrote primarily to convert my original question and answer format into personal anecdotes so that the book would be more marketable to the trade. Six months later, the finished book, now renamed, "Start Your Own At-Home Child Care Business" was on the bookstore shelves.

Meanwhile, another book idea

After experiencing the success of writing my first self-published book (before Doubleday got involved), I thought of another related topic that I felt would fill a need. Since I had owned a commercial day-care center in the mid-seventies, I felt that another how-to book in the same format would sell well and offer additional income as a self-published book. Once again, I approached adult evening non-credit schools and offered a course description on "How to Start a Profitable Day Care Center." Once again the handouts that I compiled for the students became a second self-published book titled, "So You Want to Open a Profitable Day Care Center." This course was targeted for people who wanted to open a day-care center in an institutional setting. As I did with "Child Care and You," I conservatively printed quantities of about a hundred at a time. The cover price varied with each printing, but I finally settled at $19.95 for each of the self-published books. (When Doubleday published "Start Your Own At-Home Child Care

Business" later, it was listed for $8.95 for the paperback edition and is certainly a vastly improved product.)

I didn't make a great deal of money on the books, but the whole business was fun for me and I enjoyed all of the new experiences associated with publishing. One of the best outlets for marketing my books was through the seminars I taught. If twenty people in the class purchased the books during the one-evening seminar, I made about $100, or $5 on each book. The schools paid me between $17 to $25 per hour. Although, at first that might sound like a fair amount for a few hours of work, in reality, that sum didn't compensate for the hundreds of hours behind the scenes calling printers, traveling to the typist, running to the stationery store, and trying to stir up publicity with newspaper editors and TV show producers.

Writer's passion and nemesis

The latter part of putting my books together—dealing with the media— has been the most enjoyable aspect of the process for me. In that regard, I found that I am different than most authors. For most authors, writing is their passion and the marketing of the work is their nemesis. During the first year of my marketing campaign—a fancy name for trying to find friendly newspaper editors who would be interested in my story—I received six local newspaper feature stories and one magazine article in *Lady's Circle*. This initial success buoyed my confidence in my chosen topic of child care and I was encouraged by the media's interest. I tried to make at least two contacts for the book each day.

Then as now, the fruits of my marketing efforts aren't realized immediately. On many occasions, I see positive results years after making the initial contact. The most exciting example of this delayed reaction was when the producer from the "Oprah Winfrey Show" called in June 1988. She said that she was responding to my letter of August 1987.

To be truthful, sometimes responses to my marketing approach make me a little nervous. There have been occasions when a producer or reporter requested a review copy of my book in advance. During the initial conversation or mailing, I would tout myself as author of "Child Care and You" and "So You Want to Open a Profitable Day Care Center." The question inevitably came up, "Oh, and who published your book?" My typically enthusiastic tone lowered as I said "I did" and finally had to show them my home-made edition. But for the "Oprah Winfrey Show," my home-made book got me on the show!

At times, when I am in a library, I will see my earlier self-published efforts on a shelf and I always stop to see how many people have checked it out over the years. There is a part of me that wants to steal the home-made versions and replace it with the "real" Doubleday book with my by-line and book title on the spine, with the professionally designed cover. Although the Doubleday-published book is certainly a first class product and a credit to professional editing and know-how, learning the hard way by doing it all myself proved an invaluable experience. My mistakes in regard to pricing, packaging, and publicity have all helped me in some way. One important lesson that I have learned is that book buyers rely very much on visuals—the cover must have pizzazz. If the cover looks dull or amateurish, the prospective buyer may not pursue the information within it. An impressive cover is absolutely critical for book sales.

If only the cover were the only difference between the self-published book and Doubleday's. However, it will become quickly obvious in the paragraphs that follow just how many more lessons were to be learned in successfully self-publishing.

Endorsements pay off

Another important boost to marketing a book is having some testimonials from key people in your book's field of interest. Since I am not an organization joiner by nature, I did not become an active member in child care related associations. Having three little kids under four years of age and attending classes three nights a week in a graduate MBA program left little time for outside interests. The hours in my day were pretty much accounted for and I did not pursue many extra activities. As I look back, I know now that books sell in greater quantities when they are endorsed or pushed by an organization or association.

Often, organizations are looking for funds to support themselves. Offering a special discount to group members provides a great opportunity for bulk sales for the self-publisher, and profits to the organization. Testimonials from the group's officers or key spokesperson can do much to propel a book's sales.

(Self-publishers should seek these remarks while in the process of writing the book so that flattering remarks can be printed on the cover of the book.)

The "Hula Hoop Syndrome"

When approaching organizations, be prepared for professional jealousy. After all, the person who is the "president" of the group may think that he or she could have written the book and done a better job. But little old you wrote the book! Becky Barker, (see chapter three) has called this phenomenon the "Hula Hoop Syndrome." So many people have thought how easy it must have been to invent such an inexpensive toy, which brought fame and fortune to the inventor. Millions of people have said "I could have done that! It's so simple an idea." But Becky and I always say in unison, "They could have, but they didn't."

Remember the topic of your book will be of interest to thousands of people who do not belong to trade organizations, and there will be plenty of alternative markets for book sales. I visited several day-care organizations, in a "dressed for success" suit, with copies of my home-made editions proudly packed in an official-looking briefcase. The reception to the books was "cool" to "cold." The reason for this was because of the many similar books on the market, published by major publishers. These other books looked like real books, with four-color glossy covers and perfect binding (glued inside to the book's spine).

When I tried to sell to members of various day-care organizations and I got to my closing, where I offered them my treasure for a mere $19.95, very few took advantage of my bargain. I then began to research what was already on the market and found that a great deal more pages and an overall better book could be purchased for about half the price. A small publisher, like myself, could not compete because I printed in such small quantities, making per-unit costs high. It was at those times that I went back to the comfort of my husband, parents, and sister who all convinced me that it was certainly the best book that they had ever seen or read. (Thank goodness for the family's rose-colored glasses!)

Over the next year or so, I sold about 500 copies of each book through seminars, mentions in newspaper articles and by word of mouth. Many other copies were given away gratis to reporters, newsletter editors, and others who, for some reason, I felt would be able to herald the good news of my book. During the three-year period of selling both day-care books, before I found a major publisher, I wrote an arts and crafts activity book, "Robin's Play and Learn Book—How to Entertain Children at Home or in Preschool," which I named after my oldest daughter. Since all three titles were related, I found that my workshop participants often purchased all of them. I was also advised by another author to try confining my books to specific topics so that they would appear as books-in-a-series.

Catching an editor's eye

I continued sending mailings and press releases that were neither in the proper format or especially professional. My first goal was to arouse the editor's curiosity when my envelope appeared on her desk. I always tried to do something to the exterior of the envelope that would make a busy producer or reporter interested in opening it. My rationale for decorating the envelopes rather than using the more professional choice of business envelopes, was that I wanted mine to stand out.

One of my colorful efforts was using bumper stickers that said "I Love Collies," even though I've never been an avid dog lover. The reason I used them is because I had about a hundred of these stickers, which I found at a garage sale from a box labeled "FREE."

In a local odd-lot discount store, I bought gummed stickers in all sorts of shapes and sizes. The neighborhood kids and my three daughters had a ball painting and jazzing up the envelopes with stickers. Although it's never been determined how successful the bumper stickers were in capturing responses, it was an interesting trip to the postal counter with my potpourri of 500 envelopes!

Since media contacts are continually swamped with notices of local events and celebrities, it probably is in an author's best interest to have a different approach in attracting attention. I have been fortunate in attaining a lot of media attention. My very first TV attempt was a popular morning show based in California. Gary Collins was the host of "Hour Magazine." I contacted our local TV affiliate and asked for the show's address. On plain white copy paper, I sent a brief five-sentence letter with the salutation, "Dear Producer." You can imagine how surprised I was to find myself with airline tickets in hand and registered as a guest in an exquisite hotel in Beverly Hills, California. (All expenses paid by "Hour Magazine.") This all happened within a week of mailing the letter. This was beginner's luck because it was never this easy again! Last summer I sent out more than 200 press releases and only received two invitations for TV appearances, CNN and CNBC.

Appearing on national TV

Since "Hour Magazine" was a national morning TV show with at least six million viewers, I was certain the resulting book sales would be better than winning a lottery. I was told the interview would last about ten minutes and I was instructed to give the viewers some tips about starting a child care business. I had visions of Gary Collins holding my home-made book on the screen for the full segment and of course he would probably laud it as the best in the world. In my dreams! The address to order, I thought, would be emblazoned on the screen with special effects so that all six million viewers and their friends and relatives could get the information readily.

It was with great disappointment that I was told that Gary Collins, the host, would not be mentioning my book. The focus of the show, they explained, was about mothers at home with the kids! Well, at least I had the chance to sit in a major network "green room," eat from a scrumptious specially-prepared buffet, and nervously sit next to newscaster Linda Ellerbee and Donny Osmond.

Since the show had been taped and would be aired three weeks later in Philadelphia, I made several pleading phone calls to the producer to please just list my address for the six million viewers who might desperately be seeking my book.

Reality sinks in

As I flew home, my mind focused on the two stacks of 250 books each piled neatly in my laundry room next to baby diapers and a yet-unpaid for computer, which I still hadn't learned to use. (The book, at this time, had now been bravely printed in quantities of 500 in anticipation of the expected avalanche of orders presumed to be forthcoming after this national debut.) Up until this point, most libraries and bookstores had never heard of me, or my books. I stepped up my efforts to appear on a few local TV shows. The first respondent was "AM Philadelphia." They invited me to be a guest on their show and asked me if I could round up participants for their studio audience to ask questions during the audience segment. My loyal relatives and some neighbors filled up the seats and, once again, the emphasis was not on my book, but the topic of "women leaving the corporate world to start their own businesses." I was disappointed but from other previous experiences I realized any type of exposure is invaluable and is really free advertising for your product or service.

For me, I was beginning a business as a corporate child-care consultant and this type of coverage enhanced my credibility. News broadcasts and feature articles, using my quotes or excerpts from my books, did much to assist promotional efforts and distinguish me as someone with newsworthy knowledge of the topic. Since I was introduced as an author of day-care books and as the president of Gallagher, Jordan & Associates Child Care Consultants, the introduction opened several opportunities for paid speaking engagements and corporate consultations. I still hadn't found a quick and easy way to unload the books that loomed larger than the laundry in my laundry room. As the laundry piled higher, I swear the books were multiplying too, and I wondered how I would ever sell them.

Months before this, I had started a telemarketing plan while the kids took their naps. I called libraries throughout our tri-state area and sold quite a few copies, but this was very time-consuming and expensive due to long distance calling. I probably sold four books an hour and made a profit of $5 per book. Twenty dollars an hour might sound OK initially but you must take into account the administrative time of looking up contact names and numbers of acquisition librarians, creating invoices for books ordered, shipping and handling, taping, stapling, and waiting in lines.

For about the first year, I was not even aware that UPS picked up packages at home and tortured myself, and the line of people that filed behind me, while I juggled six packages and three little children. I always avoided looking at anyone behind me in line as I scurried out of the UPS depot. I would drive miles out of my way in order not to be causing some sort of scene and visited UPS counters in a twenty-five-mile radius of my home. Finally, some frustrated businessman yelled to me "Hey lady, why don't you let them pick your stuff up at home?"

Librarian's key to selling books

Luck came to me in the form of a local librarian, Mr. Peter Manakos. As the director of our local library, he took a personal interest in my spiral-bound books. He was very supportive of my project and saw my books as a valuable acquisition for libraries. I told him how I had been selling single copies here and there and how even TV exposure did not move my book on to *The New York Times* Best Seller List or even out of my laundry room in great quantities.

Mr. Manakos had been a publisher in his native country of Greece. He unlocked the key to marketing large quantities of books to libraries. If your book is reviewed by a library-reviewing source such as Library Journal or Booklist, you will most likely receive hundreds of purchase orders from individual libraries, library systems, and wholesalers. I followed his suggestion and was thrilled to find well over 1,000 orders in my post office box for each of my books that had been reviewed by Booklist. Even though the review was excellent and recommended my books as a natural acquisition for public libraries, it ended with: Warning: Spiral Binding. They reviewed both day-care related books but passed on the arts and crafts manual. When I heard that the review was carrying such a warning to librarians, I contacted several library directors in my town. A few libraries said that spiral binding was a death sentence for library purchases because such bindings did not meet their durability standards. Luckily, that didn't deter the many libraries that did order the books, spiral binding and all.

Getting past the "discard pile" with book reviewers

Since I had personal success with library reviews, I mailed my mother's book, "Mother Teresa's Someday"—the story of the young life of the Nobel Peace Prize Laureate. With great hope and expectation, we sent her beautifully crafted book to the Children's Reviewing Source of the same journal, *Booklist* (American Library Association). Her book is absolutely beautiful in every way with an award-winning illustrator's cover design. The content of the book has been well received by archbishops, superintendents of schools and the elementary children in our tri-state area. She was even invited to visit Rome and present one of her books to the Pope.

When I called to follow-up as to when her book would be reviewed, the person told me that the book had not been considered due to the staple binding. Their policy is to review only bound books for the children's reviews. We have now made a few revisions to the story, applied for a new copyright date and plan to resubmit according to their very particular guidelines. (Always contact reviewing sources for specific guidelines and advice before mailing review copies.)

I'll never forget the first time I heard that one of my submissions to a reviewer was in the "discard pile." I dearly hoped that it didn't mean what I thought but, sure enough, it had two strikes against it—it was not submitted at least three months in advance of publication and the copyright date was 1985 and I submitted it in 1986. Once again, I made some revisions, applied a current copyright date and was thrilled to receive a tear sheet in November indicating that my book would be reviewed the following February. Orders poured in, with no checks or payment accompanying the request since libraries and wholesalers work on a purchase order system and expect to be billed. For the most part, the libraries paid within three months but the same can not be said for many bookstores. Even after reminder notices are sent for small orders of one and two books, you often wait six months for payment, if it ever comes. (I have probably lost about $500 due to uncollected debt from bookstores and individuals who took a book at a seminar but failed to send the promised check.)

In the midst of all this, my third baby, Kristen was born. I no longer ran a child-care business from my home but spent all available time trying to publicize my three self-published books, resolve my cash flow problem and redesign each book to give them a more professional bookstore-quality appearance. They now all have glossy covers and are perfect bound. I increased my run size to 1,000 at a time to take advantage of cost reductions for larger quantities. Since books are an investment, you make your profit when they are all sold but the printer expects his money when the job is completed. My credit card cash advances and credit union debt increased as I speculated that someday soon, my ship would come in.

A new marketing approach

About this time, I got a lead about a small radio show, located about an hour from my home. I contacted the host and was invited as a guest. The whole time I was driving there, I questioned why I was putting myself through all of this—making arrangements for a baby-sitter, driving a few hours round-trip and using gas. About this time, I wondered if I shouldn't just let some leads pass.

This turned out to be one of the best opportunities in terms of important contacts. The host, Louise Collins, of Newtown, Pa., was extremely nice and very interested in my topic. When she saw that the book was self-published, she went into her files and retrieved a press kit from a Becky Barker. Becky had originally self-published her book "answers.," along with her sister, Suzi Hart.

After several appearances on "Donahue" and "Good Morning America" and a few years of really creative marketing and exhaustive work, Harper and Row and Becky negotiated a very substantial contract. Although she did not have an agent, she used the counsel of a highly regarded CPA and attorney. I called her and she told me things that I could never have learned if I read a thousand books about publishing. She generously shared her tricks of the trade. She introduced me to the importance of ISBN numbers and bar codes. When she presented an idea to a producer she stated in many ways how it would "benefit" and "help" their viewers and she would speak of the negative consequences that could happen to people if they were not aware of her topic.

Discount schedules for bookstores, wholesalers, and distributors were all a maze to me however, with her help, I prepared my price breaks for multiple orders. At her suggestion, I added re-order coupons in my books, which I find contribute to a significant number of new sales because people borrow the book from a library or friend and decide they want their own copy. We have kept in touch almost weekly by phone for five years. Although we have never met in person, we have seen each other on TV shows and I consider her a very good friend. She is my telephone mentor and without her expert advice and willingness to help a fledgling writer, I would never have experienced the publishing satisfaction that has come my way. The value of networking with other writers cannot be overemphasized.

A new strategy

There came a period of time when the home self-publishing business started to become difficult. With three children, I found it difficult to manage my prior routine of calling for publicity, answering requests for information, trying to collect accounts receivable payments, offering seminars and all of the thousands of little things that need to be done when you are trying to balance a book and family. On a visit to my local bookstore, the owner, Gary Dahl, mentioned that he was going to the American Booksellers Convention in Washington, D.C. He told me that it was a trade show for everyone related to the book trade—bookstore owners, publishers, distributors and wholesalers. It didn't take me long to decide that I wanted to be there despite the fact that I had invited relatives from Iowa for that weekend. Since Washington is only a few hours by train, I took a few home-made copies of my book and copies of all of the publicity I had garnered thus far.

While at the convention, I made some great contacts. One was the producer of "AM San Francisco" and the other was a senior editor of Doubleday. I talked briefly to the producer and when I returned home, I decided to call her and say that I was going to be in California making a library presentation and would love to be a guest on her show. There were a few calls back and forth, two packages of background materials sent by Federal Express to her and I got a confirmation date. Then I contacted several libraries in the San Francisco area and asked (pleaded) if they would be interested in a two-hour seminar that would help people in starting child care programs. Since I was going to be there for three days, I arranged two radio shows and three newspaper interviews. The radio and TV shows did not begin to pay my expenses so I decided to publicize my book through the media prior to my free presentation at the library in the hope of drawing a larger turnout that might buy my books.

Book sales at the library did not cover the expenses for my husband, baby and me. Books were still in my laundry room and not in bookstores. I began to wonder if this was one lead I shouldn't have pursued. However, as in most cases, I discovered later there was a purpose.

The "AM San Francisco" show went very well so I sent a letter to the "Oprah Winfrey Show." I explained that the theme of the California show was about day-care nightmares and that I was the panelist (or supposedly author expert) who could shed some light on how such tragic things could happen. More importantly, I could give advice to parents about how they could evaluate quality child care. I mailed the letter and some newspaper articles and promptly forgot about it. Again, it wasn't until nearly a year after that, I received a call from the producer and within four days, I was in the elegant Hotel Nikki in Chicago, with all expenses paid, finding it hard to fathom that I was really riding in a chauffeur-driven limousine on my way to be a guest on the "Oprah Winfrey Show."

Once again, I thought that my ship had come in. In a publishing magazine I read that a plug by Oprah could sell 50,000 books. Well, Oprah could not have held my book more prominently. The camera zoomed in on the cover and she even stammered over the title so she repeated it. What was I ever going to do with all of the money that would be generated from this once in a lifetime exposure? Crash!!! Reality set in. Nobody would be able to buy my book because it still was unknown to bookstores and if anyone wanted a copy, they were more than welcome to the many stacks of books in my laundry room.

Within days of appearing on that program, I sent a similar letter to the producers of "Sally Jessy Raphael," "Geraldo," "Donahue" and other major shows. Within six weeks, I found myself once again on a plane to Connecticut, at no expense to me, for a taping of "Sally Jessy Raphael." (So far, I've been on this program three times.) During the next few months, other shows called, such as "People Are Talking" (Boston and North Jersey), and also a local show in Philadelphia. The other mothers who were guests on the original show with me continued their mission and were guests on "Joan Rivers," "ABC Nightly News with Peter Jennings," "Geraldo" and many others. For me it was too hard to relive the tragedies of these mothers as they shared their heart-breaking stories about what had happened to their little children in a day-care setting. I decided not to accept invitations for shows that focused on negative day care experiences.

Contact to contract

At the same ABA convention where I had made my contact with the "AM San Francisco" producer, I met the Doubleday senior editor who expressed interest in publishing my book. I couldn't believe it when she asked if I would send her a copy of the book along with newspaper articles and a list of shows that I had been on so far. Since I had sold several thousand of my self-published book on home child care, I photocopied hundreds of orders that I had received on large sheets of paper and sent everything off to New York. As editors frequently move on, I received a letter saying that another editor would be handling my book. The convention took place in May 1987 and it was not until the next September that a contract was signed. There were many phone calls and letters in between to discuss issues such as whether or not I'd have time to revise the book with three young children and getting permission from the original sources of some materials that would be reprinted.

It was a year after the contract was signed that I was asked to begin the revision process. Nine months after that, my book "Start Your Own At Home Child Care Business" was on the bookstore shelves. Half of the advance was given at the time of contract signing and the second half was after the book was completed. Since I did not have an agent or a lawyer to negotiate the fine print, I found that I made a few mistakes. For example, I agreed to discontinue marketing my self-published book at an agreed-upon date and not to appear on any more TV shows until my Doubleday book came out. The purpose of this, from a publisher's point of view, was to create a market for the book. If I continued to sell my version in a big way, then the reviewers and individuals would not be interested in their edition. This agreement caused a financial loss to me because during that interim, I was invited to be a guest on "Oprah Winfrey," the "Home Show," "Hour Magazine" and at least ten other shows, which I had to decline.

I also made my income from teaching workshops on day care at local colleges and I sold my book as the text. Since I could no longer sell my book, it did not pay for me to offer the course as the instructor's fee was minimal.

Despite these disappointments, I felt proud that my book was being published by a major publisher and looked forward to June 16, 1989, which was the official publication date. So revisions were made between October and January and then I heard from a new person in the book publishing process, the publicist. A beautiful press kit was prepared and this was mailed out to the media about a month in advance of publication. I was surprised to learn that even though the publicity departments mail out materials, it behooves the author to get involved in the publicity effort.

Although I know that the effort I put into the book promotion is not for everyone, what follows is one chapter in my odyssey of letting the public know about my book. If your name is Lee Iacocca, Jacqueline Onassis, or Nancy Reagan, you will probably never have to move a finger to let the world know about your book. However, if you are not a well known person or you have written a book about your "Best Gift Ideas," "How to Plan a Party," or "My Best Family Recipes," you might want to get your creative juices flowing and plan to market your book in conjunction with your publisher's efforts.

The promotions track

What did I do to promote my book "Start Your Own At Home Child Care Business," which was published by Doubleday in June 1989?

In December 1988, after recovering from the initial shock that my publisher was not going to give my book the first class treatment via publicity that they give to other prominent authors' books, I put my own marketing ideas into gear. Due to making my own contacts, I was a guest on "Oprah Winfrey Show," "Sally Jessy Raphael," CNBC, CNN, FNN, "Hour Magazine," "People Are Talking," "Evening Magazine," and many others. I also decided to promote my book through a nationwide Child Caring USA Tour. The following is an encapsulated version of my promotions strategy.

January 1989

The decision was made to travel around the United States with my three little girls, ages two, four and six to promote my book. I contacted major auto manufacturers in Detroit, trying to convince them to give me a new van for my travels. In return, I proposed promoting their vehicle in all my media interviews and would laud the safety features and reliability of their van. I spent about $250 to Federal Express letters and copies of my forthcoming book to auto union leaders, public relations managers and the presidents and vice presidents of General Motors, Chrysler, Ford, etc. (In addition, about $100 was spent for follow-up phone calls). I even sent Lee Iacocca flowers via FTD hoping to get his attention. His staff probably thought that it was "Fatal Attraction" from an admirer. I made an appointment with a Chrysler regional manager, but still no luck. They donate vans to non-profit causes such as "Muppets On Tour" (for car safety) and Mothers Against Drunk Driving. I finally bought a brand new Plymouth Voyager, which cost $18,000.

February 1989

I figured that in order to get media attention and interviews, I needed a "cause" or a "mission." I dubbed my self-styled tour "the Child Caring USA Tour" and offered to present seminars on child care related topics at libraries around the country. The van was custom- decorated so that it was covered with hundreds of multi-colored teddy bears and the words on the side panels said, "Do you love children? Start Your Own Child Care Business—Ask Us How!"

I also had the phone number of the New Canaan Bookstore of 1-800-ALL-BOOK and the publisher's name, Doubleday, clearly visible on all sides of the van along with the name of the book. The van was a traveling billboard for my new book. The graphics were bright and attractive and cost me about $550 for a professional graphic designer to custom decorate the van. After a six-month period, the same sign company removed the graphics for $150. The tour actually lasted three months, but I kept the copy on the van for six months. Pressure to remove the teddy bears and balloons from the van came when my second grader became embarrassed to have me drive to school. The kids in her class thought I was a clown.

March 1989

I contacted three companies that were mentioned in my book and asked if they would be interested in supporting my Child Caring USA Tour "cause" by sharing the expenses of the tour. The cost to each was $2,500. All three responded positively and in exchange for their financial participation, I promoted their products in my handouts to the seminar attendees and also had their names on the back panel of my van. They received exposure for their companies and mention in the media interviews. I also enclosed their advertisements when I mailed out books. A major hotel chain and I worked out a mutually beneficial arrangement whereby my family and I received free lodging and meals.

April 1989

In this phase, I mailed 300 cover letters and brochures pitching the Child Caring USA Tour to radio and TV producers as well as newspaper editors listed in "Book Marketing Update." I then scheduled fifty media interviews and thirty library presentations during the summer to be done as I traveled around the country.

May 1989

I placed a full-page ad in "Radio-TV Interview Report," which is a magazine-format publication distributed throughout the radio and TV media. The ad included sample interview questions, a black and white photo of me and another photo of the cover of my book. Before I signed with "Radio-TV Interview Report," I called ten authors who had advertised in previous issues to verify that the publication really generated lots of interviews. I was thrilled to receive calls from producers after my ad appeared and from this source alone, I did twenty phone interviews over a six-week period.

June, July, August 1989

Travel time! I toured around the country with my children, and oh yes, one other detail... I was expecting my fourth child.

What else did I do?

For the trip, I had adhesive-backed stickers printed (the size of an index card) that said "Ask me about my mommy's book," with a picture of my three little girls sitting on a six-foot white stuffed bear. Also included on the sticker was the price of the book and ordering information. I put the sticker on all envelopes that I mailed out to the media (producers remembered my mailing because the photo was unique). Since I had 2,000 black and white stickers printed, I placed them on all bills that I mailed out during 1989. I figured maybe even a postal worker sorting the mail might know someone interested in starting a child care business.

My three children had tee-shirts and jogging suits with a cute picture of a bear and words imprinted on the front. Printed on Robin's shirt, "Ask me about my mommy's book." Katelyn's shirt read: "Have you read my mommy's book?" Kristen's read: "My mommy wrote a book."

The large white envelopes I used to send media press kits and pitch letters were especially "eye-catching." The return address was Child Caring USA Tour, Box 555, Worcester, PA, 19490 printed in blue ink. On the lower left corner, I had printed—"Support Quality Child Care, It's a Great Reflection on You!" I had silver stickers which were circles the size of a silver dollar attached. The silver stickers looked like a mirror and "reflected."

I contacted "Publishers Weekly" and they ran a great human interest story about my forthcoming odyssey with the kids. It was three columns wide, complete with a photo of the kids and me standing in front of the van. The bold headlines read: "Savvy marketer learns about Publishing... and Vice Versa?" (I could have never afforded an advertisement like that).

I also had a nice story written in the American Booksellers Magazine. The "hook" that tied me into them was the fact that I met the Doubleday editor who contracted with me for the book at the ABA convention in 1987. (I didn't have an agent.)

All in all, it was a great trip and we did sell some books. The service at 1-800-ALL-BOOK said that she probably sold about 500 copies and I sold about 500 through the library seminars. The real pay-off was not the quantity sold, but the name recognition and the other opportunities that have come about from the publicity. I have been invited to speak at many conferences and I am the product spokesperson for "Skintastic," a new insect repellent introduced this year by Johnson Wax, who are the manufacturers of the well-known "Off" insect repellent. Deborah Durham and Associates, the public relations firm that initially contacted me heard of my venture through a UPI story. (Thanks to the contact that I read in the "Book Marketing Update.") And Doubleday has just gone into a second hardcover printing so we did generate interest in the book for the bookstores.

Well, what is in store for our family travel this year? Yes, I am doing it again, but this time, I will have my new baby with me. Four kids under eight years of age in a van! Since the teddy bears are gone, we have the opportunity to be creative. Our new publicity campaign is "Who cares—for KIDS?" The graphic designer will place pictures of frolicking children on the side panels along with "KIDS"—the four legged, shaggy, horned animal type that are usually found on a farm, not traveling with a family along the nation's highways.

We are traveling with our four children and we will be pulling a new red trailer complete with hay, a feed trough, and two pet pygmy goats—also known as "The Kids!!" This is going to be our "hook." I hope for some national attention. As bizarre and painful as this new idea may sound, I think we have a unique "angle" for our summer trip. There's a lot more to this year's publicity campaign. Hopefully, we will make it into People Magazine or "CBS Morning News." Then you will hear the rest of the story!

ASK ME ABOUT MY MOMMY'S BOOK!!!

START YOUR OWN AT HOME CHILD CARE BUSINESS
Great for day care centers
and
lots of ideas for mothers at home too!

(Doubleday)

$8.95 plus $2.00 for postage
ORDERS: Gallagher, Jordan & Associates
Box 555
Worcester, PA 19490

SATISFACTION GUARANTEED OR MONEY BACK!

```
DOUBLEDAY PUBLISHING CO BY KARA
666 5 AVE
NEW YORK NY 10103 16AM
```

Western Union **Mailgram**

```
4-0062085167003 06/16/89 ICS IPMMTZZ CSP PHAB
2 2124929773 MGM TDMT NEW YORK NY 06-16 0935A EST


PATRICIA GALLAGHER
301 HOLLYHILL RD
RICHBORO PA 18954



THIS IS A CONFIRMATION COPY OF A TELEGRAM ADDRESSED TO YOU:

WELL CONGRATULATIONS AS OF TOMORROW YOU'RE AN OFFICIALLY PUBLISHED
DOUBLEDAY AUTHOR, WE ALL VERY PROUD, BEST
   KARA
   (DOUBLEDAY PUBLISHING CO 666 5 AVE NEW YORK NY 10103)
   666 5 AVE
   NEW YORK NY 10103

09:34 EST

MGMCOMP
```

TO REPLY BY MAILGRAM MESSAGE SEE REVERSE SIDE FOR WESTERN UNION'S TOLL FREE PHONE NUMBERS

GALLAGHER, JORDAN & ASSOCIATES
— Child Care Consultants —
P.O. Box 555 ● Worcester, PA 19490
Telephone 215-584-5304

A DAY CARE NIGHTMARE

—How did three beautiful, healthy infants become blind and paralyzed while in the "<u>unloving</u> arms" of child care providers? (Three infants, in separate cities, were <u>severely shaken</u> by stressed out caregivers who could not cope with screaming babies).

A SHOCKING STORY?
A TERRIBLE TRAGEDY?
HOW COULD THIS HAVE BEEN PREVENTED?

—Why was my personal experience with day care an extremely positive one? (The woman who watched my 3 month old made her clothes and loved her like her own).

As the author of several books related to Day Care, I was recently invited to be a guest on a morning talk show on the West Coast. As the "expert" on evaluating "Quality Child Care," it was my position to help the viewers to sort through the myriad of options available: IN-HOME CARE, FAMILY DAY CARE, GROUP HOMES, DAY CARE CENTERS and NANNY SERVICES.

What I was <u>not</u> prepared for were the shocking experiences of the other three panelists. They were all well educated, intelligent, career oriented women. One by one, they told their story. The tragic common denomination that bonded these families were that each of their babies was the victim of "Shaken Baby Syndrome" (which results in brain damage and loss of vision in an infant). They left their "precious bundle of joy" with babysitters who could not cope with the frustration of a screaming baby.

The tragedy is that these youngsters, now four years of age, went from bouncing, beautiful and healthy children to being blind, paralyzed and with seizures.

During the show, there wasn't a dry eye in the audience (Talk Show Host Included).

I would like to give an "<u>INSIDER'S VIEW OF DAY CARE.</u>" My unique qualifications are: 1) That I have owned a large Day Care Facility; 2) I have also provided child care in my home for eleven children and 3) That I left my three month old in a day care arrangement.

I would like to be a guest on your show so that we could help other parents to avoid what happened to these three families. I would also be able to arrange for these mothers to tell their stories.

I will look forward to speaking with you soon so that we can offer guidance before parents place their <u>most</u> <u>precious</u> <u>treasures</u> into the wrong set of extended arms!

Sincerely,

Patricia C. Gallagher

Start Your Own At-Home Child Care Business

Find Out How To:

$ Set up and advertise your business

Build a good relationship with parents

Plan exciting play-and-learn activities

Make your play area accident-proof

and much, much more!

PATRICIA C. GALLAGHER

Lou Alpert

There are days filled with fun and excitement and days filled with exhaustion and frustration—but it's never boring.

chapter **2**

Family Vacation Inspires an Illustrator's Publishing Career in Children's Books

by Lou Alpert

Three years ago at this time I had never written a book and knew absolutely nothing about the publishing business. Now I have my own publishing company, Whispering Coyote Press. I've written, illustrated, published my first seven children's books, and I have plans in 1992 to publish twenty new books (four of my own as well as sixteen by other authors). The great part is that I love it all and feel truly fortunate to have come so far, so fast.

In the summer of 1987 my husband and I took our then five children to the south of France for two months. This was my Christmas present, one that I "opened" with both interest and extreme reservation. The idea of flying to the south of France with children ages eleven, ten, eight, two and one; moving into a villa with no TV, VCR, or radio; and coping in a small French town when I spoke virtually no French (I was limited to asking for the restroom, counting to ten, and ordering a glass of wine) seemed a little overwhelming. But, married to a man who sees all these challenges as part of a fun-filled adventure—off we went.

It turned out to be one of the most wonderful two months I ever spent, and the place that I began writing and illustrating my first books. It was so quiet.

With no TV or outside distractions of friends and activities we all began doing a lot more reading and writing. My husband became the tour guide. Almost every day we would pile in the van to explore some quaint French town...I'm not a very good "sitter," and although I did OK at first, I eventually started getting restless in the car. I really am worse than the kids, so I started writing stories. I began by writing on the backs of paperback books, scribbling on napkins and anything else I could find as we drove through the countryside. It was in this manner that I wrote my first three books: "The Man in the Moon and His Magic Balloon," "Emma Lights the Sky," and "Emma and the Magic Dance." I bought some good paper and watercolors to start my illustrations. It was a very peaceful time, sitting in my room overlooking the Cote d'Azur and painting.

When we returned to the United States in August, we went directly to Long Island where we were moving from Florida. The books became a real lifesaver as I adjusted to a new life and a new community. Once again I had few distractions since I didn't know anyone and was basically focusing my time on getting the kids settled in and unpacking.

I had grown up in Texas and lived there for thirty-five years before we moved to Miami for a year and then on to New York. I knew from my first move that it would take a good year to form new friendships, and I also knew the unpacking might happen slowly. As my children became involved in new schools and activities, I became more and more involved in writing and illustrating.

As I always tell the children I speak to in schools about writing and publishing books, I don't get up in the morning and spend hours at a typewriter—I normally don't bother typing my stories until the very end. I'm like all other moms. I drive carpools, fix dinner, clean the house, and do all those things that have to be done when you're raising a large family. Fortunately, I think most of writing is thinking—so while my body moves through the day, my mind works out stories. Once I get going on an idea I can move pretty fast. When the idea is pretty well worked out in my head I can usually sit down and write it out in fifteen to twenty minutes. Of course, that's just the first rough draft. Before it goes to press I will have re-written it five to ten times and have sent it off to be edited by other people.

I used a very strange editing process on my first seven books. I would show the manuscripts to a local writers' group for valuable suggestions and also sent them to a couple of professional children's editors. My best editors turned out to be my husband and my mother. Both are very good with the spoken word and they seemed to be more in tune with the feeling I was trying to maintain with the books.

I illustrate throughout the writing and editing process. From the time I begin to develop a story idea, I also begin to visualize the illustrations. I see the two together. I think that's why it would be so difficult for me to illustrate another author's manuscript, and visa versa. After coming back from France, most of my illustrating has been done at the kitchen table. The reality is that there is very little time without children in my house, and illustrating is something I can do with them around. They can talk to me, comment on what I'm doing, and I'm available to stop and get juice and snacks, and quite often they sit and do their own illustrations as I work.

I use mostly watercolor or gouache, a little pencil or pen, sometimes crayon, and really whatever else is readily available in the kitchen. Once when I was drawing a group of school kids, a little girl asked me why Emma's hair was a different color in each book. I had to confess that it was because I was just too lazy to walk upstairs and get the right color, so I used what was available at the moment.

I love to illustrate, and for me it's a joy, not a chore. When speaking with children in schools and libraries, I try to emphasize the fun of illustrating. It's one place where there are truly no rules. Trees aren't green, skies aren't blue, and the most important person to please is yourself. My drawing and painting have a real sense of freedom that the kids seem to enjoy. I don't have a need to stay in the lines, I don't think I ever did even as a child. To me it's all a process where mistakes only exist until you fix them to your liking. If I accomplish nothing else with these books, I hope that I teach a few kids along the way that we can all be artists and how to let go and enjoy the process of expressing themselves with art.

After I had finished writing and illustrating the first three books and had begun writing the fourth one, I began to start thinking about how to get them published. Having absolutely no idea of where to start, I headed for my local bookstore to get "how-to" books on writing and publishing a children's book. I discovered there are many available. I also bought a copy of

"Children's Writer's & Illustrator's Market." This book lists all the children's publishing houses, how many books are actually published each year, the average length of time it takes after the books are accepted to be published, the type of books they publish, and what they are looking for currently in manuscript material. It also includes how manuscripts should be presented, terms of contracts, percentage of books by first-time authors, and more. I spent a lot of time weeding through these books and finally began to send off my manuscripts.

I met personally with a number of people in the children's book business, including some at the large publishing houses. They were all very nice and offered suggestions to fit the current market needs: take out the rhymes, change the illustration style, tighten it up. I definitely got my share of rejections with those cold form letters that arrive in the mail. It's a good skin-toughening process.

The problem was I'd go home and re-read the stories and look at the illustrations again but I just couldn't change it all. Editing was one thing, but to change the whole concept just to get it published made no sense to me. I had been reading to my own children for eleven years at this point and had taught art and worked with kids most of my life. I really felt like I knew what kids liked and wanted and I wasn't finding it too often in the current marketplace. Quite often the books my kids wanted to read were the stories I'd read as a child, ones published in the 30's, 40's, and 50's. There were illustrators that I would kill to be able to paint like, and writers who I loved, but they weren't me. The kids seemed to really like my rough, free illustration style, and truthfully they were the ones I wanted to please. The books were for children. I wasn't trying to teach anything heavy with the books or change the world. My goal was to give kids books that they wanted to touch, to pick up, and to read again and again. I call the books "child friendly." I fill them with bright colors, free illustration style, and fun upbeat stories with characters the children want to keep as friends.

So, being a relatively hard-headed person who wanted to maintain artistic control over the books, I went back to my local bookstore to get books on "how to do it yourself." The book I used like a bible for the next few months, although it wasn't really geared to children's books, was "A Complete Guide to Self-Publishing" by Tom and Marilyn Ross. I read this book cover to cover and used it as a reference for answering questions throughout the process.

My first step was to get my books printed. I knew that if I focused on all that was ahead of me, it would be overwhelming. I simply took it one step at a time and did each day what was absolutely required to get to the next step. By this time I had another child who was just a few months old. I wasn't really getting enough sleep to start writing anything new, so it was a good time to start making phone calls.

I first called a friend in Dallas, my hometown, who had a commercial printing press. He said he would be happy to bid on the project, but it would be really tough for him to compete with a book manufacturer. He gave me a couple of names and I moved on with my calls. I found after my first four or five calls that not everyone prints full-color children's books. Each book manufacturer would ask me a few questions and then send me to the next person. After a half dozen more calls, I ended up with a book manufacturer in New Jersey and dealt with a terrific company representative. I told him up front that I had no idea what I was doing, knew nothing about publishing or the proper terminology involved, but I had seven children's picture books that I wanted to print and could he give me prices. He worked with me and put up with my naivete. I would send things off and he would call me back and nicely say, "I really need a mechanical," and I would say, "what's a mechanical?"

The rep kept telling me as we got into the printing process that he would turn me over to someone else. He never did. When we finally met face-to-face after the books were on press, he confessed that no one else would take me because I knew so little and they thought he was a little nuts to have agreed to the project. The company runs its presses twenty-four hours a day, seven days a week, if I hadn't come through on schedule it would have been costly to them. It's people like that, who are willing to take a chance on you, that make it possible to succeed in this business.

A contact through my kid's school led me to a graphic designer in my neighborhood. This designer was actually willing to meet me at home amid six children, fixing dinner, construction workers ripping out windows, and my carpool schedule. Things were moving very fast now.

At the same time I was speaking with printers and graphic designers, I was setting up my publishing company. This mostly involved meeting with a lawyer to do the paperwork, picking a name, setting up a bank account, ordering stationery, business cards, and starting to focus on my bookkeeping. After studying the options, I chose to incorporate, although an individual proprietorship would have worked fine. Once again my book on self-publishing dealt with a lot of these issues.

The self-publishing book helped me to find out what needed to be included in my book to make it acceptable to the bookstore market. Particularly useful were the tips on having correct copyright information, ordering ISBN numbers, and the importance of ordering bar code scanner bars. The expense of self-publishing is too great not to take the extra steps to make it marketable.

It was the first of July 1990 when I made the decision to publish the books myself. Although I had decided on a 1991 copyright for the books in order to give myself time for promotion, I wanted the books published before Christmas 1990 so I could do some pre-publication mail order business to defray some of the costs that were building up.

The book manufacturer needed six to seven weeks for printing and binding. I had agreed to get everything to them by the second week of October and they agreed to have the books to me by Thanksgiving. It was about mid-September when it hit me that doing the final editing, layout, and cover design for seven books at once could make a person a little crazy. I had no idea how many steps would be involved and how many decisions would have to be made. It wasn't just choosing type, I had to decide how it would fit on each page, cover design, picking the artwork and deciding on the color of the book, picking end papers. This was a whole new creative process.

We kept Federal Express busy for the first three weeks in October as color separations and blueprints went back and forth between New Jersey and Long Island. Inger, my graphic designer, helped me learn to read the "blues" and showed me what to look for. By the third set, I felt confident enough to look at them alone.

As the end of October neared, I was notified that I needed to start being "on press" in New Jersey at 8 a.m. October 31. I panicked. How could a mother of six be gone on Halloween? My mind filled with scenes of my children and their therapist at twenty-five: "It was all because she left me on

Halloween when I was five—she didn't care enough to see me in my pumpkin costume." The guilt was overwhelming. After a significant amount of begging and whining, I got the schedule changed and the manufacturer let me come on November 1.

The next six days were like walking into a new life. The people working for my manufacturer, from the receptionist to the pressmen, were terrific. I was able to spend a lot of time sitting and listening to other people who had come for press approvals. People who actually seemed to know what they were doing. The first time they brought out a sheet for my approval, they laid it out on the table and said, "What do you think?" "Well," I said, "it looks pretty good to me." Then my education began as I was made aware of all the things I should be looking for, such as little holes, color variations, etc. It was amazing to me that they could do so much on press. After I had initially sent the books to the manufacturer, I had designed my mail order flyer and had it printed. I now used my waiting time to address the mailers. I also used this time to do the bulk of my Christmas shopping by catalog and over the phone. I wasn't really used to sitting so much and even though I was getting up really early, I'd be bouncing off the walls when I got home at night. I even got to have leisurely lunches—something relatively foreign to most stay-home mothers. At home, my husband, my housekeeper, and friends drove my carpools and kept up with my house and kids. Being away from the kids and that part of my life was then, and still is, the hardest part of the business for me. I want to be both places at once—but it's just not possible.

The day before Thanksgiving I received 1,000 copies of each book on my front porch. I had printed 5,000 copies of each book, but the manufacturer rep I had been dealing with convinced me that I should store the other 30,000 books with the company until I needed them. I had no real concept of how much space 35,000 books took. I had them moved to the basement of my home and then had the unmatched pleasure and satisfaction of holding my books. It's hard to describe how you feel when you actually see the finished product with your name on it. As my children would say, "it was awesome!"

I had told myself that I wouldn't market the books, other than through mail order, until after Christmas. Christmas is a really special time in our home with lots of traditions, and I was way behind in "creating those childhood memories."

Once again, I knew absolutely nothing about how to market the books. The only thing I can really compare it to is having a baby. No matter how much people tell you or how many books you read, nothing prepares you for the joys and frustrations of having a baby other than living through it one day at a time. If I had known then what I know now about all that would be involved with marketing and distributing the books, I might never have started. I somehow just trusted and believed it would all work out.

Regardless of the vow I had made not to do any additional marketing, I just couldn't resist going to my two local bookstores. I was dying to see if I could sell the books, and I wanted to see them on a store shelf. So with the baby on my hip and a diaper bag containing a copy of each book, I went to meet my first appointment.

I hadn't really planned to take the baby, Max, but my sitter cancelled and I didn't want to take a chance on cancelling my appointment and not being able to get another one. I was nervous. The owner came out and I proceeded to empty my diaper bag of books as Max began removing books from the shelves of the store. It was truly a ridiculous scene as I tried to give my sales pitch while chasing Max around the store. Coreen, the owner of "Oscars" in Huntington, was great. She had children of her own. She bought two copies of each book and explained to me the basic guidelines of discounting to bookstores. I went out to the car, got the books and she handed me a check. It was a real high, and I found I couldn't stop with just one bookstore.

Right after Christmas, my husband and I took all the kids to Florida for a few days. While they swam and played on the beach, I went to six bookstores in the Miami area. Once again, they all ordered books.

I decided it was time to approach one of the major bookstore chains, so I put calls into both Walden and B. Dalton. The local stores wouldn't even give me an appointment; they said everything had to go through the main office.

Most of the bookstores I had seen were small, individually owned stores. Although the people were willing to buy directly from me, they almost always asked if the books were available at Baker & Taylor or Ingram. Baker & Taylor and Walden were both within two hours of driving from my house, so I decided to start there.

When I called Walden the women said, "You're not doing this out of your kitchen, are you? I mean, we have 1,000 stores!" I said, "Oh no," hung up and looked at my husband. "I'm not going to tell her I'm doing it out of the kitchen." But the bottom line was that I realized that even if I got an order from a large chain that it would be virtually impossible for me to fill it out of my basement.

I called Baker & Taylor and made an appointment with a wonderful woman who dealt with the children's books. She was very positive about the books, but also explained that Baker & Taylor wasn't really what I needed. She said Baker & Taylor was a wholesaler and what I really needed was a distributor with a sales force out there knocking on doors. As I sat there wondering what to do next, she told me she had a friend who was a distributor and that she thought these would be perfect for him. With that, she picked up the phone and told his office to have him call her in the next twenty minutes.

She then sent this distributor copies of my books and told me to give him a couple of days and then call—if it didn't work out to call her back and she'd see what she could do next. It required persistence, but a week later I met with Eric Kampmann. He explained that he handled distribution for National Book Network, a Maryland-based distributor with a national sales force. He read the books, showed them to his own kids, then called me back and said he was interested.

After a couple of meetings and some negotiating I signed a contract with NBN to handle all bookstore distribution. I kept specialty store, catalog sales, a few other rights for myself. I couldn't give up total control! It was a relief to give up the bookstores. I had begun scheduling talks at schools, book signings, and a couple of promotional trips to Miami and Dallas. I was having a hard time just keeping up with the dozen stores I had.

Eric didn't handle a lot of children's books and so suggested that I meet with someone who could put together a marketing plan for me. It was only at this time that I began to truly understand what I had gotten myself into. I had done a promotional trip to Dallas and gotten a number of nice articles in the local papers, and I had a nice article in Long Island Parenting —I thought things were moving along pretty well.

Soon my marketing education began when I met with a consultant who had been involved in various areas of children's publishing and selling for twenty years. Library market, reviews, "pub" dates, ABA —a whole new world was opening up and I had to decide whether to promote and market the books all out or go back to selling store-by-store. Advertising, marketing, and conventions are expensive items. It was time for a real business plan that would show me what it would actually take to promote the books like a regular publishing house would and when I could reasonably expect to make money.

It was pointed out to me the importance of continuing to publish three to four books a year to keep up the momentum. In devising a business plan, my marketing consultant asked if I was going to publish only my books or was I interested in taking on other people's books. I really didn't know. I wasn't sure I wanted the risk or responsibility of publishing another person's material, but it became clear that it would be financially difficult to only publish thirty-two page, full-color picture books and make money.

Finally, we arrived at a plan that involved publishing twenty books in 1992: four of mine and sixteen others, varying in audience age-range and price range. We decided to begin moving forward. I now had a distributor, a marketing team, a publicity person, and the American Booksellers Association convention coming up in June.

My husband had reserved me a booth at the ABA months before. This was going to be my first real opportunity to show the books to a mass market. Although I had resisted going to the ABA, he insisted. As usual, he was right. Before the convention Sally Hertz & Associates sent out promotional materials to 400 children's bookstores.

The ABA was a fun and exciting experience. Not only were people incredibly positive about the books, but I had a chance to see what else was coming out in 1991, to begin meeting other people in the business, and to start looking at products Whispering Coyote Press can publish in 1992.

Things haven't slowed down yet. Since the convention, I've booked four more stores for signings, scheduled a trip to London to look at product there, had books listed two weeks in a row in New York Magazine's children's section, sent out 2,500 follow-up promotional letters to bookstores, and approved the next set of press releases that will announce my sixth and seventh books' publication dates.

I don't know where this new venture will lead me. I think I'm best off continuing to deal with it one day at a time. There are days filled with fun and excitement and days filled with exhaustion and frustration—but it's never boring. I look forward to seeing where life leads me next.

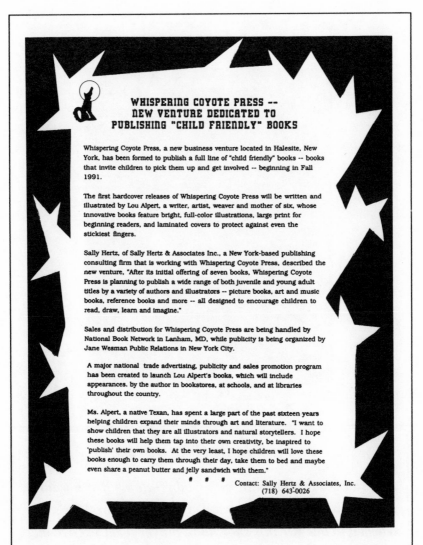

WHISPERING COYOTE PRESS -- NEW VENTURE DEDICATED TO PUBLISHING "CHILD FRIENDLY" BOOKS

Whispering Coyote Press, a new business venture located in Halesite, New York, has been formed to publish a full line of "child friendly" books -- books that invite children to pick them up and get involved -- beginning in Fall 1991.

The first hardcover releases of Whispering Coyote Press will be written and illustrated by Lou Alpert, a writer, artist, weaver and mother of six, whose innovative books feature bright, full-color illustrations, large print for beginning readers, and laminated covers to protect against even the stickiest fingers.

Sally Hertz, of Sally Hertz & Associates Inc., a New York-based publishing consulting firm that is working with Whispering Coyote Press, described the new venture, "After its initial offering of seven books, Whispering Coyote Press is planning to publish a wide range of both juvenile and young adult titles by a variety of authors and illustrators -- picture books, art and music books, reference books and more -- all designed to encourage children to read, draw, learn and imagine."

Sales and distribution for Whispering Coyote Press are being handled by National Book Network in Lanham, MD, while publicity is being organized by Jane Wesman Public Relations in New York City.

A major national trade advertising, publicity and sales promotion program has been created to launch Lou Alpert's books, which will include appearances. by the author in bookstores, at schools, and at libraries throughout the country.

Ms. Alpert, a native Texan, has spent a large part of the past sixteen years helping children expand their minds through art and literature. "I want to show children that they are all illustrators and natural storytellers. I hope these books will help them tap into their own creativity, be inspired to 'publish' their own books. At the very least, I hope children will love these books enough to carry them through their day, take them to bed and maybe even share a peanut butter and jelly sandwich with them."

Contact: Sally Hertz & Associates, Inc.
                          (718) 643-0026

Joan Wester Anderson

And so I made a bargain with God. "Tell me if you want me to be a writer," I commanded (over the years, He's learned to tolerate this shorthand prayer form.) "Give me a sign—two quick sales if it's 'yes,'"

chapter 3

Two Quick Sales and I Became a Writer

by Joan Wester Anderson

I was always going to write "someday"—when the kids grew up, the goldfish died, or I got my can goods arranged in alphabetical order. I know now that my excuse was simply fear; if we can avoid testing ourselves, we can avoid the possibility of failure—and hang on to our dreams indefinitely. "Someday" was a secure place to stay....

Until something happened that propelled me to the typewriter. We moved, to a handyman-special house. Only later did my husband and I realize that the house did not come with a resident handyman. Each square inch of it needed attention, including the bilious mustard-colored paint covering almost every wall (somehow I hadn't noticed this during our initial inspection). One thing was certain: We were going to need plenty of extra cash. My husband was doing a yeoman's job supporting what had just become a seven-person family, and I couldn't ask him to work any harder. I, on the other hand, was simply lying around the house looking after four small boys and a newborn daughter; I had plenty of time.

And so I made a bargain with God. "Tell me if you want me to be a writer," I commanded (over the years, He's learned to tolerate this shorthand prayer form.) "Give me a sign—two quick sales if it's 'yes,'" I then sat down and dashed off two family humor pieces, one to a diaper service magazine, another to a reader-generated column in a Chicago newspaper. Within a month, I had two checks for $25 each. It seemed a princely sum in 1974.

Visions of House Beautiful danced before my eyes. And after our abode was stripped of mustard yellow for all eternity, I could provide college educations for the entire neighborhood... but it didn't work like that. God had certainly honored my plea in His usual indulgent fashion, but I soon came face-to-face with the reality of the publishing world I had so blithely entered. I collected twelve rejection slips before I got my third sale, and another eight or nine before I managed to place number four.

Somehow, however, this was all right. Because I had been graced with two immediate sales, I was able to work my way through the feelings and doubts that often cripple a novice, making her conclude that she probably ought to pursue a degree in accounting instead. That first and second sale, in short, were the touchstones that propelled me through the "no's" and helped me believe that another "yes" was just around the corner.

Since those days, some sixteen years ago, I have published seven books and almost 1,000 articles and short stories. My work has appeared in many of the major women's magazines, as well as Reader's Digest and obscure religious periodicals. For ten years, I juggled two monthly columns, one for which I still write. I have a busy lecture schedule providing humor talks on family life to women's clubs and convention wives. At a local junior college, I teach beginners to market their free-lance writing, and give one-day seminars on the same subject on request. In short, without actually planning it, my temporary quest to beautify my environment turned into a permanent lifestyle.

Very few of these steps were planned or even anticipated—on the contrary, I seemed to lurch along on a rather bumpy and often perilous track.

"Let's write a book together." "Can you come and speak to our organization?" "We need a teacher on humor writing for the conference." And the phrase most dear to any writer's heart: "We would like to assign our lead article in the June issue to you..." I kept responding, "why not?" then racing like mad to catch up, and learn to do what people kept assuming I already knew how to do. And, in the trying, I became knowledgeable in those very areas.

Thus, when sharing ideas about the publishing world, especially with you the novice, I find myself falling back on the importance of those first sales— and my wholehearted belief that this is what you must try to do first: See yourself in print. Never mind that your byline appears in Gerbil Digest or the American Journal of Cereal; it's a sale, complete with a tiny paycheck, and it allows you to glimpse at yourself with a subtly-altered perspective: If I did it once (or thrice), I can certainly do it again.

This viewpoint, in turn, begins to carry you through the lean days when the mailbox bulges with "no's," when your idea font has dried up, when you made a mistake and an editor is angry, when no one answers your queries and when you don't know how to change the printer ribbon. It carries you through when you hear that voice whispering inside you, "It's a fraud—and what if the world finds out?" You get through all of it—and more. Why? Because it isn't a fraud. The sales prove it, after all. You are no longer would-be, it is no longer "someday." You have begun. So do whatever it takes to get your byline into print, and your hands on a little check. Scrutinize "Writer's Market," and look for the small periodicals, the ones that pay a few cents a word; there's less competition there, and at this point, you don't care about the money or the fame. Yes, maybe your college English professor told you to submit your short story to Redbook. But Redbook gets about 20,000 unsolicited fiction submissions every year, and may buy twelve or fifteen (professors don't usually know this). And you need better odds. You need a sale.

Write it to the best of your ability, and then send it out. This step is very important, for novices seldom know when something has been done as well as it can be, seldom are willing to turn their literary child into the cold cruel world. I critiqued a clever article for a student at a conference in 1989. With a few minor changes, I told her it would have a good chance at being accepted. In 1990, I met the same woman at the same conference. She was still working on the same article. This is not the way to become published. Let it go and get on to your next piece. The odds increase with each submission floating around Magazine Land.

And when you get that sale, buy a gallon of paint, like I did. Or frame the check. Or make copies and show them to your relatives, the ones that said you'd never amount to anything as a writer. But most important, get another sale, as soon as you can. Because like bricks building a house, each "yes" increases your confidence, gives you the impetus to take a chance on something new, to say "why not?" to a suggestion you hadn't considered until now, to run like crazy to catch up and learn to do what the world thinks you already can do.

There will be time, someday, to hone your markets, to specialize, to make contacts, move up, target carefully written query letters, branch out into speaking or teaching or column-writing. There will be time to catch your breath (at least for a few minutes) and decide where you'd like to go from here. But as for now, your job is clear: You have to get published first, before any of these other good things can happen.

So go ahead and do it. Millions have, and you can too. It just takes an idea, a piece of paper, a deep breath, and a beginning line. The rest will surely come if you keep at it. Do. And we'll be watching for your byline!

Joan Wester Anderson
811 N. Hickory
Arlington Heights IL 60004
(708) 394-9598

Wife and mother of five, ages 29 through 18.

Born Evanston IL, attended Chicago-area schools and Mount
  Mary College, Milwaukee WI

1973 Began a "temporary" kitchen-table freelance writing
     career. Has since sold over 900 articles and short
     stories, covering family topics, how-to, humor and
     Christian themes. Features have appeared in McCall's,
     Family Circle, Modern Bride, Income Opportunities,
     Christian Science Monitor and many others.

1976 The first of seven books, Love, Lollipops and Laundry
     was published (OSV Press), followed in 1979 by Stop the
     World--Our Gerbils are Loose! (Doubleday), both co-
     authored collections of family humor. The Best of Both
     Worlds, A Guide to Homebased Careers (Betterway 1982),
     Dear World, Don't Spin so Fast (Abbey Press, 1983) and
     Teen is a Four-Letter Word (Betterway, 1984) followed;
     Teen was re-released in 1990 in a second edition.
         As Jeanne Anders, two Christian paperback romances:
     The Language of the Heart (Zondervan 1985) and Leslie
     (Bethany 1987)

1979 Began two monthly columns: "Your Baby," a how-to health
     feature for True Confessions, discontinued in 1988, and
     "Hangin' In There with Joan," a humor commentary for
     Marriage and Family, still running.

1979 Launched a public speaking sideline as a result of local
     media appearances. Spoke in Chicago exclusively until
     1981. Represented by The Leigh Bureau, 1981-86, Potomac
     Speakers Bureau 1986-, American Program Bureau, 1989-.
     Offers humorous speeches on marriage and family.

Frequent guest on media, including The Today Show, The 700
Club, local and national radio talk shows. Adjunct Professor
at Harper Junior College in Palatine IL, teaching Write to
Publish!; teaches publishing classes regularly at library and
writing seminars. Active in church, school and community
affairs.

Member of the American Society of Journalists and Authors.

Becky Barker

She, who at the time was a housewife, pretty much grabbed me and said, "Wake up and smell the coffee. There's a whole country out there who needs this book!"

chapter **4**

How I Arrived at My "answers."

by Becky Barker (as told to Paula DuPont-Kidd)

I had no knowledge of the publishing business whatsoever. I didn't do any research before I started out, didn't ask for anyone's advice, didn't care about profits, after all, I was just going to "put together" twenty workbooks for my family and friends as Christmas gifts in 1980.

In October 1980, my husband was killed by someone who chose to drink and drive. My two daughters were also in the car, one critically injured. Between dealing with the pain of my husband's death and the recovery of my children, I found myself totally unprepared to handle all the questions and decisions that were plaguing my life. My husband had handled everything: our money, insurance, bills, bank accounts, etc. "I don't know" became my standard reply whenever I was asked a question about our business and personal finances.

All I knew in November 1980 was that I wanted my family and friends to avoid the experience I was encountering—being totally unprepared to handle the practical side of a crisis situation. I searched bookstores and office supply stores for some sort of workbook that would allow my family and friends to prepare ahead for an inevitable event. I wasn't trying to be morbid, it's just that I knew then, as I do now, that I was not the only person who would find herself in this confusion. Someday these dear people in my life were going to face what I faced.

There was no such book on the market, so I decided to make one. I bought loose-leaf binders at the grocery store and bought pocket folders, which I cut down and labelled, indicating the status of such household information and family information such as property, insurance, finances and business. My book became a workbook to be completed and could be updated annually and could hold virtually all the answers needed for a family crisis situation. After all, we plan for all the major events in our lives—weddings, birthdays, vacations—why don't we prepare for the one event that is not an *if,* but a *when?*

How did "answers." get from under the Christmas tree and into bookstores?

The response to that initial book was so positive and inspiring that I was more or less forced to print more copies for all the people who had seen the book and requested it. People I didn't know were calling me, telling me they'd seen my book and would like to order it for themselves or friends.

In the spring of 1981, I used $10,000 of insurance money to self-publish 1,000 copies. I never expected it to go very far. All I wanted to do was to help these people who loved their own families enough to want to buy this book and prepare it for them. I still wasn't thinking of profit—more of an "at cost" service. But I couldn't afford three-ring binders at the retail price (never even occurred to me to contact a binder company directly). I took the book out of the binders and into spiral binding. An advertising agency coordinated the layouts, typesetting, and printing with a few instructions from me.

I could handle the costs to this point, but this workbook had to be hand-assembled because of the binding, pocket folders, and dividers. The labor charges blew me out of the water. No problem, I could buy a spiral hole puncher and binder and 1,000 rings and do all the work myself and stay within budget. I didn't have anything else to do but cry and sleep. Those first books cost about $8.50 per unit to publish and $9.95 was all I felt I could charge—after all, it was just a book of questions with space to write each family's unique answers. I never realized how long it would take to assemble all the boxes of printed material into a finished product. Nor did anyone else who volunteered to help with "Becky's little project."

Name and direction for "Becky's little project"

I have my mother and all her wisdom to thank for the title of my workbook. Like most writers, I spent painstaking hours in my head trying to come up with a poignant name for this book. At one point, I churned out several ideas to my mother over a long-distance phone call, each long title containing the word answers. I'm not sure if she was just weary of my complicated semantics or if the title was clear to her, but she blurted, "Just call it answers period." (Thanks mom, it worked.) The name of the book then and now is "answers."

Most of the books sold by word-of-mouth. At that point, I still hadn't really thought to make money—certainly not a living—printing this book. There were times I didn't want people to call—my hands hurt from punching the heavy stock paper that I had insisted on.

A lot has changed since then and largely through the help and guidance of others. I formed a business partnership with my sister, Suzi Hart, in June 1983. A major part of the success of "answers." is due to her drive and determination. This was a time for me when I needed to go back to work financially, and emotionally. She, who at the time was a housewife, pretty much grabbed me and said, "Wake up and smell the coffee. There's a whole country out there who needs this book!"

We were off and running. Well, for a while we sat and finished putting together the rest of those books, making plans and sharing goals and dreaming of the day when we would have offices instead of my spare bedroom and how we would react when Phil Donahue's staff would call to book us on his show.

We placed the remaining books into a local gift shop and appeared on the local morning talk program and began revising "answers." for its new printing and its first launch for profit.

Instincts made good business sense

When we look back now, we find that a lot of our instincts made good business sense without realizing it at the time. We followed our intuition and when we found ourselves going the wrong direction down a one-way street, we just backed up and tried another street.

We weren't happy with the format of the book. The fact that it was bound prohibited new pages from being added. After all, the original concept for the book was for it to be a source-book that could be updated and added to by the individual to meet his or her changing needs. Back to the three-ring binder. The bookstores hated us (and probably still do) because "answers." didn't stack neatly on a shelf. This did not affect us too much because we weren't in this to please the bookstores, we had families and their needs to think about. This proved a good move as the public loved the three-ring binder.

Nothing but common sense told us to be sure and use large print because some of the consumers would be elderly, who often have trouble reading smaller print. When the first twenty books were made, of course the print was black, and the plain binders available at the grocery store were black, gray, and red. When the first 1,000 were printed I decided to steer clear of black for the cover and pages; buyers might associate it too much with death and find it morbid. For this reason, I chose royal blue ink on white pages. I wanted every aspect of the design of the book, particularly the colors to convey a more positive tone. To me, the book *is* positive because it gives people a sense of security and organization. Suzi and I stayed with the blue.

Revisions made, we wanted to be thorough in our approach and make sure we had all our bases covered in regard to content. We sought feedback from professionals. We talked to attorneys, real estate brokers, insurance agents, stock brokers, bankers and even car dealers to make sure nothing was missing.

Because we wanted a quality product that would stand the test of time, we chose to use heavy stock paper, which could be more easily erased as information was updated. It cost more, but we knew in the end it would pay off. Another good move, as we found people are willing to pay for quality.

We were as conscious as the next person with trying to pay the least for the best quality. In shopping for a printer, we once again followed our instincts and didn't go with the cheapest bid. Checking out printers in Texas and a couple out of state was interesting. We made personal visits to as many as possible. If they had trouble putting their hands on paper samples we wanted to see, they were crossed off our list. If their desks looked like ours, we crossed them off our list. Probably not a sound reason, but if we didn't like the way they "looked," they got the big "X."

Of course, personalities played a significant role too, because we had to like the people, knowing that we would be working closely together to successfully publish "answers.," our baby. This project was going to require the printer's special attention. We found just what we were looking for at the Premier Company in Houston, a well-organized and meticulous printer, willing to afford the care needed on producing a book comprised of pages and folders intermixed, which had to be hand-collated and inserted into a three-ring binder. We have never regretted our relationship with Premier. From printing to warehousing, to handling fulfillment, to printing an occasional mail order piece, they always give 110 percent.

Making the most of opportunities

Using our instincts saved us from many expensive mistakes and propelled us to make the most of opportunities. We made some mistakes, after all, self-publishing was new to us and we were learning as we went along.

During the time we revised and printed runs of 5,000 and 10,000, we tried to sell to distributors like Baker & Taylor and Ingram. Neither was interested. They didn't want to deal with "single-title" publishing companies. Instead, we did a lot of footwork, selling the book one-on-one to bookstores. Not the ideal way of handling sales, they are slow in paying. We did manage to place the book with a couple of small regional distributors. One would only take it on a consignment basis, but we were desperate. Bad move. We wouldn't place any books anywhere on consignment ever again!

By this time, we were into offices, had hired one of the best secretaries on the face of the earth, and were using the skills of two friends who were paid on a commission basis. One was great with contact and "angles" and one was great with putting together press kits.

In 1984, we made a call to a "Good Morning America" producer. We sent a letter with a copy of "answers." that said in so many words, "Take a look and give us a call." And, they did. We could never have predicted the kind of response that would follow. According to a source at "Good Morning America," they had the largest number of viewer responses for my segment than any other with the exception of Jill St. John, who appeared regularly with cooking segments. That response led them to book me for another appearance within a couple of months from the first.

This would seem a fantasy for an author trying to sell books, except for one thing: the books weren't readily available in nationwide bookstores. We were aware of these limitations, but we had to gamble with our instincts and take the cart before the horse. Another good move. While "Good Morning America" wouldn't or couldn't give out our address over the air, they did slip viewers some helpful clues such as "Becky Barker and her new book business mail order out of Corpus Christi." It didn't take the local post office long to figure out all the strange mail addressed to "Becky, Betty, Beverly, Publisher, Book, or answers" belonged to us. We were thrilled, but frustrated, knowing the potential of other buyers who couldn't find us in the bookstore and didn't remember where we lived. Despite this frustration, "Good Morning America" opened other doors.

A few months later, Suzi and I went to the American Booksellers Association convention in Washington, D.C. We set up a booth to sell our book and hopefully get the attention of some book buyers or distributors. This was when we really discovered the impact of my TV appearance. Bookstore owners came up to me and said, "Here you are, we've been looking for you for months." This kind of response to our book would have been enough to make our trip to Washington a success, except we were still dealing with individual bookstore owners. If we wanted to get the book out nationwide, which the market seemed to be receptive to, we needed a distributor.

So, naturally, our next move was "crashing" a private cocktail party in town thrown by Ingram. Actually, we weren't totally uninvited, we went as guests of someone who was invited. As we tried to blend in as invited guests, Suzi looked up and the chairman of the board of Ingram was standing there. She took a deep breath, said a prayer, and "went in for the kill."

"Did you know that your company does not carry my sister's book, 'answers.,' a book that generated the highest number of phone calls from 'Good Morning America' viewers than any other guest spot on that show?" It was a short conversation, but it proved effective.

The next morning, back at the convention, a vice president from Ingram paid a visit to our booth, inquiring about *our* terms. That began a successful relationship with Ingram. We happened to be in the right place at the right time and unfortunately, many times it isn't the quality or the material of a book that predicts its future, talking to just the right person on just the right day at just the right time plays an important role. There are too many titles every month competing for shelf space in the bookstore. Bookstores don't want to order a book through an individual, they want a distributor where orders for many titles can be placed. Once Ingram began carrying "answers.," the other major distributor, Baker & Taylor began listing us. And, fortunately, I have had two other cracks at the "Good Morning America" audience, with a total of four appearances.

That first appearance, in 1984, has led to appearances on nearly every talk show between New York and Los Angeles. I have appeared on "Donahue," the "Today Show," "Hour Magazine," and the Lifetime Channel's "Regis Philbin Show." Television exposure is great and fairly easy to obtain if you will remember one thing: the purpose in appearing is not to "hawk" your book, you are there to provide information and help to the audience. The book sales will follow!

By far, the best responses with regard to media have been from print articles. We have had three beneficial articles written about us in *Guideposts, Better Homes and Gardens,* and *The New York Times.* Even though these articles are now years old, they still generate orders for us, with *Guideposts'* article clearly being the leader in resulting book sales.

Media attention aside, the biggest breakthroughs in publishing seem to have come from the ABA conventions. We landed a book co-publishing contract with Harper & Row (now Harper/Collins) as a result of the convention we attended in New Orleans in 1986. Like the valuable connections we'd made before, this one did not land in our laps.

We had been looking for a distributor to handle the Christian book market and we had been told that Harper & Row did a good job in this area. We made contact and the next thing we knew the director of marketing wanted to know if we could talk, not about distributing to the Christian market, but working out a publishing arrangement. After several months of negotiating, we finally arrived at contract terms agreeable to all of us. We didn't use an agent, we already had a publisher interested, but we did rely heavily on the advice of our trustworthy attorney and accountant. We would have made some costly mistakes without them.

One bad move we made at our first ABA convention was using an outside consultant to help in the designing and setting up of our booth that very first year. It cost us a small fortune and she didn't do anything that we couldn't have done on our own. A better move would have been to talk with several other small publishers who had booths in previous years.

Since Harper & Row signed on "answers." in 1987, it has progressed to its fifth printing and is considered in the trade to be an "evergreen" book. Evergreen means that the book will stay in bookstores for an indefinite period of time because it can continue to sell for years.

Was the decision to quit self-publishing a wise move? It's a gray area. On our own, we published and sold more than 56,000 copies. Harper/Collins has certainly toppled that mark, but no one will ever be as interested in our book as we are. Even though they promoted us heavily initially and continue to publish "answers.," we are considered "old hat" to them and any further promotion will come from our work and not theirs. We can generate the interest but Harper/Collins is in total control of the distribution. We pull our hair out every time we get a letter from someone who says, "I cannot find 'answers.' in the local bookstores." Of course, if a bookstore doesn't stock it, they can certainly order it for the customer—unfortunately most bookstore employees aren't trained to service the customer. This is by far our biggest frustration.

Despite the book's success and status, I'm no Danielle Steele and "answers." won't compete with the Bible in sales. We are luckier than many self-publishers with one book still selling after ten years. However, it takes a lot of books to make money and it takes a lot of money to sell books. People are always remarking about all the fame and fortune we have received. Suzi and I both laugh—we could use a lot less of fame and a lot more fortune! Don't go into publishing to get rich—your odds are probably better winning the lottery.

We have made some good moves and some bad moves in our publishing career. But here we are today, being published by Harper/Collins, with a retail price of $24.95 and "answers." can be found in just about any bookstore in the country. "answers." is also a main component of my speaking engagements, a primary source of income. Sharing my story with others has been good therapy for me but because I re-live the tragedy each time I speak, I also have to withdraw from it at times.

For me, the success of my career is not measured by how much money I make from the book, but rather the people whose awareness I've sparked.

My very motivation from the beginning is still my motivation now, loved ones faced with the grief of someone's death should not have to compound their despair with untangling legal and financial matters.

Our book, "answers." hasn't been the solution to all of my questions or problems. It doesn't brighten my wash, improve my tennis game, or help me deal with raising two teenage girls. But it has been an experience that I wouldn't trade for anything else. I have met people from all walks of life, from all parts of country, from the mega-personalities in TV to everyday folks, like Suzi and me. Publishing has provided this opportunity. For as long as life remains complicated, people will search to simplify it, hopefully with "answers."

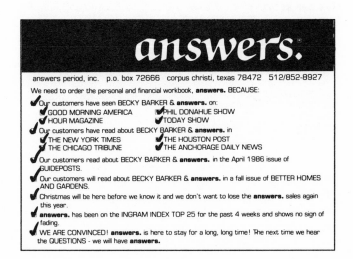

answers.

answers period, inc.   p.o. box 72666   corpus christi, texas 78472   512/852-8927

We need to order the personal and financial workbook, **answers.** BECAUSE:

✓ Our customers have seen BECKY BARKER & **answers.** on:
  ✓ GOOD MORNING AMERICA   ✓ PHIL DONAHUE SHOW
  ✓ HOUR MAGAZINE   ✓ TODAY SHOW

✓ Our customers have read about BECKY BARKER & **answers.** in
  ✓ THE NEW YORK TIMES   ✓ THE HOUSTON POST
  ✓ THE CHICAGO TRIBUNE   ✓ THE ANCHORAGE DAILY NEWS

✓ Our customers read about BECKY BARKER & **answers.** in the April 1986 issue of GUIDEPOSTS.

✓ Our customers will read about BECKY BARKER & **answers.** in a fall issue of BETTER HOMES AND GARDENS.

✓ Christmas will be here before we know it and we don't want to lose the **answers.** sales again this year.

✓ **answers.** has been on the INGRAM INDEX TOP 25 for the past 4 weeks and shows no sign of fading.

✓ WE ARE CONVINCED! **answers.** is here to stay for a long, long time! The next time we hear the QUESTIONS - we will have **answers.**

answers.

answers period, inc.   p. o. box 72666   corpus christi, texas 78472   (512) 852-8927

QUANTITY DISCOUNT

answers.
ISBN 0-06-859808-4
Retail Price: $24.95

QUANTITY DISCOUNT GIVEN ON CASES ONLY, 16 BOOKS PER CASE.

40% OFF RETAIL
$239.52 PER CASE
18.48 POSTAGE, HANDLING, INSURANCE

$258.00 TOTAL

* TEXAS RESIDENTS PLEASE ADD AN ADDITIONAL $17.96 SALES TAX

* 1/2 OF TOTAL BALANCE DUE WITH ORDER. REMAINING BALANCE
TO BE PAID WITHIN 10 DAYS OF DELIVERY.

* PLEASE ALLOW 2 TO 3 WEEKS FOR DELIVERY.

A Practical Survival Kit
To Help You Organize Your Personal
and Financial Matters

* Prices effective April I, 1990.

answers.

answers period, inc.   p. o. box 72666   corpus christi, texas 78472   (512) 852-8927

In 1980, Becky Barker was the typical American housewife, caring for her husband and two young daughters in a casual, Texas lifestyle. Life was good. In a matter of seconds, her world was turned upside down when Billy was killed by a speeding, intoxicated driver.

Becky felt the jagged reality of being ill-prepared for personal emergency when she was called upon to answer the many questions following Billy's death......

"Where was the will?" "Keys to the safe-deposit box?" "Insurance policies?" "What income would there be?" "What debts were there?"

The list goes on. Thus begins her remarkable story...

Sifting through all the confusion, pain, and grief, she slowly began putting her life back together, not realizing how a handmade Christmas gift in 1980 would change her life.

Becky Barker in 1990, is president of answers period, inc., a single-title publishing company responsible for the creation of the personal and financial workbook, <u>answers.</u>, a family organizer that is now being co-published with Harper & Row Publishers, Inc.

Becky has told her story to millions, appearing four times on GOOD MORNING AMERICA, two appearances on HOUR MAGAZINE, and has also been a guest on THE TODAY SHOW and THE PHIL DONAHUE SHOW, as well as countless talk shows across the country. Articles have appeared in BETTER HOMES AND GARDENS and GUIDEPOSTS magazines.

From housewife to publisher, talk show guest, public speaker, and time-juggling mommy, Becky has grown through the years, learning through her experiences. Terribly shy as a child, she now speaks before hundreds and surprises herself that she is able to do so without fear. She still has many goals to reach but is proud that something good has developed out of a tragedy. She has learned to live again, laugh again, and love again -- a very different person from the woman in 1980 who stood in the shower screaming that life was so unfair.

Jean Horton Berg

Hooray! Because of my experiences I really believe I'm a writer. And I like it. Also, I believe my work in the field helps me to help students in my workshops. And I like that, too.

chapter 5

Write from the Beginning

by Jean Horton Berg

I learned to read when I was about three and a half. My mother had a studio in our house where she made designs for painted china. I spent a lot of time there with her. I still love the smell of turpentine. I had blocks to play with and I loved to look at the pictures on the blocks. One day mother gave me new blocks. I couldn't figure out what the pictures were. "They're pictures of sounds," mother said.

She held up one that looked like this: S. "That picture says 'ess', " mother said.

"What does this say?" I held up an "L."

"It says 'lllllllll'," mother answered.

I had a great time sounding out the letters. And before long I was reading.

About this time I began to exaggerate a lot. (Lie.)

I'm grateful to my parents for not saying, "That was a big fat lie you just told!" They said, "Wow!" (or words to that effect) "That's some story. Why don't you print it out, and then we can all read it."

That's how I started. I'm grateful that my parents didn't make me feel guilty or embarrassed about these whoppers.

When I was in third grade I decided I was a writer. Our class had been assigned to write a poem. Mine, which cost me much time and effort, was:

There was a goat, a calf, a horse.
The horse's hair was kind of coarse.
The goat's hair was kind of wooly,
And the calf, too, felt a little bully.

I remember my teacher, Miss Chamberlin, very well. She said, "Jeanie, that's a real poem. It rhymes, and it has a good meter. You keep on writing."

So I did.

From that time on, I wrote. I never dreamed of having anything published in a book. But I wrote. I didn't save my early writings, but I wrote.

And I read everything I could lay my hands on. I read poetry and fiction—adult and juvenile. My father came home one night to find me reading "The Genius," a novel by the newly popular Theodore Dreiser. I was eight years old. My father put the book in the furnace. After that I took a flashlight to bed with me, and read under the covers. I didn't understand much in the books, but I loved the words.

And I kept on writing.

Many of my college professors encouraged me, and I began to feel at home writing. Still, I never considered it my profession. I majored in Latin and English with a minor in French, and prepared to teach.

I did teach Latin and English in a consolidated high school in southern Delaware. I taught for two years until my fiance finished dental school.

We married when he was an $80-a-month intern. But we weren't worried about money because I was going to get a job teaching Latin in the Philadelphia school system. I was pretty good in Latin, but not so bright about other things. For instance, I didn't bother to find out the requirements for teaching a language in Philadelphia. It was a real shock when I learned teachers had to take a special exam to teach a language in the city's school system! They were given in alternate years. And this was the off year. I couldn't teach.

I was frantic. Who could live on $80 a month?

"I'll have to get some kind of a job," I howled. But what? And where?

"Don't get so excited," Jack said. "You've been writing little things since you were a kid. Why don't you stay home and write three hours a day—five days a week. Treat it like a job. Don't do anything during those three hours but write. And act as if you're going to sell what you write to a magazine or a newspaper. I bet you'll like it."

That's how I started. And I was serious about it. I had loved all the writing I did in college, but I was writing to please a professor. Now I was writing to please an editor.

I began buying The Writer magazine, and Writer's Digest. There were good articles in the two, and lots of markets were listed. After several months of rejections I sold an article and a couple of verses.

This was very exciting, and the real beginning of my writing. I sold to a few other publications—Woman's Day and The Christian Science Monitor. I became a stringer for the Monitor, and continued in this area for some time. I sold a lot to juvenile magazines—stories, verses, and some nonfiction. And in due time I began to consider writing solely for juveniles. I really loved it.

After a few years I sent three short manuscripts to Grosset and Dunlap for possible publication in their Wonder Book series. They bought all three! Although I was pregnant with my third child, who could consider such an ordinary happening as a pregnancy when I had sold three manuscripts to a major publisher my first time at bat.

Well, I was now assured of constant success. I didn't have anything more to learn, I had arrived. And I tried very hard (not with unmitigated success, however) to be modest—well, fairly modest—and not to speak too loudly nor too often about how easy the whole thing was.

I was greatly helped in my efforts in modesty by getting nothing but rejections for the next two years. I sold very little—even to the magazines and newspapers that had been so friendly for so long. It finally dawned on me that I might not actually be God's great gift to readers, and that there were possibly a few things I might do well to study and to practice.

This I consider my real beginning. I was eager to learn what I began to realize was a craft as well as a profession. And I am grateful for and to editors all along the way who realized I really wanted to learn.

I learned to write and to rewrite with good grace. I was genuinely eager to do it properly. (And I learned I didn't have to be a stick in the mud to do it right.)

Margeurite de Angeli became my dear friend. She worked for a long time on her autobiography, "Butter At the Old Price."

One evening she telephoned me. "My dear," she said, her voice triumphant, "I've finally finished the book."

"Wonderful!" I said. "I'm so happy for you! Now you can take some time off."

"Time off?" she practically shouted. "Now I must go over the whole thing and get on with revisions and rewriting! I want it to be perfect, you know!"

I learned to understand and to appreciate what she meant. One of my books, "The O'Learys and Friends," I wrote in an afternoon, and never had to change a word. I sent it to Follett. They bought it immediately, and a couple of months later told me they had given it the Follett award for the best beginning-to-read book.

In contrast, "Miss Kirby's Room," bought by Westminster Press, took me nearly ten years to finish to my satisfaction. It did, however, become a First Cadmus book.

"Miss Tessie Tate," a story in verse about an old lady who won't do anything but roller skate, went to thirty-six publishers over a period of six years. Each time it came back I wept bitterly, and wanted to go behind the front door, and quietly slit my throat. Then I set to work to read it again and try to make it perfect. Finally, on the thirty-sixth time out it sold and eventually became a Junior Literary Guild selection!

Hooray! Because of my experiences I really believe I'm a writer. And I like it. Also, I believe my work in the field helps me to help students in my workshops. And I like that, too.

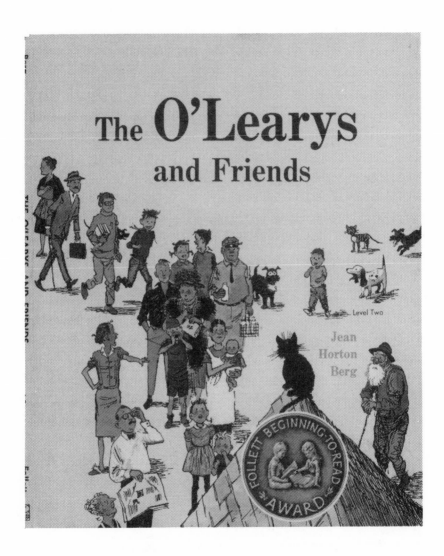

Jane Bluestein

I'll close with a quote from Goethe (hanging on my wall) and a wish for you for the persistence, resources, and guidance to happily and successfully fulfill your own mission: "Whatever you can do, or dream you can, begin it. Boldness has genius, power, and magic in it."

chapter 6

Don't Most Fourth Grade Teachers Turn Into Writers, National Speakers, and Publishers?

by Jane Bluestein

If you want to get technical, my writing "career" started with a 1963 diary that I got in the middle of sixth grade. Over the years, I had hoped that the entries detailing what I ate, who I had a crush on, and what was wrong with my hair would eventually give way to the Great American Novel. Perhaps one day.

In the meantime, I did end up a writer almost by default, as no one else had bothered to write the particular book I needed as a supervisor of first-year teachers in a graduate training program. What started out as a series of handouts, frantically prepared before each weekly class, quickly evolved into a forty-four-chapter workbook.

For the better part of 1982, three years before my Macintosh came into my life, I carried my yellow tablets and pens around wherever I went. From the spare bedroom that served as my office to motels on field supervision trips, from the campground after a rafting trip to the back seat of the car on the way home, I jotted, noted and revised.

Late that summer I started to type and by the middle of fall I had more than 400 pages cranked out on what was then a fairly state-of-the-art (having mylar ribbons and interchangeable type balls) Olympia typewriter. My initial vision for this "Beginning Teacher's Resource Handbook" didn't go much farther than helping the twelve students in my program. For that particular purpose, the typewriter seemed well suited and overwhelmingly preferable to a $2,500-typesetting job, even though the final product *did* look an awful lot like a cheap cousin to my dissertation.

The school year had started and I was in a bit of a panic to get this book out so I dispensed with the little publishing details like editing and proofreading (a major flaw of many self-published books, I've since discovered). Around Halloween, I took the manuscript down to the university copy center. There was some kind of a price break if I got twenty-five copies, so I went ahead, figuring I'd have a few extra to send to the folks and keep on hand for whatever.

The printing and comb binding (those plastic jobs they use on a lot of cookbooks) cost me $300, which, at the time, I simply didn't have. I wrote a hot check, begged the guy at the copy center to hold it for a few days, and charged each of my twelve students $25 to cover my expenses.

Despite the plain manila cover, crooked—and occasionally mixed up—page numbers (typed on tiny little stickers and put on after the entire manuscript was typed), and tacky hand-drawn illustrations, I remember staring at my first box of books as though they could do dishes.

Fortunately, my students were far less concerned with the cosmetics and were thrilled to have the information they needed. In addition, other instructors at the university, program coordinators at the local school district, and several other teachers and student teachers requested copies, which meant I ended up selling just about the entire first printing in about a week. Not too bad, especially since I now had enough money to pay for the second printing with a check that wasn't quite so hot.

I figured if the book was such a big hit with my colleagues and friends, why not try marketing it? Since my background in education offered little in the way of business acumen, I made things up as I went along, although I was smart enough to ask questions and follow up on leads and suggestions from anyone who was a step or two ahead of me.

For starters, I went to the library and got a list of colleges that had teacher education programs and found a directory of every school and district in New Mexico. I bought my first computer (an annoyingly difficult and primitive IBM clone) with a data base that eventually yielded a mailing list.

I made up my first flyer to send out. It had black ink on dark green paper, and with a dozen different type styles, it looked a bit like a ransom note. Although I cringe whenever I come across a copy today, at the time I thought it was great. I sent out about 1,200 copies of the flyer, which, a year later, was verbally torn to shreds by an advertising expert at a conference dinner. I was devastated by his criticism and, in my ignorance, conceded that was probably why I only got a 13 percent-return. After recovering his composure (and dropped silverware), he explained that 3 percent would have been terrific—13 percent was unheard of.

I then set about cleaning up the manuscript by laying out a *real* cover (with rub-on letters and an optical-illusion illlustration from an old *Mad Magazine* that eventually became my company logo), nicer illustrations, and divider pages. I also got busy establishing two businesses, Instructional Support Services for my speaking and consulting work, and I.S.S. Publications for the publishing and mail order component. I did all the business things I was told to do, from setting up a separate checking account and mailing address, ordering letterhead and business cards, and filing the necessary tax forms.

My business vocabulary and management skills began to grow. I was now getting "purchase orders" that I had to "invoice" and keep track of in an "accounts receivables" file. All new territory, but I was learning. With the money that started coming in I could manage a larger print run, which got my unit costs down, and step up to perfect binding with the title on the spine so that the books could be displayed and sold in bookstores.

I completed a second book on an individualized, prescriptive handwriting program to go with a workshop I was starting to do, and a third book, "Parents in a Pressure Cooker," was born within the year. These two titles, along with a couple of stationery items for parents and teachers, not only gave me a "catalog," but the parenting book also gave me a mainstream topic for promotion and marketing. I received wonderful feedback on the contents of the book, but the general consensus from the professionals (including other book and magazine publishers, bookstore owners, and marketing specialists) was that it looked like it was "thrown together on somebody's kitchen table."

My co-author and I hired a graphic designer and invested about $8,000 in a new cover, cartoon illustrations, typesetting, and a 5,000-piece first printing. The investment paid off, although we would have benefited greatly from editorial support, which we did seek for the latest revision.

In 1984, I went to my first American Booksellers Association convention, sharing a small-press booth back at the tail end of a hall, next to a garbage bin in the basement of the Washington, D.C. convention center. My display was tacky and home-made, but I made important contacts as well as a few sales, and I took lots of notes on how to set up a trade-show exhibit.

I started running education conferences and, here and there, met other self-published authors with excellent materials that I offered to include in my catalog on a consignment basis. I set up agreements using terms I "borrowed" from Kathy Baxter at Children's Small Press Collection, who was distributing my books at the time. Although the majority of sales come from my own titles, often in association with my workshops, building a larger catalog has provided additional income and credibility for I.S.S. Publications. This also offers greater exposure and income for the authors whose books we distribute. Currently, our catalog advertises 130 items from thirty-seven different publishers plus books, games, and stationery items that I've published or co-published myself.

In addition, my friend, associate, and publishing "guru," Judy Lawrence, had stimulated an idea for promotion when she took off in the middle of the American Booksellers Association Convention to do a talk show she'd set up a few weeks before. On her urging, about a month prior to a publishers' conference in Utah, I called the Salt Lake City media and timidly asked if they had any interest in interviewing me on parent-child relationship issues. Those contacts led to an article in the local paper, a spot on the evening news, and a half-hour radio interview that aired at 5:30 a.m. on a Sunday. What I mainly got from these contacts was the beginning of a media promotion speaking resume and the confidence to continue.

I began to arrange media interviews whenever I had a speaking engagement either on a contract with a school district or organization, or as a part of a conference—in another town. One particularly successful trip, media-wise, was a visit to Minneapolis for an early childhood convention. While I didn't get paid for the speaking or reimbursed for the traveling, I did sell just about enough books there to justify the trip. Plus, about six months later, I got a call from one of the producers of the "Oprah Winfrey Show," who had heard about me through a producer of a similar format show I had done in Minnesota. (A lot of the "results" I've seen in this business happen months—or even years—after initial, often protracted, footwork).

The weird thing about the call was that they didn't actually need me for a particular show, but just wanted to check me out. Despite my disappointment and frustration, my only option was more footwork: some follow-up with the producers, a photo of Oprah on my office wall to remind me of my goal, and a focus on the work that was in front of me every day. I had plenty to do until they called back, which they eventually did, about a year and a half later.

I've *done* "Oprah" twice and I would love to report that my appearances have blown my book sales out of the water. They haven't. Although I've turned printing rights over to other publishers, the books simply hadn't received the distribution necessary to have them in all the chains when the shows aired. Things are improving, but we still have a lot of work to do in this area. The exposure has helped, however, if for no other reason that my appearances on that show seem to be the strongest line on my resume, giving me more credibility and stature than all of my writing, degrees, and experience. Sigh.

About being published versus self-publishing

In 1985, someone from Fearon/David S. Lake Publishing approached me about publishing the teacher's "Resource Handbook." I grabbed the copy, held it to my chest suspiciously, and told them it was *already* published. After months of negotiations, I finally signed a contract that gave me escalating royalties and, most important, a significant discount so that I could buy the books at a low cost to resell them at my speaking engagements. I figured I'd let *them* take out second mortgages on their houses, and decided to concentrate on my writing, speaking, and the highly-targeted marketing I was already doing.

The benefits have been tremendous, if only in editorial support. My first book, which has since been retitled "Being a Successful Teacher" to reach a broader audience, came back with a two-word cover letter from the editor that said, simply, "Don't faint!" It took me nearly two months to emotionally be able to look at the 400-plus pages that came back with lots of yellow sticky notes plastered on each page, none of them telling me what a great writer I was. And I was only able to do so by convincing myself that their comments were only the impetus and guidance by which I was going to make this very worthwhile mess into a real, much improved, grown-up-looking product. Their resources brought about a book that was far more attractive, in both what it says and how it looks, than anything I did or could ever have afforded to do on my own. Likewise, they've been far better at reaching the market than I've been, plus turning over the production aspect has left me free to do what I do best: writing and speaking.

Since the mid-eighties, I sold "Parents" to a second publisher and wrote "21st Century Discipline" (from scratch) for a third. I co-published four books with other authors (with their money and my advice, editorial work, production, and distribution) that has worked out pretty well. Although a creative way to build the business back in the beginning, I've since quit accepting manuscripts as I no longer have time to read them, let alone turn them into books.

I've gotten increasingly busy with presentations around the country and spend a great deal of time "on the road." My husband Jerry, who was laid off in 1986 from a construction job that allowed us to eat while I was getting things off the ground, has since taken over the mail order company and most of the "business" part of the business. All of this growth has allowed me to sharpen the focus of the work I do, which revolves around co-dependency issues in adult-child relationships. In my "spare time"—don't say it—I'm the associate editor of *Families in Recovery,* a new parenting magazine for adult children from dysfunctional families.

And in the frequent chaos of day-to-day details, I find the first casualty to be my perspective, with balance and sanity running a close second. When things get muddy, I have a phenomenal network of friends who are doing similar things, most of whom I've met at professional conferences and publishing conventions. These are the people whom I call for guidance, support, and the assurance that I'm not completely insane to be doing this work. They're the ones who remind me that I have indeed grown, that the products, money, and recognition have gotten better, and that I am incredibly well-supported by the Universe.

In between, I rely on inspirational and motivational materials that range from professional tapes and magazine articles to "Dear Abby" clippings and fortune cookie fortunes.

Had anyone suggested to me that I'd be doing what I'm doing when I was still back in Pittsburgh teaching fourth grade, I doubt I'd have believed a word of it. By writing this chapter, I've had a rare chance to regain a moment of perspective, and with it a great deal of gratitude. I'll close with a quote from Goethe (hanging on my wall) and a wish for you for the persistence, resources, and guidance to happily and successfully fulfill your own mission: "Whatever you can do, or dream you can, begin it. Boldness has genius, power, and magic in it."

PARENTS IN A PRESSURE COOKER

**JANE BLUESTEIN, Ph.D.
and LYNN COLLINS, M.A.**

...what do children need? Parents
in a Pressure Cooker takes us a
giant step forward in understanding
the answer to that question. It's an
encouraging practical book that
explains how to share healthy
behaviors with the whole family,
how to have families that "work".
Melody Beattie

Extra Bonus Note

Dr.Judy Kuriansky
Author of How To Love A Nice Guy

Always believe you can accomplish whatever you dream of. Write without editing yourself at first-just to get it down on paper. Enjoy telling your story. Pretend you are telling it to someone who loves you and loves to hear what you have to say. Network with everyone you know to get references to agents, publicists, and even other writers to get feedback on your manuscript, references and tips. If you have the time and passion, get involved in all aspects of your book being published. Stay on top of it, there are many snags such as in distribution. Don't hesitate to do some aspects yourself. I did four months of publicity on my last book. *You* know what you want to say best!

Barbara Brabec

From experience I've learned that average writers become good writers only with considerable effort and attention to detail. And good writers don't just write, they become specialists in the art of rewriting, which is the real secret to good writing.

chapter 7

Keep an Ear on the Marketplace While Your Fingers Are Flitting on the Keyboard

by Barbara Brabec

Iliterally fell into writing when my intense interest in selling my craftwork led my husband to suggest that we ought to publish a crafts marketing magazine for people like me. "But I'm not a writer," I said, and he said, "Try!"

We launched *Artisan Crafts* magazine in 1971, and it had a good run. In time, however, profits did not justify the amount of time I was giving it. Although I edited the magazine and wrote much of the material in it, I didn't think of myself as a writer until the magazine ceased publication in 1976. At that time, a book publisher asked me to write a crafts marketing book. (Another writer, too busy to take the job, referred me to him.) "Just string all your old magazine articles together, and you'll have a book," he told me.

I knew there was more to writing a book than this, and since I didn't want to be embarrassed by poor writing, I began an intense period of self-study as soon as I had a contract in hand. (No advance was offered, by the way, and I was too dumb then to question this policy, and too thrilled by the idea of being an author to care.)

That first book was "Creative Cash," which has had a successful, though speckled life. Now in its fifth revised edition with sales of 70,000 copies, it has had six different covers and four publishers. I have twice self-published it on the two occasions when the book went out of print and rights reverted back to me. Presently, I have the rights and plan to keep them from here on.

I have written four books to date: two trade paperbacks and two companion books I published in 1986 and 1987. Curiously, both trade books came about when publishers approached me, and I sometimes wonder if I ever would have written a book without this nudge. My second book, "Homemade Money," is now in its third revised edition with sales of nearly 60,000 copies.

Like most writers, I work at home, full time since 1981 when I launched my newsletter, now a quarterly known as *National Home Business Report.* While profitable by itself, the newsletter is doubly profitable to me in that it serves as a wonderful marketing tool, adding to my credibility as an expert in my field, and giving my books constant national visibility. I sell my books and newsletter primarily to individuals, but do have a few mail order dealers and a library distributor. I sell through a sixteen-page, two-color catalog that is sent free to anyone who requests information about my publications. Later, these people receive additional mailings from me—a series of inexpensive self-mailers that emphasize individual publications in my line. From experience I've learned the importance of constantly remailing information to my entire mailing list, which I keep in pristine condition.

Speaking as a promotional tool

Most of the successful writers I know end up speaking sooner or later and, for many, "back-of-the-room sales" generate even more money than the speaking fee. This is not usually the case with me, but speaking is nonetheless profitable. Since 1982, I have done two kinds of speaking engagements:

✍ Keynote speeches for home-business/entrepreneurial/trade conferences, often coupled with a short business or marketing workshop. (A speech, by itself, isn't as likely to generate book sales as an intensive workshop that focuses attention on your book.) At such events, I ask for free display space so I can be on hand to answer questions and sell my books and newsletter.

✍ Day-long workshops, on a variety of topics, where one of my books is the recommended text for the day, and is either included with the workshop fee or offered separately at day's end along with all my publications. If I sell my books at day's end, I generally expect to sell one or more books to at least 70 percent—sometimes 90 percent—of the total audience. The profitability of such workshops depends greatly on the number of people who show up, and this often depends on the sponsor's ability to get publicity. (I do not have time nor the inclination to sponsor such workshops myself, although a lot of writers do.)

I would encourage all nonfiction writers to branch out by offering workshops. They provide a great way to learn more about your reader-market, build your mailing list, and improve both your speaking techniques and marketing strategies.

Obtaining media attention

I have built my business and my reputation as an expert in the home-business industry through a combination of networking, publicity, word-of-mouth advertising, speaking, regular direct mailings, my newsletter, and a monthly magazine column I've written for *Crafts* since 1979. I have rarely purchased traditional advertising space but have invested in some cooperative mailings, and even produced a couple of them myself. Nothing has worked as well for me as free publicity. My first book was published in late 1979, and there hasn't been a month since that I haven't received publicity in one or more publications, including newspapers, consumer, business or trade magazines, newsletters, and home-business periodicals. Major mentions in *Family Circle, Woman's Day, Parade,* and *Time,* have put thousands of dollars into my pockets, both directly and indirectly.

All my public relations (PR) efforts were crowned in 1989 with a week-long appearance on ABC TV's "Home" show, where I was the home-business expert on their "Homemade Money" series, titled after my book. For a few minutes each day, my book and I were in the limelight, and my royalty checks a few months later proved the enormous power of a few minutes of television exposure. It's difficult to know for sure, but I estimate my appearance on that show sold between 12,000 to 15,000 books at the bookstore level. I know it added enormously to my satisfaction level and credibility as an expert.

To keep my publicity ball rolling, I periodically send press releases to newspapers as well as all the editors and writers on my regular PR list. In addition, I make regular promotional mailings to another list I call my "educator list." The latter includes the names of teachers, extension specialists, directors at small business development centers, Small Business Administration (SBA) and Service Corps. of Retired Executives (SCORE) personnel, economic development directors, libraries, schools and organizations—all special contacts made through the years. This is my "word-of-mouth army," individuals who may never order anything from me, but have indicated an appreciation for my work and a willingness to tell others about it. Such people are in a position to influence other buyers through their personal recommendations, and many issue bulletins, resource lists and workshop handouts that are distributed at conferences, seminars, or local networking groups. Some of these people are also dealers for my books and newsletter.

If you plan to publish your own books, I cannot emphasize strongly enough the importance of building and using promotional and "key contact" mailing lists. It took me years to develop such a list, but it now gives me an enormous edge over new competitors entering my field.

One of the most successful strategies I've used through the years is to identify and work with other successful business writers—syndicated columnists, free-lance writers and authors. As a member of two writers' organizations (American Society of Journalists and Authors, and National Writers Club), it's easy enough to connect with writers, but my best contacts have come merely from reading a lot of publications. Whenever I spot someone writing about topics related to my business, I make contact with a press kit or telephone call. As writers have been helpful to me through the years, so too am I helpful to them, by giving their books or other publications visibility in my own books or newsletter, mentioning them in workshops, etc. I also help editors and writers connect with interesting people in my network who can be interviewed for articles or books in progress. In return, they give me additional "editorial mentions" in their magazines. (Remember the old saying, "What goes around, comes around.")

Choosing a title

A good book title makes all the difference when it comes to getting publicity. When I wrote "Creative Cash," there were at least a dozen other books in print on the general theme of "how to make money with your arts and crafts." But by giving my book a unique and memorable title, it stood out from the crowd and has, in fact, outlived all those other titles. I chose "Homemade Money" for my home-business guide because I figured the media would love the idea, and I was right.

In addition to a crisp two- or three-word main title, every book needs an explanatory subtitle that immediately tells buyers what they're going to get. While cover design is important in selling books at the bookstore level, a catchy title will increase sales from book reviews and other publicity mentions. That title has to grab the reader by the throat and say, "Buy me! I'm just what you've been looking for." In a bookstore, it's got to make them reach for their wallet or purse. In an article or review, a great title will motivate them to tear out the article and track down the book.

In trying to find the perfect title for your book, try this: write down every single word or phrase that comes to mind when you think of your book, including words that spell out the book's benefits or purpose. Read through the list daily, trying first one combination of words, then another. After awhile, your subconscious will begin to work for you. Would you believe that I got the titles for both of my trade books at 4 a.m. when my subconscious woke me up screaming, "I've got it, I've got it!" Sure enough.

Importance of contracts

If you elect to work with a trade publisher, *be sure* to include some special clauses in your contract (an agent or attorney familiar with book contacts can help you here):

1)   You should have the right to sell your book at workshops and by mail to your own list of readers. It may be tough to get some publishers to accept this clause since they seem to fear competition. Try to get a 60 percent-discount on case lots, but be happy if you can get at least 50 percent. Some publishers won't give more than 40 percent. Explain that this discount will enable you to do a lot of

promotions that will ultimately sell more books to bookstores and libraries. My experience proves this fact. If all else fails, set yourself up in business as a mail-order dealer and order books at wholesale prices the way everyone else does.

2) Someday the publisher will decide to let your book go out of print. (The less you promote your own book, the sooner this will happen.) Prepare for that day by including a clause that enables you to *immediately* acquire the rights so you can offer the book to another publisher or take it to press yourself. Also include options to acquire the text as well as cover negatives if you don't have the facilities to re-create the book yourself; and the right to buy the publisher's remaining stock *before* it is offered to one of the "remainder houses" at about ten cents on the dollar. (Such books usually turn up at half-price in mail order book catalogs like *Publisher's Clearing House.)*

3) Try to get a graded royalty scale, one that starts at the level first offered by the publisher, and gradually increases as the book becomes more successful. Try for quantity breaks at 10,000, 25,000, 50,000, and 100,000 plus. If you are willing to work to help promote your book to achieve a higher sales level, I believe you should be compensated accordingly.

Advantages of trade publishing

Some books ought to be given to trade publishers, while others should be self-published. When an author can identify a huge market for a work, the book ought to be offered to a trade publisher with good mass-distribution capabilities, particularly with libraries and bookstores. True, an aggressive self-publisher can get similar distribution, but the *time* this takes is beyond description and before long, the writer is spending all his or her time on marketing—leaving no time to write new books. And nothing is quite as aggravating as dealing directly with major bookstore chains, who have a tendency to order 500 copies, delay payment for three to six months, then return 250 for credit. . . only to reorder the same book thirty days later.

For this reason, I do not solicit bookstore orders from chain distributors. Each time one of my books is reviewed in a major magazine, however, I get purchase orders from independent bookstores and wholesalers alike. I fill them, of course, invoicing accordingly. Libraries are another story. I work with Quality Books, one of the best library distributors in the country. They actively solicit books from self-publishers and work hard to get them into libraries, paying promptly. You do need the right pricing structure to make a decent profit, however.

Books that should be self-published

Books that should be self-published are those with a tight focus for which only a modest audience can be identified—ideally, one the author can reach through publicity, word-of-mouth, workshops, or speaking engagements, and direct mail efforts. Take my two self-published books, for example. While both are loaded with useful information, it is recycled information unlikely to be of interest to a trade publisher. Yet I have sold several thousand copies of these books to individuals on my mailing list. Because I now have "a following," all I have to do is announce a new book with a press release, or just add it to my catalog. Sales are automatic.

Printers and print quality

Shop carefully. Get several quotes. Prices vary dramatically depending on where a printer is located.(Access to paper mills has much to do with pricing. For this reason, printers in Michigan will be less expensive than printers in Illinois.) Be sure to get quotations on several quantity levels, too.

I would advise new authors to print no more than 500-1,000 books the first time around, depending on the number of copies that will be moved through dealers or distributors. Better to go back to press in three months when you've found your market than to end up with 1,500 books that have to be stored in the basement or garage for a year. Tying up your cash for this long a time is not cost-effective; better to pay a little more per copy on the initial run. Besides, after the book is printed, you may decide you want to make some minor changes. Until your book is actually off the press, it's hard to envision what the finished product will look like.

Publishing through a vanity press

What a total waste of time and money! There is nothing a "vanity press" can do for writers that writers can't do for themselves. All they have to do is buy and read a couple of the excellent self-publishing manuals on the market and follow instructions.

Advice for beginning writers

Anyone can write a book. The trick is to write a book *that people want to buy*. To be published by a major book publisher, you must be a capable writer with a clear understanding of your book's market. Publishers are not interested in publishing "good books." They want titles that will *sell*—books in keeping with the times, books the general reading public (or at least an identifiable chunk of the population) can relate to and will be eager to buy. The most successful writers are those who keep one ear to the marketplace while their fingers are flitting around on the keyboard. They consistently deliver books that offer real benefits to the reader—whether it's nonfiction that addresses specific business or consumer interests and problems, or exciting fiction that merely provides entertainment.

I learned to write well through practice coupled with the reading of dozens of books and magazines on how to write well and be paid accordingly. I then applied the things I learned to my writing and marketing strategies. The book that helped me most in the beginning was William Zinsser's "On Writing Well," now a classic in its field. (Fourth edition by Harper Perennial.)

From experience I've learned that average writers become good writers only with considerable effort and attention to detail. And good writers don't just write, they become specialists in the art of rewriting, which is the real secret to good writing. Test the quality of your work by reading it aloud. Whenever you stumble, you can be sure some reader will stumble, too. Make whatever changes are necessary to make your copy flow.

Agents and new books in the works

I am now working on a major book that will probably take two years to complete, given my already busy schedule. After that, I'd like to do a new book every other year. I'm not at a loss for ideas, but lack of time for writing is a big problem. If anyone had asked me three years ago if I planned to use an agent, I would have said no. With my considerable experience in publishing, and the many publisher contacts I've formed through the years, finding a publisher is the least of my problems. I'm comfortable with contract negotiations, too, so why give an agent a percentage of my royalties for doing what I could do myself?

That was my argument until this year, when I finally accepted the fact that one person can do only so much. The demands of my business, coupled with the memory of frustrating publisher experiences in the past, have made me realize that I need a break. It is the tendency of entrepreneurs to want to do everything themselves, but after several years, burnout is a serious problem. So I figure the time has come for me to ease up a bit and accept help from someone else. Now the idea of giving an agent a chunk of my advance/royalty income doesn't bother me because time and experience has shown me that the benefits will far outweigh the cost.

Although my immediate interest is in working with trade publishers, I will probably self-publish a few titles in years to come. I do enjoy the creative process involved in making a book, and some of what I have to say will be of interest to only a limited audience. And some day I'd like to write a book to encourage the average person to write and self-publish family histories, personal experiences, cookbooks, and other collections of material. I've even got the title ready and waiting. I'll call it:

"How to Write a Book
When You Say You're Not a Writer,
But You Wannabe an Author
Awful Bad"

HOME-BUSINESS "BACKGROUNDER" - Use at will during 1991; Thereafter, write for updated material from National Home Business Network, P. O. Box 2137, Naperville, IL 60567.

This article will be helpful to anyone who is currently doing a story on the growing work-at-home movement. Radio show hosts may use it as a guide to questions that might be asked in an interview, while reporters and free-lance writers may quote it directly in newspaper or magazine articles...*so long as all quotes are properly attributed to:* **"Barbara Brabec, founder of the National Home Business Network in Naperville, Illinois," or "Barbara Brabec, a Home Business Development Specialist and author of *Homemade Money*** (Betterway Publications).

HOME-BUSINESS ADVICE FROM
INDUSTRY EXPERT BARBARA BRABEC

Q: How many people now work at home in businesses of their own?
The latest National Work-at-Home Survey conducted by LINK Resources indicates there are more than 30 million "homeworkers." Because this figure includes everyone who works at home, including employees who merely bring work home in the evenings, no one can say for sure how many of these individuals actually own their own businesses. HOWEVER...the best estimates at present are that between 13-15 million individuals may now own homebased businesses. The important thing here is not just the numbers...it's the fact that working at home is now an important economic trend, and the wave of the future.

Q: What has prompted the work-at-home trend, and why are so many people now considering their entrepreneurial options?
Several things come into play here. First, technology has certainly fueled the entrepreneurial movement. Affordable computers and business software has made it possible for many individuals to perform as employees in home offices, while other individuals have simply opted to quit their jobs in favor of self-employment.
Because one-income paychecks no longer seem sufficient for the needs of most American families, more women continue to enter the workplace... but large numbers of these women also yearn to be at home with their children. So, while many hold full or part-time jobs, they may also be trying to get a homebased business started on the side, just as many employed male workers are now "moonlighting" -- offering the same type of services performed in their job to a small-but-growing clientele being developed on the side. (Needless to say, employers frown on this sort of activity, and if discovered, could lead to the loss of one's job.)
As many companies continue to lay off employees, thousands of individuals live in fear of losing their jobs and have thus started a homebased business as a hedge against an uncertain future. Those already unemployed may find self-employment their only logical choice, particularly if they're past the age of 50. Still others start homebased businesses with the idea of using this income to supplement social security and simply give them something meaningful to do in their later years.
Finally, the desire for a better way of life is another important reason why millions want to work at home. It's one of the few really safe places to be these days, and when one is self-employed, it allows for more selectivity in where one lives.

Q: What are some of the important advantages of working at home?
Speaking for myself and the many home-business owners in my NATIONAL HOME BUSINESS NETWORK, I would say that being one's own boss is high on the list of "perks." Being able to control your working hours is another. Everyone who works at home loves the time they save in transit to a job, fighting traffic jams, or commuting on trains and busses. How wonderful to look outside at the blizzard or torrential downpour and know you don't have to go OUT to work! Homebased workers also save a bundle on travel expenses, wardrobe, and lunches out, and daycare expenses.

Q: What special advantages do homebased business owners have over others who merely work at home for an employer?
First, there are good tax advantages. A small business at home is the best tax shelter left for average Americans, and it's a good way for a family to achieve financial independence while also keeping more of their hard-earned dollars safe from income taxes. Legitimate home-business owners can cut their taxes simply taking advantage of the many special deductions available to them. (These are outlined in detail in my popular book, *HOMEMADE MONEY--The Definitive Guide to Success in a Homebased Business* (Betterway Publications).

GALLAGHER, JORDAN & ASSOCIATES
– Child Care Consultants –
P.O. Box 555 • Worcester, PA 19490
(215) 364-1945

START YOUR OWN AT HOME
CHILD CARE BUSINESS

<u>JUST PUBLISHED!!!</u>

HOW TO START A PROFITABLE
DAY CARE PROGRAM IN THE HOME

This comprehensive guide to organizing a profitable home based Day Care business is invaluable for setting up a successful program. Everything that you need to get started is included. Licensing, Insurance, Zoning, Arts & Crafts, Safety Tips, Emergency Procedures, etc. are discussed. You can start your own program within a few weeks ($12.95).

<u>SO YOU WANT TO OPEN A PROFITABLE DAY CARE CENTER. . .</u>
(Within A Corporation, Hospital, Nursing Home, College or Outside Facility)

For Teachers, Nurses, Corporate Personnel, Hospital Staff, College Students, and anyone who asks "How Do I Get Started?" This manual will provide vital information on: Where To Begin; Guiding Principles; Development Needs; Educational Plans Activities; Suggested Equipment and Supplies; Program Cautions (potential problems and how to avoid them); Tips From Experienced Directors; Free Information Resources. . . and much more! ! ! ($19.95)

ROBIN'S PLAY & LEARN BOOK
CREATIVE ACTIVITIES FOR YOUNG CHILDREN

Preschool Teachers, Parents, Early Childhood Students, Babysitter, Grandparents, Scout Leaders, Student teachers will appreciate the hundreds of ideas for: Simple Crafts, Games, New Party Themes, No-Bake Cooking Recipes, Field Trip Ideas, Songs, Finger-Plays and Learning Activities. The book is chock full of creative ideas. It will show you what to do when a child exclaims, "But there's nothing to do!" ($12.95).

Name: _____

Address: _____

City _____ State_____ Zip_____

Number of Books Ordered:_____ Number of Copies:_____

Amount Enclosed:_____

Please add $2.00 postage per order.

Julie Adams Church

At last the books arrived—2,500 of them! Dozens of my friends and relatives, even the mayor of Oakland, Lionel Wilson, (whose dog frequented Pride 'n' Groom Beauty Salon) attended a gala book party. We were launched!

chapter **8**

Joy in a Woolly Coat

by Julie Adams Church

Words and dogs—two major loves of my life! These two seemingly unrelated interests became integrally entwined when my beloved dog, Lady, died. Her death, and the days surrounding that event, transformed my life, emotionally, spiritually, and practically. Within hours of her passing I tried to capture my feelings on paper. "Lady," I wrote, was "a look that said 'I love you. I am joy in a woolly coat come to dance into your life to make you laugh.'"

Although I did not know what would follow, I already had a title for my book, "Joy in a Woolly Coat." I next developed a roll of film that included recent pictures of Lady, and there it was, the cover of my yet to be conceived project. A voice within would not be stilled as it gently and repeatedly urged me to write more of my experience that I might bring to others a measure of the understanding, comfort, and hope I had just known. "Write a book," said the voice. A startling idea! Many years before, in the midst of a teaching career, I had earned a masters degree in English education. I continued to teach school for several more years until, facing "burnout," I left education to form "Pride 'N' Groom," a dog grooming and boarding business. Now, prodded by my unseen mentor, these two divergent careers seemed to be coming together to have a new united purpose.

My deep, personal, joyful, and gut-wrenching memories and experiences poured onto the yellow legal-sized tablet. I would pause and wonder what on earth I was doing. The voice within continued to guide. "That's OK," it said, "just write." Truly, I can say the entire production of "Joy in a Woolly Coat" was backed by this guidance I came to trust implicitly. Each stage of the journey brought just the right people, the needed word processor, the pertinent information for the next step.

A trip to the bookstore introduced me to Dan Poynter and Mindy Bingham's book "Is There a Book Inside You?" uncanny in its direct application to my project. I then attended their three-day, self-publishing workshop in Santa Barbara, California. Although I recognized the excellence and value of this workshop, I felt overwhelmed, out of my league. However, just like pieces of a puzzle, another vital element fell into place. While in Santa Barbara I had arranged to meet with internationally-known animal portrait artist, Constance Coleman. We were immediately drawn together by our mutual interest in and advocacy of animals in our lives. Constance offered valuable advice on the presentation of my material and then offered to illustrate the book. I felt both thrilled and validated.

The next months entailed writing and re-writing and more writing with supportive and valuable assistance from friends and relatives. My network brought me in touch with Marian O'Brien, a free-lance producer of books who, with me hanging over her shoulder, designed and coordinated the technical aspects of production—layout, including seventeen illustrations, typography, and printing. I wrote letters, sent galleys, applied for a copyright etc., etc.

At last the books arrived—2,500 of them! Dozens of my friends and relatives, even the mayor of Oakland, Lionel Wilson, (whose dog frequented Pride 'n' Groom Beauty Salon) attended a gala book party. We were launched!

A call came. "I've been looking for a book like yours to publicize," said a woman at the other end of the line. We talked and agreed to meet. I felt inadequate to promote my own story and had not, in fact, received affirmative replies from distributors, so I welcomed assistance. Thus, what turned out to be a hard lesson commenced. In my inexperience, I signed an expensive and not very comprehensive contract with this person and over the next month had only one newspaper review, one radio interview, and no distributors to show for it. I had no more money to offer her and I felt very discouraged.

How, having followed my inner guidance, could I find myself at this crossroad, not knowing where to turn? The road sign appeared. My publicist had introduced "Joy..." to friends of hers, publishers, who had expressed a possible interest in producing a second edition of the book. This seemed to be the break I needed. H.J. Kramer, his wife, Linda, and I met. They thought "Joy..." showed much potential. They wanted me to make it longer, change the format and, to my dismay, replace the cover. They offered a contract, which I passed on to my lawyer. With minor changes, all appeared to be in order and we signed the deal.

Now I had supportive people in the business and a professional editor who not only knew her stuff, but loved animals. We added forty pages, shifted the emphasis, and added chapter titles. Constance Coleman agreed to re-do all illustrations, thirteen of them. The Kramers insisted on a cover change and contracted with Constance to illustrate it. I held out for my title, agreeing to add the subtitle, "Living With, Loving, and Letting Go of Treasured Animal Friends." Sticking with "Joy in a Woolly Coat" as my title was not my automatic option; the Kramers reluctantly acquiesced to my desire—both the professional publishers and the people I met at the self-publishing workshop were skeptical about my chosen title. They questioned whether it adequately expressed what the book was about. However, I very often hear unsolicited favorable comments from non-professionals, even to the point of saying they picked up the book because of its title.

A year from the initial birthing of "Joy..." the second edition came out. Now I had someone else's resources and promotional capabilities to take over what I found nearly impossible–selling my product. I believed completely in my subject, I felt totally comfortable with any audience, regardless of make-up, in person or via radio or television. I can speak in response to another's prompting and, indeed, love to do so. However, pushing my own product, creating my own publicity required marketing knowledge and skills foreign to my personality and experience. The Kramers' belief in me, support of me, and professional expertise behind me has been invaluable. Obtaining both national and international distribution was a major and necessary plus. They advertised in pertinent publications, arranged for thirty radio and TV interviews and talk shows, and sent review copies throughout the country.

Financially, they did what I could not do. Still, I found relinquishing control of promotion to be a "Catch-22." I often hear from people who've looked all over and can't find "Joy..." in the local bookstore. I find I have had less exposure in my local area than in many other places in the country. I don't have the resources, nor for that matter the actual books in hand, (I now have to buy them myself) to go door-to-door with my wares. My publisher says people can order the book from any store, but that we can't dictate to the store what they should carry. This tells me we've missed the boat somewhere along the way. With 40 million dog owners and 50 million cat owners in this country, bookstores should be begging to stock "Joy..." to reach this vast audience. One consideration affecting the salability of my book is the fact that it reads easily (albeit emotionally) and can be passed on to people in need of its message. Readers say, "I'll have to lend so-and-so my copy" rather than buying a new one for their friends. I am not sure exactly why this is so.

The response from those who do find and read this book has been greatly rewarding. The personal letters I have received from readers have been worth every hour and every dime I spent to tell my story. It amazes me that people actually take the time to write to me, a stranger, their intensely personal testimonials. I used to think that if I touched one heart it would fulfill me. That so many have been touched is a tremendous blessing.

I do not know whether or not this book will lead to my writing another. I consult with people all over the country by phone or letter in response to specific questions concerning the human-animal bond. Possibly there is material for a second book in these communications. I am exploring other avenues for reaching, via the written word, the millions of people who share this love and bond with their animal friends.

To anyone interested in venturing into the exciting field of book publishing I would encourage them to do so. My understanding from my many friends who have gone with a publisher is that there is very limited follow-up in terms of promotion. You should be prepared to do this yourself or hire a very competent publicist at an expense which may be well beyond your royalty payments.

Self-publishing, too, costs money. I have a garage stacked with 1,700 first editions, meaning I am out a pretty penny and 1,700 people are missing out on a couple of hours of poignant reading! Had I not self-published there would be no second edition. However, I wish now I had printed fewer than the 2,500 copies. Would I do it again given what I now know? Unequivocally, yes. I learned (thank you, Lady-Dog)—about myself, about others, and about a fascinating business.

H J Kramer Inc

P.O. Box 1082
Tiburon
California 94920
(415) 435 5367

AT LONG LAST,
GRIEF SUPPORT FOR PET LOSS

Joy in a Woolly Coat: Living with, Loving and Letting Go of Treasured
Animal Friends is Julie Adams Church's hearfelt story of her relationship
with her animal companions. Beginning with her first dog, Shadow, who
entered her life when she was only six years old, Julie's growth as a spiritual
being becomes intertwined with the many beloved pets that she has the good
fortune to bring into her life. In exploring the significant bonding which
occured over a lifetime of experiences, Julie is challenged to ask many
questions. Does spirit manifest in animals? What opportunities do our
animal friends provide for human growth? How does one deal with the
death of a companion animal? Are there indeed eternal qualities and values
embodied within the woolly coat?

In this beautifully written and illustrated book, the answers will speak to the
heart of all animal lovers. The feelings are universal, easily recognized and
will bring fresh insight and awareness to the cycle of grief.

We at H J Kramer feel strongly that this book has an audience of people who
are hurting for a book that will acknowledge the deep emotions
accompanying the loss of a pet. Joy in a Woolly Coat is such a book. We
know of no other book that addresses this aspect of the interdependence of
people and pets and offers so much in the way of comfort.

Julie Adams Church, a native of Madison, Wisconsin, resides in the
Montclair hills of Oakland, California with her three beloved dogs and their
friend Sammy Cat. Animals, people, travel, the ocean and music weave their
way through Ms. Church's enthusiastic embrace of life. Her compassionate,
outgoing nature has drawn her to teaching elementary school children, to
establishing and operating her own canine "spa" and more recently to grief
counseling on the subject of pet loss.

Joy in a Woolly Coat   Contact: Julie Adams Church
by Julie Adams Church   33 East Circle
Pub. Date May 1988   Oakland, CA 94611
Quality Paper, 144 pages, $9.95   (415) 339-1937
ISBN 0-915811-08-1

                                              Uma Ergil
                                              H J Kramer Inc
                                              (415) 435-5367

Gloria T. Delamar

For several years I wrote a weekly column for the Richmond Metropolitan Observer. "On the Soapbox" was a wonderful opportunity not only to express myself on any number of issues, but to apply the craft and techniques of changing style, mood, or tone to suit the particular subject of the column.

chapter **9**

There's Editing and Then There's Editing

by Gloria T. Delamar

Perhaps the most basic tenet the writer must learn is that "everything counts." Assuming, first of all, that you have something to say, you must learn to say it well for the market you're trying to reach. Research compulsively; information has to be verifiable. The slant, the tone, the voice, and the language have to be appropriate. What's more, the syntax, grammar, and punctuation have to be correct.

Many naive beginning writers take the attitude that "the editor can always fix up spelling and grammar." The fact is that when editors spot such basic errors, they can't help but react negatively to the entire piece. They wonder if there are other, less detectable errors—faulty information in nonfiction pieces, for example.

Writing a first draft is fun. But don't forget that the re-writing is just as creative as an initial spurt. Some writers hold that "the spontaneity will be edited out" with re-writing. That's nonsense. It's when re-writing and polishing that you know in your bones you're a writer, capable of pushing and molding the material so it best does what you want. One doesn't take out spontaneity; what one does is leave in the parts of the spontaneous first draft that work well, and change or delete the parts that don't, and add what's needed. Re-writing, is, in fact, both creative writing and editing.

In nonfiction, clarity and information have to be examined. In fiction, logical plotting and believable character motivation must be re-examined. In both, language and organization of the material have to be re-assessed. Also in both, extraneous sections have to be ruthlessly deleted. This is the most difficult part of editing for writers to learn. No matter how lovely, no matter how interesting even, if sidetracks appear in your writing, they've got to be taken out.

Part of that re-writing process is double-checking grammar, punctuation, spelling, syntax, logical paragraph breaks, transitions, and general rhythm. That's editing your own work before it goes to an editor.

Another part of editing is knowing how to work with an editor when you have one. That can take a variety of forms. For several years I wrote a weekly column for the *Richmond Metropolitan Observer*. "On the Soapbox" was a wonderful opportunity not only to express myself on any number of issues, but to apply the craft and techniques of changing style, mood, or tone to suit the particular subject of the column. I can't recall that there was ever any actual editing done on my finished copy.

But there were other things I did to maintain a professional relationship with the editor. First, my copy was always in before deadline. Then, just in case the paper had to go to press early or I was too ill to write, I kept two universal-issue columns on file with them. Only one was ever used; the editor was called out of town on an emergency and wanted to set everything up before leaving, so he pulled out one of the on-file columns, which I immediately replaced. Another thing I did, was to indicate what could be deleted if it was necessary. Of course, my material was always submitted to conform to the length allocated to it, but if space should unaccountably run short, I wanted to control where the cuts would be made. Newspapers have a terrible tendency to cut off the end of material that doesn't fit, but when you're writing editorials and essays, this can seriously affect the way you want to conclude a piece. This technique, however, should only be used where you have a standing arrangement; never submit an article with options. Write it as it should be, know what the publication's subject, length, and style requirements are, and submit a completed piece. Convey a sense of confidence about your work.

Integrating life experience and formal education

Although I had grown up wanting to write, I opted for a career in Kindergarten-Primary education. After several years, I quit to have a family and be an at-home mother. Caring for my five children at home, watching them develop, sharing all the aches and pains as well as the joys and high points, was a different education for me. And as I seriously began setting aside time to write, I drew from both my formal and informal education for my first published writings.

I wrote articles about family life and sold them to local newspapers and national magazines. I should mention that I also took several writing classes and read a lot of books about writing. I wrote twelve plays based on Aesop's Fables for my own kids and submitted them for publication. My little paperback, "Play Aesop," is still in Eldridge Publishing Company's catalog.

With my publishing credits mounting, I was accepted into the National League of American Pen Women and the Author's Guild, and to my amazement, was listed in "Who's Who of American Women." Those are nice validations, but I believe that learning should never cease, so I founded a writer's manuscript critique group, something I've done in each city I've lived.

The give-and-take of such a group is helpful not only for specific revision suggestions on your own material, but invaluable for learning from what you critique and hear critiqued in the work of others. But perhaps the most important aspect is the companionship of other writers. This is probably most crucial for those who don't get caring support at home. I've been fortunate, as my husband is not only a writer himself, but my biggest fan. Being with other writers helps you through the inevitable rejections from publishers. Even good work gets rejected for various reasons—timing, overlapping subject with another project, even the editor's mood on a given day. Non-writers just think your stuff must be bad; writers understand that having work accepted is most often simply a matter of having your work land on the right editor's desk at the right time. Rejections can't help but batter the writer's sensibilities; sharing with others who understand the marketing process helps to soothe the psyche.

Having moved from beginner to professional, in time, I was asked to give writing workshops myself, and have been lecturing and teaching for a number of years. The adult schools, which have shorter terms, allow me time for my own writing and keep my editing skills honed. I enjoy working in schools with children, either talking about how one of my books came to be, or conducting creative writing workshops. Talking to adults has different compensations; teaching beginners how to shape their work and watching them grasp the essentials spurs me to always keep my own work in control.

My first book grew out of my notebooks as a Kindergarten teacher and playing with my own children. I knew I had a unique collection—all available reference books held only bits and pieces of the extra-curricular material that teachers and day-care workers use with children. I had enough for a valuable reference book. Once it was accepted, I learned how to work with someone else editing my work.

Turning it over to an editor

First there was the title. I had what I thought was a catchy short title, "Rhythms Galore." The publisher called to say that, though he'd leave the choice of a title up to me, he thought something more descriptive would sell better. Although I was the author, I figured he certainly knew more about marketing than I did. What he suggested, in effect, was that I choose a title that said exactly what was in the book. Together, we decided on "Children's Counting-Out Rhymes, Fingerplays, Jump-Rope and Bounce-Ball Chants and Other Rhymes: A Comprehensive English-Language Reference" (McFarland & Co. Publishers, 1983). (Whether the title was a factor or not, I don't know, but the book became one of the publisher's best-sellers.)

The book contains anthologized pieces, as well as a good portion of my own original material, categories mentioned in the book's title, plus other sections like responsive readings, tongue-twisters, and staircase tales, with detailed descriptions of how to use the pieces. Each section has an introduction that explains the educational applications for the benefit of teachers, parents, and counselors. Internally, the book was lightly edited, but I quickly decided that there was a technique to accepting and/or objecting to changes. This was reinforced with my next three books for McFarland, which publishes heavily in the reference and scholarly area. The publisher prints all books on acid-free paper with cloth binding because their books are intended for archival use and marketed heavily to libraries and other educational institutions. Sloppy writing just wouldn't do.

My second book took roots from the same notebook that spawned the first, but grew far beyond that. "Rounds Re-Sounding: Circular-Music for Voices and Instruments: An Eight-Century Reference" (McFarland, 1987) gives the historical perspective on more than 600 rounds, discusses types and uses, and has popular rounds, rounds by classical composers, and parodies. It has both collected rounds and my own original compositions. The pieces are arranged under 18 subject categories. The proofreading was massive, as both words and music had to be proofed. The editing again was light, and any objections I had were readily agreed to by an editor who loved her assignment to work on the book. She even sent me a round I hadn't known about that could be fit in—it wasn't presented as a "must-do," but as a "what do you think" suggestion. She moved one section that I had at the end as an appendix and incorporated it at the end of an early chapter; I agreed that the change improved the presentation.

The third volume, "Mother Goose: From Nursery to Literature" (McFarland, 1987), is a literary treatment that gives the history of nursery verses, in particular those that are traditionally designated as "Mother Goose" rhymes. There's a general analysis and also comments about relevance. The rhymes themselves are given along with historical allusions and derivations; the authorship of specific rhymes is recorded. The book concludes with a chapter about the uses and abuses of nursery material. The publisher himself edited this one. I recall one section where I was determined to make a point so made it, made it again, and then again. He took out the last comment, writing in the margin, "Enough already, Glo!" I wrote under his comment, "You're absolutely right. I was beating a dead horse!"

The fourth book was another editing situation altogether. A new young editor was assigned to "Louisa May Alcott and 'Little Women': Biography, Critique, Publications, Poems, Songs, Contemporary Relevance" (McFarland, 1990). It's a reference book about the life, career, and influence of Louisa May Alcott. The book consists of a history of "Little Women" in print and film, a history of changing reviews over the years, and offers Alcott sites as literary mecca. It concludes with a chapter that offers a number of professional opinions about the contemporary relevance of "Little Women" (from several scholars, a children's literature professor, librarians, teachers, writers, an editor, along with some "grass roots" comments from several general readers.) When I first saw the massive changes in structure and editing that deleted important information, deviated from consistent presentation, and even made some points ungrammatical, I went from anger to tears to panic and finally to calling the publisher calmly. After three books, he knew me to be literate and professional; I was assured that any objections would be addressed.

I decided to tackle the project of undoing the incorrect editing as though I were training this person for her job. Yet, I wanted to develop a working relationship while still repairing the damage done by her inexperienced editing. I often wonder if there wasn't some kind of serendipity in the publisher assigning my book as her first chore. Now, I'm fully aware that there are editing tasks that the author doesn't ever need to worry about—setting up manuscript page ratio to the typeset page or calculating the type sizes for headings and body—she had no trouble with these technicalities. But the copyediting had eluded her; it had now become my job to get that book back into logical, literate shape. To do this, I felt that each editing change I objected to should be explained. Where my meaning or my own voice was violated, I wrote in the margin the reasons for wanting my original wording. Every time I edited back to the original, whether for grammar, consistency, or anything else, I explained why. It made the proofreading task unnecessarily tedious, but certainly made me think about exactly what I was doing. In retrospect, it strengthened my own skills.

Successful collaborating

As I begin work on two very different projects, I find myself reaffirming the differences and yet the similarities between nonfiction and fiction. My nonfiction project is a long-term, down-to-earth book about creativity, which is still to be marketed. The other is a mystery series, which my husband and I are co-authoring. As my collaborator and I work at writing and editing together, we've both been learning new things, not only about writing, but about each other. The creative mind at work is a constant wonder. We've preserved our collaboration as well as our marriage with our early agreement that if one of us absolutely wants a section deleted, it's out. The other writer is naturally open to persuade, but failing a convincing argument, the editing caveat is firm. It is, in effect, having two in-house editors on the job.

In the end, editing consists of several points. First, there's the self-editing that organizes the material, checks research (nonfiction) or plotting and characterization (fiction), adds, deletes, polishes wording, and eliminates grammatical transgressions.

Then, in working with an editor, there are three phases. First, a writer should gratefully acknowledge editing changes that improve his or her work. Next, if a change doesn't really substantially matter, accept the editor's wording. (The first two actions, then give you leverage for the third.) When editorial changes truly violate your presentation, argue against them, but argue knowledgeably. In the end, it's your name that appears with the material, so its your concept, your credibility, and your writing talent that will be judged.

Writing something you believe in is rewarding. But you can't just drop words onto paper and assume that your first efforts are your best. Do whatever back-up research is needed, and more. Learn to edit. And foremost, have something to say, because "everything counts."

Tips on Getting the Most Out of Writers' Conferences

These helpful hints, written by Ms. Delamar, first appeared in "Pen Point," the newsletter of the Philadelphia Writers' Conference, P.O. Box 7171, Philadelphia, PA 19117. Spring 1990 edition.

1) Don't forget to pack your "conference lifesavers," (aspirin, bandaids, regular medications, etc.)

2) Bring briefcase or tote bag for handouts and magazines.

3) Bring plenty of notebook paper and take good notes that you will understand when you look at them later.

4) Don't be shy about starting conversations with other conference attendees. Many helpful tips come out of impromptu meetings.

5) Invite others to fill your table at the dining-room.

6) Before leaving home, write out short, specific questions you want answered in specific workshops.

7) The atmosphere in a conference is stimulating; bring along an idea notebook so you can jot down inspirations.

8) As soon as possible, implement something new you've learned.

9) One month after the conference, go over all your notes and handout materials to reinforce the effectiveness of what you've learned.

On conference etiquette

Be in your seat a few minutes before conference time; stay through the session. Late entries and early departures are disrupting.

Ask questions that are general enough to benefit all, and keep your questions short. Other conference attendees want to hear the leader, not a blow by blow report of your personal writing problems.

Louisa May Alcott
and *Little Women*
Biography, Critique,
Publications, Poems, Songs and
Contemporary Relevance

Gloria T. Delamar
[368]pp.   LC 89-42710
Frontispiece, photographs, illustrations, music, appendices, chronologies, bibliographies, index
ISBN 0-89950-421-3 $29.95 library binding   1990

Louisa May Alcott—abolitionist, suffragist, early feminist—moved in the literary circle of Thoreau, Emerson, Hawthorne, and others. This fascinating reference shows her struggles while she authored a broad range of material from fairy tales to "blood and thunder" stories, philosophical adult novels, and music lyrics.

Included are a lively biography, many of her little-known poems, a history of *Little Women* since publication in 1868, and a discussion of the Alcott legacy. Wonderful illustrations.

Gloria T. Delamar lives in Melrose Park, Pennsylvania.

McFarland & Company, Inc., Box 611, Jefferson NC 28640

Also of Interest

Mother Goose: From Nursery to Literature. Gloria T. Delamar. 332pp., 1987. $25.95 library binding, illustrations, bibliography, index. "Commendably inclusive... annotated bibliographies... a good acquisition"—*Choice;* "looks at the rhymes as important contributions to Western literature, analyzes their effects on children, and traces their evolution in the literary tradition"—*AB Bookman's Weekly;* "a wealth of information"—*Emergency Librarian.* 0-89950-280-6. 87-42504.

Children's Counting-Out Rhymes, Fingerplays, Jump-Rope and Bounce-Ball Chants and Other Rhythms: A Comprehensive English-Language Reference. Gloria T. Delamar. 224pp., 1983. $19.95 library binding, author, subject, title, first line indexes. "Busy librarians will find it helpful"—*Booklist.* Hundreds of old favorites (and some new—"also worthwhile"—*Booklist*). 0-89950-064-1. 82-24904.

Rounds Re-Sounding: Circular Music for Voices and Instruments: An Eight-Century Reference. *Compiled and written by* Gloria T. Delamar. 347pp., 1987. $35 library binding for 8½ × 11), appendix, bibliography, index. "By far the most extensive compilation of rounds yet collected, with historic annotations"—*Come-All-Ye;* "fun to have so many rounds in one place"—*Sonneck Society Bulletin;* "600 rounds...scholarly"—*Reference and Research Book News.* 0-89950-203-2. 85-43576.

Louisa May Alcott and *Little Women* $29.95 _____
Mother Goose $25.95 _____
Children's Counting-Out Rhymes ... $19.95 _____
Rounds Re-Sounding $35 _____
Shipping/handling ($2 first book, 75¢ each additional book) _____
Canadian and foreign shipping/handling ($4 first book, $1.50 each add.) _____
N.C. residents add 5% _____
TOTAL $_____

Canadians add 25% and pay in Canadian funds
Foreign orders: please pay in U.S. funds drawn on a New York bank
VISA and MasterCard accepted

Name _____
Address _____
_____
_____

McFarland & Company, Inc., Publishers
Box 611, Jefferson NC 28640 (919-246-4460)

Extra Bonus Note

Marguerite Kelly
Author of The Mother's Almanac

You have to believe in your message to start a book and to believe in yourself to finish it. You have to put more into substance than fine writing and forget about the glory you might find at the end of the road; it's the getting there that matters. Above all, you have to be willing to make a fool of yourself, because sooner or later, you will.

Mary Flower

While most publishers say they are trying to be fair to their authors/illustrators as well, it only makes sense that the contract generally protects and favors the publisher especially where finances are concerned.

chapter **10**

Championing the Legal Rights of Writers

by Mary Flower

L awyers! Who needs them! When I decided to go to law school after ten years of working for various publishing companies, the comment I most often heard was, "You hate lawyers. Why do you want to join their ranks?" Since I worked in rights and permissions and contracts I had to deal with lawyers fairly frequently and I got tired of dealing with people who knew less than I did, were paid much more, and were arrogant into the bargain. I figured, why not me, at least I would be pleasant to deal with.

So exactly twenty years after graduating from college, I graduated from law school and went immediately into a job as head of the contracts department for a major publisher. I very quickly learned that I would rather be representing authors than publishers and after some soul-searching (I was a single parent with a child ready to go off to college), I decided to take the plunge and go out on my own. That was nearly four years ago.

My original client base was drawn from writers and illustrators published by the company I worked for and from writers and illustrators I met at writers' conferences in which I participated. Now those people are referring more people to me and my base has expanded to include a number of self-publishers as well. I hasten to add that I'm not a literary agent, but a literary lawyer and only come into the picture once a publisher has indicated that it will publish a book. My original clients were (and are) children's book writers and illustrators as they rarely have agents.

One of the first things I did when I set up own business was to check to see what books were available on publishing contracts as I wanted to have a basic library of reference books. I discovered that there wasn't much on the market that had more than a passing word to say about contracts or negotiating them. As most of my clients were and are children's book writers and illustrators, I wanted something that would help deal with them specifically. Unfortunately, none of the books I consulted dealt with the particular problems of children's books. It seemed that no one thought these people important enough to even mention what a reasonable contract would provide. I knew from experience that these provisions would not be the same as those for an adult trade book.

I was having dinner one night with a close friend who is a nationally known quilter and designs a line of "designer" fabrics sold mainly in quilt shops. He has written a number of books on various aspects of quilting, some of which he published himself. I was lamenting the lack of material in my field and his response was "so you write a book." All well and good, I said, but I would then have to find a publisher, etc. "Nonsense came the reply. Publish it yourself."

So it was with that I plunged into first writing and then publishing my book, " A Writer's Guide to a Children's Book Contract." I decided to write the book as a self-help and explanatory guide to a book contract with special emphasis on the ways in which a children's book contract can differ from one for an adult trade book. I wanted users to understand how publishers figure what they will offer as an advance, what royalty rates really mean, how author/ illustrator splits work, and most especially what all the legalese in a contract means. I drew sample paragraphs from the contracts of a number of publishers citing both good and bad examples of what you can expect to find in a contract.

Right from the beginning I decided not to seek a standard publisher. I wasn't sure I could find one who would market the book more effectively than I. I then had to figure out how much I could afford to spend on printing and binding (not much) not to mention design, etc. I decided to stick with what my computer was able to do in terms of typefaces and to leave the book in an eight and a half by eleven-inch format because I thought readers would find that more usable. For the same reason, I also decided to use a spiral binding so the book could open flat. The cover would be card stock. Those decisions made, I turned to a friend who had a laser printer and turned my diskettes over to him. After producing on his printer, it was then camera-ready copy for the printer.

Meanwhile, I decided to set up a publishing company for this book. Naming this company proved to be harder than anything else about the book. I wanted a name that was botanic (to suit my name) but also had a literary allusion. No easy task. I rejected such suggestions as Garden Path or Flower Bed. My first choice was Columbine Books, however no sooner had I chosen it than a new paperback line was announced with that very name. I thought and thought. No names came. Then one day when I was thinking about something completely different the right name popped into my mind: Fern Hill Books. ("Fern Hill" is one of my favorite Dylan Thomas poems and it certainly is botanic.)

While I was working on the book, I had a number of ideas about how to market the book to reach its target audience. I still think they're good ideas and one of these days I will get around to trying them. Meanwhile, the book sold out its first printing and now much of the second, mostly by word of mouth. At the time of publication it was reviewed in the Society of Children's Book Writers Bulletin. Ordering information accompanied the review (which was laudatory). I bring copies with me when I speak at writers' conferences and people who have bought the book recommend it to friends who in turn buy a copy. I have no distribution system to get the book to bookstores but that doesn't seem to matter. (This was not part of my unused marketing plan.)

My book was a good idea and I'm glad I did it. Some of my clients are people who bought copies and some of my clients buy copies. It works both ways. The per copy cost of the initial printing was high and I met some price resistance but as prices for books have risen generally and this has stayed the same, that has abated.

I'm now getting ready to revise the book since the first edition was published in 1988. The new edition will, I hope, contain even more information than this edition. I still intend to publish it myself in the same eight and a half by eleven-inch format. The format and the binding have made it usable in the way I hoped. But I want the book to have a less dense-looking appearance. I have a new computer with many typefaces and greater capability as well as a laser printer. The new equipment should facilitate a less dense look and still produce camera-ready.

This time I will try to use some of my marketing ideas—a mailing to Society of Children's Book Writers members, ads in writers' publications, etc.

Now, for some tips from a legal view, just imagine that after months, maybe years, of support groups, submissions, and revisions, Zippo Publishers has decided they want to publish your book. You are told what your advance and royalty rate will be and the contract arrives in the mail. But once you try reading it, you realize that almost none of it makes sense. Do you shrug your shoulders, figure the publisher is being fair, and sign on the dotted line? Do you figure that because you are a first-time author and/or illustrator that you have no power to change anything in the contract anyway, even if you did understand it? Wrong!

You should try to understand what the various contract provisions mean, especially the ones that deal with money and what happens if you get sued. They directly affect your pocketbook. And, despite this being your first book, you do have the power to negotiate better provisions in the contract. Don't get me wrong—you can't change everything to just what you want it to be but you can make it more fair.

What should you be aware of? Royalty rates for one—is the rate based on the retail price of the book or on net sales, i.e, is a rate of ten percent of net a better deal than five percent of retail? The former may look better on the surface because ten percent is higher than five percent. But perhaps what you should really look at is what the ten percent is from. If you are an illustrator (or an author where the illustrations will be done by someone else) be sure you understand how those splits work and be aware that author and illustrator contracts will have to agree in their basic provisions or the publisher will have its hands tied when trying to sell the book.

Check the warranties and indemnities clause. Who pays if you get sued? How is money withheld and then held if a suit is brought. Lawsuits rarely, very rarely, almost never are brought where children's books are concerned but that doesn't mean you shouldn't be concerned with what the contract provides.

Remember that publishing contracts are written by lawyers, either the in-house counsel or whatever outside counsel the publisher uses. While most publishers say they are trying to be fair to their authors/illustrators as well, it only makes sense that the contract generally protects and favors the publisher especially where finances are concerned.

If you don't have an agent, it is a good idea to either have your contract reviewed by a lawyer or better yet, have her/him negotiate it for you. NEVER use the lawyer who drew up your will, did the closing on your house, or represented you on other matters. Try to find a lawyer who knows the publishing industry and who specializes in literary or entertainment law. They don't come cheap (no lawyer does) but your regular lawyer will probably know even less about a publishing contract than you do. If you can't find a qualified lawyer, you are better off doing it yourself. Publishing law is a specialty just like anything else. You wouldn't go to a general practitioner for open-heart surgery, so don't go to a GP lawyer for advice on your book contract.

If you want to do it yourself or can't find a qualified lawyer, try to find a book that will help you understand a book contract and read it carefully before you begin dealing with your publisher.

A WRITER'S GUIDE TO A CHILDREN'S BOOK CONTRACT
  Mary Flower
  The only publication available that specifically addresses the special problems of children's book contracts. This work is designed to
help both writers and illustrators understand
their contracts by explaining general contract
provisions found in most book contracts as well
as the kinds of provisions found specifically
in children's book contracts.
GUIDELINES ARE PROVIDED IN THE FOLLOWING AREAS:
** What every publisher's contract will include
** How to understand the legalese of the
      contract
** What to ask for and about in order to get a
      fair deal —what points can and should be
      negotiated —what points can be negotiated
      but aren't worth bothering about —how to
      know when you've gotten as much as you're
      going to get
** The special provisions of a children's book
      contract
   — the author/illustrator split
   — school book clubs and school book fairs
   — paperback originals and reprints
   — packagers
   — series novels
   — novelizations
   — merchandising
  PRICE: $15 per copy plus $3 for shipping and
handling. Send to: Fern Hill Books, 600 West
End Ave., Suite 10D, New York, NY 10024.
  The author is a lawyer who has had more than
ten years experience working in the rights and
permissions and contracts departments of
several major publishers. She currently works
with writers and illustrators, advising them on
contract and copyright problems and conducts
workshops and seminars on contracts at writers'
conferences.

For All the <u>Write</u> Reasons
Forty Successful Authors, Publishers, Agents, and Writers
Tell You How to Get Your Book Published

Order Form

(Did you borrow this book? Why not order your own so you can highlight, underline? Special discounts for quantity purchases. Why not sell these books through your organization as a fundraiser?)

Telephone orders: (215) 364-1945   (VISA or MasterCard accepted)
Postal orders: Patricia Gallagher
                   Box 555 PG
                   Worcester, PA 19490

Make checks payable in U.S. funds to Patricia C. Gallagher.

Qty.	Name of book	Price Each	in PA 6% tax	Shipping	Total
____	*For All the <u>Write</u> Reasons*	$24.95	____	3.00	____

Please expedite my order for Patricia Gallagher's book:
- ☐ I have enclosed a check or money order for $_____
- ☐ Charge the total amount to: ☐ VISA   ☐ MasterCard

Card number: ____ ____ ____ ____

Expiration date: ____/____

Phone number: (____) ____-_____

Name on card: _____

Please print your complete mailing address below:

Name: _____

Organization or Company: _____

Address: _____

_____

City, ST, Zip: _____

Phone number: (____) ____-_____

Peggy Glenn

Explain your credentials and establish your credibility. If you don't have credentials, don't fake it. Don't lie about credentials; don't invent some to fit the occasion. On the other hand, that doesn't mean you can't be just a little bit creative.

chapter 11

Off To a Good Start: Credibility

by Peggy Glenn

There are essentially three major and equally-weighted components to your pre-publication publicity plan. You first have to establish yourself as an author with credibility and credentials. You next have to title your book so that no one will mispronounce it, misunderstand it, or forget it. And third, you have to design the cover of the book so that people will find it attractive, easy to look at, and easily identified on a rack from some distance away, whether it is displayed face out or spine out. The cover design must also translate well to a black and white photograph for advertising purposes. If this is possible, prepare alternate black and white art.

Consider this carefully whether you are publishing your own book or someone else is publishing it for you. Try to have some say in what really gets done with your book after you have written the words. After all, whether you are publishing your book yourself or someone else is publishing it, this is your work and you have a right to some input into every step along the way. You know your audience or you wouldn't have written the book in the first place. How does your audience react? What excites them? What are their habits? Are they the kind who will give a book a quick look, or are they the kind of people who will take the time to read ten-point type on a book cover?

The publisher and the publisher's art and sales departments have a lot of expertise, and that expertise should be sought and heeded; but so do you have expertise and you should have a voice in what goes on with the promotion and the design and cover copy and the cover art for your book. If you have firmly decided on a title for your book and are comfortable with your reasons for the title, don't be pushed into changing the title without first detailing all your reasons to the publisher. Perhaps when the publisher knows all the reasons behind your title choice, compromise will yield an even better title that ultimately incorporates most of the information and influences that went into your decision on the original title. Your credentials and your knowledge of the book's audience will also help your bargaining position.

Credibility, credentials

Publicity for your books starts before you've written a single word—before you put that first word on paper—before you touch the first keystrokes on your computer terminal to make words on a disk. Publicity generates interest and creates a demand for your book. However, before you are in demand—before either the author or the book is sought after by hordes of readers—you must have some credentials. There has to be a reason to buy the book, to hire you as a speaker, to take your words as expert testimony or expert advice on any idea at all.

Whether your book and/or area of expertise is how to weave a basket, how to solve marital problems, how to achieve good publicity for a book, how to start a typing business, or whether it discusses fire safety, teenage parents, marketing, interior design, or how to travel, answer this question: Have you firmly established in the mind of the publisher, reviewer, or reader the fact that you possess the expertise and the credentials necessary to offer this advice and to make that advice believable by anyone who reads it? To establish those credentials, to become expert in the field, you will need to do several things.

Sometimes achieving recognition as an expert is a Catch-22 situation. Before you can be invited as a guest speaker or deliver a lecture you must already be an expert. Having written a book makes you an expert, but sometimes delivering those lectures and seminars and speeches gives you the credentials necessary to write the book or to have your book accepted as the word of an expert. Many people have gained expert status, so to speak, just by having done a job or performed a task, or by giving advice and information for "free" for many years.

For example, my husband had nearly 21 years of experience in delivering fire safety advice to consumers, to ordinary people. He also had experience in teaching other fire professionals how to give that advice. So his occupational credentials alone were enough to establish his credibility, his expertise, his reason to write the book.

On the other hand, to many people, I was "only" his wife. Yes, I had been a professional writer for several years, but what real credibility did I have to co-author this book on fire safety? My previous book was on how to run a typing business. I'd gained that experience by running such a business. For the purposes of the second book, I termed myself a critically-acclaimed and award-winning author. How dare I?

1) Critics had reviewed my previous books. The other books weren't on fire safety but the critics had acclaimed my ability to write. They had said that my books were clearly written and easy to understand. The critics had given me my acclaim in the reviews of my previous books.

2) Approximately four years earlier I had also won an award for writing. It was a minor award, but it was given by a prestigious magazine. It was an honorable mention award, fourth place, runner-up. But still it was an award and it was one of two honorable mentions given when 170 other people didn't earn any mention, so I was in the top five of 175. That made me an award-winning author.

Suppose you have written an unusual text on how to give up smoking. What makes you an expert in the new technique you write about? Did you use your technique to kick your own smoking habit or did you help someone else overcome their nicotine addiction with your particular technique? For you to be considered a successful expert, you have to have shared the method, advice, or ideas with someone else.

These are just a few examples of how you establish your credibility as an author, how you gain "expert" status. As interpreted by the court, an expert is someone with more knowledge about a particular subject than the *average* individual. I probably have more knowledge than the average individual about publicity for books and authors. I haven't worked for a major New York publicist, but I have certainly accomplished more than the average person would have; and I have more working knowledge of publicity channels than the average person. My husband is certainly an expert at fire safety and fire prevention. He had more knowledge than the average person.

You don't need to establish yourself as an expert in the eyes of the court in order to write and promote your book and yourself. You're only interested in establishing your expertise in the eyes and the mind of the person who would read your book. If you're trying to convince a major publisher to back you and your book, the editor and sales staff must be sure of your credentials in order to do an effective job of selling your expertise when promoting and publicizing your book.

Explain your credentials and establish your credibility. If you don't have credentials, don't fake it. Don't lie about credentials; don't invent some to fit the occasion. On the other hand, that doesn't mean you can't be just a little bit creative. I mentioned earlier how much of an award-winning author I was. But honestly, had I won a Nobel Prize for literature? Had I won a Pulitzer Prize? No. But I had won an award, Honorable Mention, fourth out of 175 given by a prestigious magazine in a contest that was open to everybody who attended the seminar. I would not have had the guts to call myself an award-winning author if I had merely won a third place award in the local writers' club once-a-year competition which drew five entries.

I remember picking up a book dealing with a rather trendy medical problem which was written by Doctor So-and-So. After his name it didn't say M.D., Ph.D., D.D.S, or indicate any other "doctor" status. There was no indication as to what his doctor credentials were. He could have received a doctorate from a mail order university. Nowhere in the book were the author's credentials listed. I decided against buying the book because I was unsure of both his credentials and his sources of information on a particularly explosive medical phenomenon. If I had had the disease, I would not have been inclined to follow any of his advice. I felt that because he didn't indicate his credentials, he didn't have any or that they were suspect.

Building your credentials and building your expertise takes time and thought. Many times starting at the grass-roots level—at the very bottom—is the way to establish local credibility which can be used to establish more regional, state, or national credibility. Suppose you intend to write a book on "The Woman's Easy Guide to Car Repair." Do you own an automotive shop? Are you the father or mother of five daughters and you've trained them all to be "back-yard mechanics"? And have you learned how to understand an engine to fix what is necessary? Do you already do enough preventive maintenance so that you feel that you are more knowledgeable about automobile repair than the average woman?

Start by conducting neighborhood training sessions in the basics of dipstick reading, battery cable cleaning, air filter checking, and radiator seasonal needs. Advance to teaching a one-day seminar at a community center. Try to find texts or handbooks that will be somewhat helpful. Use these texts in your seminars and make notes on what should be different or improved in the book you will write. Listening to the students in your seminars is the best way to determine their information needs and both the tone and technical level of your book.

If there are 35 books on how to raise rose bushes, what makes your book the one book that people should buy? Have you had extraordinary success at state fairs? Have you been a consultant to major landscapers? Have you established credibility in the horticultural academic world? What makes you stand out? If you don't stand out, if you aren't unusual, you really face a hard time finding a market niche for your book. Answer these questions before you ever start to write your book.

Your publicity campaign should be completely mapped out based on you, the promotable author, before you ever write your book. Books written and books published and books produced don't necessarily equal books sold. Publicity will bring your book to the attention of the person who will buy it, the consumer. Sometimes to bring the books to the end consumer, you must first reach a middleman. There's more about reaching the review media in other chapters in this book. Middlemen may be either a bookstore owner, a wholesaler, a buyer for a major chain. Or a reviewer who will bring your book to the public's attention. Or the consumer may learn of your book via a newspaper or magazine article. Again it is your credibility and your author credentials that will help your book stand out and be selected by the middleman for presentation to the consumer.

by Peggy Glenn

A do-it-yourself handbook
for small publishing firms
and enterprising authors.

Hundreds of ways to publicize a good book so that it receives
the attention (and sales) that it deserves!

Extra Bonus Note

Richard Morris
Executive Director
COSMEP - The International Association of Small Publishers

The best advice that I could give self-publishers is to always use a press name or publishing name rather than your own name. There is still a great deal of discrimination against people who self-publish. Unfortunately, there are many people who confuse self-publishing with vanity publishing and there is a world of difference between the two types. You want to make your company appear established so use a publishing name when marketing your books.

Michelle Gluckow

It is important to have the best cover you can afford, especially if you plan to distribute your book in bookstores. The first impression of your book is your cover and many will ultimately judge your book by the cover only.

chapter **12**

Tips From a Book Manufacturer

An Interview with Michelle S. Gluckow

Michelle Gluckow is currently vice president of marketing for Book-mart Press, Inc. The firm specializes in the manufacture of short to medium runs of soft cover and hardcover books. All manufacturing is done completely in house at their North Bergen, New Jersey facilities.

Q: What types of people have you come into contact with who have published their books themselves?

A: While the majority of our books are produced for a variety of the large publishing houses, we do produce a fair number of titles for the small to medium size publisher who publishes anywhere from one title to fifteen titles per year.

Throughout our fifteen years in business, we have come into contact with all types of self-publishers. They range from a professor who produces a book to be used in his class to a recovered alcoholic hoping to help others in the recovery process. We've produced various cookbooks over the years for homemakers who love to cook and have assembled collections of great recipes. Computer manuals, business directories, source books, and how-to books are just a few of the different types of books we've printed. The list is endless.

Over the years we've met self-publishers who are lawyers, doctors, psychiatrists, homemakers, professors, business people, and even people who have quit their full-time jobs to become publishers.

Q: Who should consider self-publishing? Who should not?

A: Those who should consider publishing are those that have a great idea for information that can be expressed where there is currently a void for that information or they feel they can do a better job than is currently being done by an existing book.

The key to becoming a successful self-publisher is being able to market your book once it has been printed. Have a clear strategy about how you plan to sell your book and test your idea before investing a lot of money. We have seen the most junky-looking books sell well and some really good books that never made it. It's all in the marketing. Think about it. Once your book has been printed, how will you sell it?

Q: Who should not publish?

A: Someone who feels they can get rich quick and retire after one great book should reconsider and go slower. It's actually more difficult to sell a book than people think.

Q: How can people learn about printing terms such as camera-ready mechanicals, signatures, four-color process, etc.?

A: People can easily learn about the book manufacturing process by doing a little research. First, read a few books: "The Complete Guide to Self Publishing" by Marilyn and Tom Ross, "Book Publishing: A Basic Introduction," by John P. Dessauer and, believe it or not, a children's book entitled "How A Book Is Made" written by Aliki, published by Harper and Row.

If a person lives within a reasonable distance to a book manufacturer, it is worth a visit. Seeing things first-hand is always the best way to learn about how things are actually done.

Ask questions. Any book printer will be delighted to provide you with answers. From a manufacturer's point of view, it is easier to deal with a publisher who understands what it takes to produce a book.

Attend seminars. Many trade shows offer fabulous seminars offering information on a wide variety of publishing, production, and distribution oriented topics.

Take classes. There are many colleges that offer fine courses to acquaint the self-publisher with valuable information on printing and production.

Talk to other self-publishers. If possible, make contact with others who have done what you plan to do. Learn from their experiences.

Q: How do you recommend that people proceed in self-publishing?

A: Seek a book manufacturer with whom you feel comfortable. Choose one who is large enough to get the book done properly, but small enough to hold your hand throughout the production process.

A good starting point is to find three reputable printers and talk to each of them about the project. After you have discussed your project with each of them, and asked them questions about their capabilities, you will have a feel for who you like and trust the most to accomplish the task at hand.

Q: What are some of the "success stories" and "tragedies" of your customers?

A: We have worked with some bright and energetic publishers over the years. We are proud to say that we've been able to assist many publishers by offering sound advice with regard to their publishing ventures.

We have done books for many years for a publisher who publishes "business how-to" books aimed at certain ethnic markets. His books are focused and have a distinct audience and he has been successful by selling his books via seminars and lectures that he arranges.

Another successful publisher for whom we produce books writes books that are marketed to singles. His books deal with how single people can find mates, relationships, dating, etc. Again, the books are focused and directed to a specific group of people. He has done exceptionally well selling these books via mail order. This publisher started publishing out of his garage part-time and had to quit his job to handle the publishing company.

Another one of our more successful publishers published a book of ethnic recipes that contains 600 pages. She has sold over 100,000 copies and has just released her second edition. The book is distributed via mail order and through bookstores nationwide.

On the other hand, we have seen some tragic mistakes. Usually the mistakes involve publishers who over-produce to obtain a low unit price and end up with a garage full of unsold books! The one that comes to mind immediately is a publisher who published a book of his grandmother's herb recipes. Instead of ordering 500 or 1,000 copies for his initial order, he ordered 5,000 copies. He quit a job to pursue his publishing venture. Unfortunately, the whole thing was a flop.

We have also seen cases where publishers have not proofread their camera copy thoroughly and, therefore, produced unusable books which ultimately had to be redone. Believe it or not, we have seen this happen to self-publishers as well as larger, more experienced publishers who have complete editorial and production staffs.

Q: What are some tips about book printing, cover design?

A: Whenever possible, publishers should try to utilize the materials that the printer stocks for the manufacture of his book, rather than specifying a text or cover stock that the printer will have to buy in small quantities. Doing this will save the publisher money.

Work with your book printer in setting up your book so that it works best on their equipment. Determine if your printer prints in increments of eight, sixteen, twenty-four, or thirty-two-page signatures and then whenever possible try and adjust your book accordingly.

It is important to have the best cover you can afford, especially if you plan to distribute your book in bookstores. The first impression of your book is your cover and many will ultimately judge your book by the cover only. Give people a reason to purchase your book. If you are able to obtain reviews from well known people, it can only help.

Q: Do major publishers use companies such as yours to produce their books and why don't they have their own printing presses, binderies, etc.?

A: Yes, many major publishers use us as a source for producing their short to medium runs. Years ago, it was vogue for large publishers to print and bind their own titles. However, in this age of specialization, publishers have decided to do what they do best, which is publish books, and to leave the book manufacturing to book printers. Publishing and printing are two distinctly different businesses and are best left to those that specialize.

Q: Can you explain the production process? What stages does the book go through from start to finish?

A: After the book has been written, edited, and typeset into camera-ready mechanicals, it is ready to go to the printer.

When we receive a book from a publisher it is reviewed by a member of our production staff before it goes into the plant to be manufactured. All of the manufacturing details are entered on a work ticket, which will act as instructions to each department on what they have to do to produce this particular title. After the job has been written up, it will go through the following steps. The steps include: camera, prep, plates, press, and bindery. I will attempt to explain how a book is produced at Book-mart Press. We utilize offset, sheet-fed presses for printing.

Prep. The camera-ready copy (mechanicals) will be shot. A negative will be produced for each page. The negatives, called film, are then put into position on large sheets of plastic (called goldenrod). This process is called stripping. The negatives are laid down so that when the printed sheets are folded, the books will be in consecutive page order. Depending on the final trim size of the book, pages are stripped into signatures of eight, sixteen, twenty-four, or thirty-two page increments. The negatives are then opened up and opaqued. This process is done to eliminate any stray marks that have been done during typesetting and camera work.

Plates. At this point the stripped flats can be used to produce a set of metal printing plates, or a set of proofs called blueprints, also called bluelines and silverlines. A blueprint allows the publisher one last check to see exactly what the book will look like before the paper is actually put through the press. A publisher can still make type changes at the blueprint stage. Hopefully, there won't be too many pages that have to be shot again as they can get expensive. If the publisher foregoes a blueprint, then a metal plate is made and the printing process begins. The image on the negatives is burned into a metal plate through a series of photo sensitive lights.

Press. The developed plate is hung on press and the pages are printed.

Bindery. Flat printed sheets are moved from the press room to the bindery area. Here the printed sheets are folded (into signatures) of eight, sixteen, twenty-four, or thirty-two pages. This is the case for sheets that come off a sheet-fed press. In the case of a web press, the paper is fed into the press in rolls and the signatures come off the press already folded. The folded signatures are then collated and a cover is glued on in the case of a perfectbound (soft cover) book. The book is trimmed and packed in cartons. Your books are now ready for sale.

When a book is to be case-bound and smythsewn, the collated signatures are actually sewn together using needles and thread on an automatic sewing machine. The sewn book block is then nipped, smashed, and glued to remove excess air. While this is being done, the casemaking department is producing cases for the exterior of the book. The binders boards can either be covered with cloth and foil-stamped or preprinted and film-laminated. The smyth-sewn book block is then cased into the case cover on the hard cover binding line. The endsheets that are attached to the first text page and last text page are affixed to the boards on the interior of the case cover. Head and foot bands are attached to the head and foot of the book. This process is called casing in.

Publishers should seek a book manufacturer who can best service their needs. This leads to a discussion of the various types of printers.

Q: What are the different types of printers? What is the difference between a copy center, a printer, and a book manufacturer?

A: Simply answered, there are those print shops that will accept all types of work from a business card to a fancy four-color catalog. And then there are printers who are specialists and excel in a particular area. For example, at Book-mart Press we produce books and books only!

There are copy centers (quick printers) commercial printers, book printers, magazine printers, mass market paperback specialists, juvenile book printers, etc. Some printers are set up to produce runs of 10-100 copies, others may specialize in runs of 300-10,000 copies, while other may not touch a print run of under 10,000 copies.

Generally speaking, a quick printer will have small presses and will be limited as to how many copies they can produce. Unless a copy shop specializes in short run books, they will probably contract with a trade bindery for the binding.

There are all different types of book manufacturers. There are those that specialize in short-to-medium runs and those that specialize in long runs. And within the specialty of short and long runs there are those printers who are suited for booklets (books with small page counts that are generally bound with staples, or saddlestitched), those that excel in perfectbound (soft cover) books and those that excel in casebound (hard cover) books. Hard cover books can either be smythsewn or adhesive (glued on the spine of the book, rather than sewn). There are those that excel in a combination of the aforementioned, such as short and medium runs of short and hard cover books. Some printers are best equipped to produce four color juvenile books.

Many book manufacturers do not print their own covers or dust jackets. They contract with a component printer for such printing. Some contract their bindery work to a trade binder. This can result in a loss of control in the scheduling of a job. It is suggested that you choose a printer close by and that you meet with them and visit their facilities whenever possible.

Q: How should a publisher go about requesting a quotation?

A: After your book is written and you can approximate the number of pages, you should request a quote for your project. When doing so, you should include the following information:

1) Quantity—the number of books you wish to produce.
2) Number of pages—number of text pages, exclusive of cover.
3) Trim size of book—this is the actual size of the book when bound. Some common standard sizes are five and three-eighths by eight and a half, six by nine, seven by ten, and eight and a half by eleven.
4) Text presswork—this refers to the number of ink colors being utilized for the text; i.e., black ink throughout, all line copy or prints two colors, red and black throughout with twenty photos. Be sure to advise the printer if there are any photos and what you will supply him with.
5) Cover presswork—refers to the number of colors that will be utilized to print the cover and the type of finish on the cover. Examples: Prints two colors and press varnished on covers one, four, and spine or prints four-color process and film laminated on covers one, four, and spine.

6) Text stock—type and weight of paper to be used.
   Example: 50 lb. white offset, 60 lb. natural offset. Specify whether you want an offset sheet, an opaque sheet, or a coated sheet.

7) Cover stock—the type and weight of the cover stock to be utilized.

8) Dust jacket—specify how many colors, type of stock, and type of finish.

9) Type of binding:
   Saddlestitched—generally used for booklets under 100 pages. Two or three staples are placed on the binding edge.
   Perfectbound—cover is glued to the text pages. Also referred to as softcover binding.
   Casebound—also referred to as hardcover binding. This can be either smythsewn or adhesive case. Advise whether you wish to have a cloth-covered case or a preprinted case cover. If you use a cloth cover, specify the type of cloth and how many hits of foil stamping you wish to use.

10) Smythsewn paperback—a paper cover is glued to a smythsewn book block.

11) Mechanical binding:
    Plastic comb—utilized for manuals or music books, so that a book will lie completely flat.
    Spiral wire—one continuous wire is inserted in a coil fashion on the binding edge. Typically used for college notebooks.
    Wire-o-binding—two wire rings are placed on each hole along the binding edge. Manuals make use of this type of binding.

12) Shrinkwrapping—a heat sealed plastic bag can either be wrapped around each individual book or around three or four copies at a time.

13) Split runs—specify if you wish to produce part of the run in softcover and part in hardcover. Your printer will have to have this information when production begins for your job.

More tips on book manufacturing

You must communicate with your printer. If your books are needed for a specific date, make sure that the required delivery date can be met before you award the job.

If you have a particular concern about how something will reproduce, seek the advice of your printer. If you are unsure about margin requirements, ask your printer, or better yet show the printer a sample page before you begin typesetting the entire book.

Ironing out all of the details in advance will allow your printer to produce the product you desire and will save both parties unnecessary aggravation.

As previously mentioned, we, at Book-mart Press, have been instrumental in producing books for many publishers who started out of their basements. Today, some of these same publishers have fancy offices, production staffs, extensive warehouse, etc. While our publishing clients have expanded and grown we have also done much of the same. Starting off with one press, a little over fifteen years ago, we are now producing soft and hardcover, smythsewn books completely in-house. Needless to say, we are proud to serve the publishing community.

Teresa Griffin

While attending an all-day conference of the American Society of Journalists and Authors, I had the good fortune of being introduced to a senior producer of CBS "This Morning." The producer was anxious to book me on his program but said he wanted to wait until my book was available in large quantities because he said it would probably generate large orders.

chapter **13**

How a Letter Turned a Mother into a Publisher

by Teresa Griffin (as told to Paula DuPont-Kidd)

T he irony of now being considered a writer and self-publisher does not just begin with the fact that I was once so timid, I didn't like calling information for phone numbers. Irony lies with the fact that my life is complicated enough juggling the nap, eating, school, sports, and social schedules of my six children, ranging in age from eighteen months to seventeen years. I certainly would have never projected that I might one day try to balance publishing and marketing my book, "Letters of Hope."

In a sense, motherhood launched me into my writing career, and motherhood keeps me rooted amid the flurry of excitement when ten more book orders come in the mail or when the phone rings with Joan Lunden's secretary or Barbara Bush's top White House aide on the line. Probably if it weren't for the humbling experience of diaper changings or exhausting days of driving teens to their friends' houses on the other side of suburbia—I would be on publishing cloud nine somewhere.

The irony of my new-found publishing career more regretfully lies with the fact that it was my two-year-old son Ryan's accidental drowning three years ago that forced a pen in my hand. It was something to clutch when the tragedy gave me too much to grasp. I'm still not sure what made me write, but it made me feel better. I kept all those scraps of yellow paper and would look at them as the months passed. There was something very healing about doing that because it showed me how much I improved by seeing the bad shape I was in during those earlier times. Writing, quite definitely, had become an instrument to my recovery.

Writing as an instrument to healing

Writing wasn't my first recourse, however. As an avid reader, I turned to the source through which I'd always found much comfort. It wasn't long after Ryan's death that I went to the library to try to find any books I could that would help me deal with this. To my disappointment, there were few books out there. The best one I found was one written by Harriett Sarnoff Schiff, "The Bereaved Parent," which describes each step of the mourning process. It was the Bible to me and I think I read it three times in those early months.

However, the book wasn't enough. Surprisingly, one of my greatest sources of strength came in the mail when I received a letter from a woman I never met. Eight years earlier, her five-year-old daughter, Ehrin, died in a sudden, accidental death. One of the many messages that stood out to me was this mother sharing the first time she smiled again—an event I never thought I'd personally know again.

Her letter was a catalyst. It stirred something in me and spoke to me in a way no one else could. I was hungry for more. I decided to write a book of letters for other grieving parents. After *The Philadelphia Inquirer* wrote an article about me in July 1988, I received about eighty letters from other parents sharing their stories. That newspaper article led to other local ones, thus inspiring more letters. It also led to appearances on "AM Philadelphia" and on CNBC. Oddly, I found that I received only two letters in response to my TV appearances, despite what I thought would be greater exposure.

Appearing on "AM Philadelphia" rendered another little insight that has turned out to be rather prophetic in its simplicity. Another guest on the program with me was a man who worked at a grief recovery institute and was a published author. After the show he turned to me and said, "Just make sure that you really want to do this, because it will change your life."

Around the time of the first newspaper article, I had also read a wonderful book, "Mothers Talking," a book compiled of chapters written by mothers sharing very personal and unique views about life and motherhood. It was a very special message and one to which I could relate. It was the combination of reading this book and all of those powerful letters that triggered the idea to put together a book. I thought that if these letters affected me the way they did, they probably would be an enormous comfort to that vast, often overlooked population of parents out there suffering in silence. According to the international support group, The Compassionate Friends, approximately 118,000 children and young adults under age twenty-four die annually in the United States. This is just one statistic that indicates the number of parents new to this life-changing tragedy; it hardly reflects all of the other parents who have been mourning for years or those parents whose adult children have died. As I often say, everyone is someone's child.

I guess if I had been a true businessperson, I would have seized upon the chance to meet the demands of this large audience that I identified. After all, I had the message and I had the audience. But, more important to me was and is making the same kind of comfort I found available to others in pain. No one understands more than I the desperation parents feel after the loss of a child, and no one understands better the lack of materials out there. My first intention was not to make money, but to offer support to other parents.

Publishing becomes a mission

Somewhere along the line without my realizing it, I became a woman with a mission and slowly started to learn about publishing. I read a couple of publishing books by some authors featured in this book. Of course, almost from the very beginning, my friend and then-neighbor Patricia Gallagher nudged me with undaunted encouragement and guidance.

Although I had all the raw materials for writing a book, I was a little overwhelmed by it and by all the letters I had. (At that time, I had well over 100 letters.) Deciding on the format and style of what was originally a booklet along with narrowing down the letters, presented the first challenge in getting out of the starting gate. The more I surveyed other interesting books and the more I learned about how parents get through life, the more possibilities I saw for my project. What helped me to get grounded with "Letters of Hope" was keeping it simple. Who better to express the feelings of grief and hope than the parents themselves in the way they chose to convey it. For this reason, I opted to edit the letters only for grammar, not style. I wanted each one to remain unique.

Another main objective for the project, was to offer a broad sampling of stories so that any parent who lost a child could pick it up and relate to at least one story. This is why I narrowed the letters down to the twenty that represented instances of stillbirth, accidental death, death to terminal illness, etc. Above all, I was ever mindful that the purpose of the book was to offer hope, and I chose only letters with uplifting messages.

Finally, I had the letters chosen and the format decided. It was a matter of having a typesetter design the pages and help me put together the book. I chose a very simple illustration for the cover, a rose, which bears significance to me. I like to believe that Ryan lets me know he hears my prayers to him by showing me a white rose throughout the course of my day. On more than a few occasions, when he was very much on my mind, I asked him specifically to send me a white rose, and sure enough I found them in some form, real or in illustrations.

Although I didn't and don't have any particular budget for the book, I wanted to publish it as simply as possible since I knew I didn't stand to make any money on my initial printing. With inexpensive stock and cover, I printed 150 copies all of which I probably gave away in a matter of a couple of months. It wasn't a great disappointment to me that I didn't turn a profit on that first printing, I more or less expected to give them away just to get the book out. I also used it as a promotional tool for itself as I worked up the nerve to send it to various celebrities in search for a powerful foreword for the book or, at the least, a positive review. When I say various celebrities, I really mean about a handful of actors like Ben Vereen and Mary Tyler Moore who had suffered the loss of a child.

Bearing out what the expert on the TV talk show had told me about publishing changing my life, me—the person afraid to call information— decided to send a copy of the book to Barbara Bush, whose daughter, Robin, died at age two of leukemia. I knew it was a longshot that she'd even receive it, and an even farther shot that she'd actually read it. But something inside made me try, and I sent it anyway. Maybe part of the reason I was doing things for the book that I would have never done before is because I believed in the book and its message, as if it were an entity unto itself. I was representing a book, not myself.

"Something" from the White House

Meanwhile, although I had run out of books, I held off printing more in the off-chance I'd receive a foreword from one of the celebrities. I was just about ready to go to press with another order, leaving a couple of blank pages in the front, when I received a call from Mrs. Bush's top White House aide. After the first initial minutes of shock of the phone call, I heard the words that Mrs. Bush read the book and loved it and would probably write something for it. Her aide was actually apologetic to me that Mrs. Bush probably wouldn't have time to write a full-fledged letter for the booklet, but that she would write "something."

That "something" came a few weeks later in the form of a one-page letter extolling the benefits of my booklet and sharing a very warm glimpse of how she and the President felt when their daughter died. She ended the letter with: "I welcome your new 'Letters of Hope,' and I pray that you are able to reach as many people as possible with its truly hopeful messages."

Her letter came like another beacon, once again reassuring me that "Letters of Hope" is meant to be. Her letter also validated for me the whole purpose of what I was trying to do with my "letters." As I said before, probably what keeps me from losing perspective at times like this is the reality of a three-year-old pounding on my bedroom door while I'm trying to write, demanding I come out and tuck him into bed.

Mrs. Bush's letter has pushed me into another direction. I decided to expand the booklet into a book with perfect binding which should roll off the presses about the same time as "For All the Write Reasons." I knew I leaned toward this direction of publishing a book, however, a chance meeting recently in New York City ignited the urgency of publishing it soon.

While attending an all-day conference of the American Society of Journalists and Authors, I had the good fortune of being introduced to a senior producer of CBS "This Morning." The producer was anxious to book me on his program but said he wanted to wait until my book was available in large quantities because he said it would probably generate large orders. He called two days later to confirm my publication date and I was told to call for my booking as soon as "Letters of Hope" was ready.

Still, the success of "Letters of Hope" and the discovery of all the other yet unexplored issues of dealing with a child's loss has inspired me to write another book. This book, tentatively titled "Triumph of the Spirit," I envision as a compilation of experts speaking on subjects varying from AIDS deaths to grief and addiction. I see this as being a complete source for grieving parents, covering the gaps not filled in any other single source. I'm not sure yet if I'm going to self-publish or look for a publishing company. I think I'll let the same spirit that has guided me through "Letters of Hope" direct me through my next project. All the while, I'll be looking for white roses along the way.

Psychology/Counseling

L E T T E R S   O F   H O P E

"A heartfelt collection of personal experiences dealing with the seemingly insurmountable tragedy of child loss. Authored by the families of those lost, the book profiles the pain, strength, and recovery of bereaved families. This work fills a tremendous void on this sensitive issue."

> —*Dr. Herb Kosmahl*
> *Atlanta, Georgia*

"Letters of Hope is valuable not only for the insights it will provide us as funeral directors but especially for families who have lost children . . . and are in need of the hope to know that the acute pain they suffer will subside and allow them over time to live more normal lives again."

> —*Joseph A. Quinn*
> *Funeral Director*
> *Philadelphia, Pennsylvania*

"For the newly bereaved it is essential that they be given hope in the midst of their feeling of hopelessness. This book does it beautifully."

> —*Mary Ehmann*
> *Founder and Leader of the*
> *Valley Forge Chapter of*
> *The Compassionate Friends, Inc.*

LETTERS OF HOPE—Teresa Griffin

Cedarbrook Press
Box 2
Richboro, PA 18954

ISBN 0-9629584-0-9

ISBN 0-9629584-0-9

9 780962 958403

LETTERS OF HOPE

SOFTCOVER: $9.95

Cover Art © 1992 by Susannah Thomer
Illustrations © 1992 by M. Pamela Soda

Jane Dewey Heald

In another false start, I had created some fine illustrations, based on newspaper photos, when I realized that I could not use anyone else's copyright work without permission.

chapter **14**

How I Backed into Publishing

by Jane Dewey Heald

In 1981, I was a co-founder of the National Support Center for Families of the Aging and co-author of its seminar materials, "Help for Families of the Aging." I prepared mechanicals on a second-hand Selectric typewriter, then added press-type headlines. With money from a small grant, I ordered 500 comb-bound copies from a local printer. Eventually, we connected with a major Michigan manufacturer, who reprinted the book several times, reproducing a photograph from my darkroom for the cover. In our zeal to put this helpful material into the hands of everyone who needed it, we priced it too low: $17.95 for a large, spiral-bound workbook plus three cassette tapes, postpaid.

Picking up the pieces

By the time the non-profit organization was dissolved in 1986, the second edition of the seminar materials was ready for publication. It had been piloted and enthusiastically received in churches, family service associations, community centers, and adult day care centers around the country. It was too valuable a resource to abandon.

After receiving a positive response to my query letter, I sent the manuscript to a religious publishing house in Philadelphia. Several months went by before they declared their reviewers had liked the seminar—and requested that we rewrite it as a trade book to be marketed to individuals.

This posed a problem. I felt the group experience was essential. Caregivers who are stuck in their feelings need each other, as isolation is part of the distress. So I refused to abandon the seminar format. But I wondered how many more delays I'd encounter as I made the rounds to other publishers.

About that time, I took a couple of self-publishing books along on my summer vacation. When I returned home, refreshed and energetic, I said, "Heck, I'll publish it myself." What a publisher does for an author is marketing—and I knew the aging network well. I was also committed to keeping the seminar in print over the long haul.

A crash course in book production

My sister is a bookseller, specializing in mail-order books for communicators (Tools of the Trade, 3718 Seminary Road, Alexandria, VA 22304). From her catalog I obtained books about type, book design, printing technology, authors' laws, and, of course, John Kremer's "Directory of Book, Catalog, and Magazine Printers."

I had been embedding typesetting codes in word-processed disks for a newsletter and considered producing the book mechanicals the same way. But typeset galley, even with embedded codes, is expensive and I had struggled with unpredictable numbers of lines. The layout of the new leader's manual and workbook was complicated by many charts and diagrams. I needed complete control. One self-publishing book I read recommended using a daisy wheel printer. For a couple of weeks, I experimented with different print wheels and proportional spacing. But it was a false start; I was never satisfied with the results.

Reading "Inside Xerox Ventura Publisher," by Cavuto and Berst, convinced me to purchase Ventura software for my IBM-compatible computer. One of the advantages of Ventura is that you can experiment with typefaces, each of which results in different number of lines from the same text. I wanted to end up with a number of pages that was a multiple of sixteen, as it is advantageous to manufacture books with whole numbers of signatures. Finally, I chose the Times Roman font (which uses space economically) for body text, and Helvetica headlines, adding a little extra white space ("leading," pronounced "ledding") between lines for maximum legibility.

I located a Postscript service bureau who would proof at 300 dots-per-inch, then produce final high resolution output at 2,540 dots per inch. When it came down to the wire, I saved time by transmitting some of the files by modem.

I knew I wanted illustrations, but was doubtful about getting good half-tone quality on the paper I would be using. I paid an artist to make a few sample line drawings. Unfortunately, they were too cartoon-like for my subject. So I turned to another book my sister had sent, Raymond Dorn's "How to Be Your Own Artist." My knowledgeable daughter gave me a package of Mactac, which is a clear plastic film that can be stuck over a photograph, then peeled off and reapplied to a piece of white paper. The Mactac surface "takes" either pencil or pen and ink, so that—by tracing over the dark areas of the photograph and photocopying the final result—one can produce a sketch that resembles a real human being. It was a simple matter to wax the sketches and stick them in place on the finished mechanicals produced by the service bureau.

In another false start, I had created some fine illustrations, based on newspaper photos, when I realized that I could not use anyone else's copyright work without permission. So again, I enlisted the help of friends, photographed them, then went back into the darkroom to produce my originals.

Self-publishing experts stressed the importance of an attractive cover. I couldn't afford to hire a graphic designer, so I did the next best thing. Using a silhouette derived from one of my photographs, I designed several covers, in a variety of typefaces. Then I called one of my friends who is a graphic artist, "Bob, would you be willing to take a look at what I've done and give me some constructive criticism?" In half an hour he re-arranged, enlarged, and discarded elements, giving me enough ideas that I could go home and complete a fine design.

The only step remaining was selecting a printer. I sent out about twenty requests for quotations to printers chosen from Kremer's directory, being careful to follow his sample Request for Quotation (RQ) format. I chose the least expensive bid, but would not necessarily work with that printer again. Fortunately, I had asked for approval copies before shipment. I'd specified double-wire binding, so the books could be turned completely inside out. When they arrived, the bindings were too tight; the pages couldn't be turned. To the printer's credit, they did undo the shrink-wrap on all 2,000 books and rebind them. But meanwhile my pre-publication flyers had all gone out; I had a huge stack of orders waiting when the books finally arrived. (The same printer, on a reprint, neglected to replace an updated page and had lost the negative for the cover. Always inspect each page of each printing with an eagle eye, and always nag until you get your original mechanicals back.)

Working with a different printer, on another book, I spelled out in meticulous detail the quality I wanted for the black-and-white cover photo: "crisp, clear whites and deep, rich blacks; we will not accept muddy grays..." and enclosed samples of what I consider good and poor reproduction. That printer came through beautifully. (It helps to give the sales rep concrete instructions he can pass along to the people in the plant.)

Becoming a salesman

To my surprise, I found that producing the sales flyer was almost as time-consuming—and expensive— as producing the book. I had heard about firms with enormous four-color web presses, firms that could supply 50,000 glossy flyers at a very reasonable cost-per-piece. Process color (accurate reproduction as seen by the eye) requires color separation negatives from a four-by-five-inch transparency, so I began looking for a commercial photographer. The man I selected not only made my books look good, but also took an interest in the total design and made important suggestions— including the suggestion that I consult a graphic artist. Again, I took in my best efforts, then picked her brain for an hour, which was much less expensive than asking her to furnish all the creative input. Despite my faith in my own artistic abilities, I have found that judicious use of graphic professionals is a wise investment. (Just as, despite my faith in my own words, I always run books past a copy editor!)

My market is specialized: people interested in helping care-givers. Sales letters and flyers emphasize that the materials are complete, tested, and loving. I do direct-mail marketing via bulk mailings and also provide flyers for distribution by others. I send display copies and flyers to large conferences via conference book services and letters offering complimentary copies to small conferences. My targets include adult day care centers, area agencies on aging, support groups, churches and synagogues, gerontology departments, cooperative extension services, family service associations, community centers, and others in the aging network. Lately, hospitals have shown a lot of interest, as they compete in their own marketplaces.

Since the book is intended for groups rather than individuals, I have not tried to work with a distributor. I give bookstores a forty percent discount if they prepay with a "stop order," but do not suggest they stock the book. My flyers request pre-payment; however, I will accept authorized purchase orders or phone orders. I do not supply preview copies, but will, upon request, prepare a sixty-day invoice so that people can return books found not suitable. Although all my books are guaranteed, only one or two per year are returned. The people I serve are an honest lot, and I have a very small accounts receivable file. I usually send only half a dozen monthly statements, which are produced via my DAC-Easy accounting software.

I've sent out several hundred complimentary copies. Often I don't see reviews, but become aware that I'm suddenly receiving orders from a particular market. I have, from time to time, accepted speaking engagements, but have not attempted back-of-the-room sales. "Help for Families of Aging" is not geared for impulse buyers.

On the other hand, it is the only seminar I know of that concentrates on the emotional issues of caregiving. It is life-changing for those who participate. I see no urgency to market quickly; care-givers' needs will continue into the foreseeable future. I have met all the costs; from now on the books will be profitable and should continue to sell steadily.

The enjoyment of doing it all

I still work from home. As each of our three children moved out, my office space expanded. I still answer every letter from harried caregivers. The National Support Center had an office manager, but I prefer to be the whole cat—no employee paperwork, and no interruptions. I like the variety of tasks and the independence. I have total control and enjoy taking all the risk: intellectual, artistic, and financial. Flexible hours are a big plus. One day a week I turn on the answering machine and go play with my grandchild!

There are easier ways to earn money. I'm not getting rich, but I have repaid $12,000 I borrowed and have money in the bank. Recently, I brought out a book of stories that I had commissioned my ninety-three-year-old father to write. It's delightful and has sold well in all the parishes he served in his long career, as well as to senior book groups. The joy it has brought our family is not measurable in dollars.

My next book, which is almost ready for piloting, will be "A Place to Call Home," a four-session seminar for families of nursing home residents. The market is smaller—there are only 18,000 nursing homes in the country—but the need is great.

My advice? Go for quality, insist that everything be exactly right. Study and network, you can always learn something. Start small—don't get in over your head. And be patient. Everything takes longer than you originally thought!

The leader's manual has everything you need!

Class resources

- Detailed lesson plans for eight two-hour sessions, with lecture material, examples, and discussion questions.
- Minute-by-minute session outlines.
- Readings, pencil exercises, skits, and monologues—the entire 80 pages participants receive in their workbooks.

Leadership skills

- Complete directions and publicity materials for initiating and funding a seminar.
- Criteria for selecting participants.
- Ways to establish confidentiality, confirm reasonable expectations, and create an accepting climate.
- More than 60 surefire phrases to use when explaining something, sensing resistance, pushing for a breakthrough, or trying to keep a discussion on track.
- Hints on responding to participants who try to monopolize the group or expect you to solve their problems for them.

Background understandings

- Underlying dynamics in caregiving families.
- 15 Imprisoning Forces that sometimes keep caregivers "stuck."
- Religious and cultural assumptions that can block effective problem-solving.

Who can sponsor this caregivers' seminar?

- Adult day care centers
- Area agencies on aging
- Caregiver support groups
- Churches and synagogues
- Community colleges
- Cooperative extension services
- Employee assistance counselors
- Family service associations
- Hospitals and medical centers
- Y's, community centers and clubs
- You can!

Highly qualified authors:

Carol Spargo Pierskalla, Ph.D., is Director of Aging Today & Tomorrow, a program of the American Baptist Churches, USA. Carol received the doctoral degree in counseling psychology from Northwestern University. She pioneered this seminar in 1980 and was the first president of the National Support Center for Families of the Aging.

Jane Dewey Heald, M.S., was a participant in the first seminar. She is past Executive Director of the National Support Center for Families of the Aging, where she edited the bulletin *Change*, presented seminars and workshops, and facilitated a caregiver support group. In 1986 she was honored to receive one of AARP's first National Caregivers Awards.

SUPPORT SOURCE
420 Rutgers Avenue, Swarthmore, PA 19081
Phone: (215) 544-3605

Concerned about caregiver stress?

You can offer more than a band-aid.

These books make it easy. Eight weeks of sharing — a lifetime of benefit.

With this seminar you can empower caregivers!

- It is HOPEFUL — Almost all caregiving situations can be improved.
- It is RESPONSIBLE — Its goal is to enable families to implement optimum present and future care of aging relatives.
- It is NON-JUDGMENTAL — Families have different histories, resources, and circumstances; therefore different caregiving alternatives are appropriate.
- It is GROWTH-PRODUCING — Participants receive problem-solving skills and encouragement, not rescue or advice.
- It is LOVING — The seminar gives priority to developing and maintaining supportive relationships.
- It is TESTED — This second edition is based on a seminar package published in 1982 by the National Support Center for Families of the Aging. The revision has been successfully piloted by professionals and lay persons from Connecticut to Texas.

Participants learn more than techniques:

- To understand intellectually and emotionally what happens to families as they adjust to the losses of aging.
- To use the skill of Active Listening to support members of the group, their aging relatives, and other people in their families.
- To sort problems into categories and let go of those they cannot change.
- To recognize and accept their feelings about unsolvable problems.
- To help each other generate and evaluate practical alternatives.
- To consider the needs of everyone in their families, not just the elderly.
- To ponder what's really important to them and balance the resources spent on different areas of their lives.
- To permit themselves to set limits.
- To trust their own decisions and reclaim control of their lives.

Order today!

Yes, send **Help for Families of the Aging** to:

Organization

Name

Address and ZIP

| | Leader's Manual
2nd edition, includes workbook
ISBN 0-9619558-0-5
LC Catalog Card 88-60169
224 pages, illustrated, @ $39.95 $ _____

| | Workbook
2nd edition
ISBN 0-9619558-1-3
80 pages, illustrated, @ $11.95 $ _____

Quantity discounts: 2-5 copies of single title. 20%; 6-10 copies, 30%; 11-25 copies, 40%
Bookstores: We accept STOP orders.

SUBTOTAL FOR BOOKS $ _____

Sales tax: 6% (Pennsylvania only) $ _____

Shipping charges:
☐ Fourth Class: $2.00 for the first book;
    50¢ each additional book.
    (Canada, US $2.60 and 60¢)
☐ UPS: $4.00 for the first book.
    50¢ each additional book. $ _____

TOTAL — Check enclosed $ _____

Send orders to the publisher:
SUPPORT SOURCE   Money back guarantee.
420 Rutgers Avenue   If any book isn't all
Swarthmore, PA 19081   you expect, return it for a prompt, full refund.

All orders must include payment or agency purchase order.

Enthusiastic reviews:

"It gave me a whole new outlook on life at a time when I needed it most."
Seminar participant

"The material is great. Neither the woman working with me nor I had ever led this type of group before. I will be ready for another next fall."
George Stahl, Central Presbyterian Church, Huntington, New York

"The empathy and respect shown to caregivers and care recipients are evident throughout... Your seminar is most valuable, as it helps caregivers help themselves."
Carolyn Ward, Family Caregivers Program, National Council on the Aging, Inc.

Jeff Herman

There are many ways to get an agent; determination will be one of your most important assets. The best way to gain access to potential agents is by networking with fellow writers.

chapter **15**

An Introduction to Literary Agents

by Jeff Herman
reprinted from my book,
"The Insiders' Guide to Book Editors, Publishers, and Literary Agents"
(Prima Publishing)

In a way, literary agents are like stock or real estate brokers—they bring buyers and sellers together, help formulate successful deals, and receive a piece of the action (from the seller) for facilitating the "marriage."

More specifically, agents search for talented writers, marketable nonfiction book concepts, and superior fiction manuscripts to represent. Some agents also seek poetry, plays, and teleplays. Simultaneously, agents are cultivating their relationships with publishers.

When an agent discovers material she thinks she can sell to a publisher, she signs the writer as a client, works with the writer to perfect the material to maximize its chances of selling, and then submits it to one or more appropriate editorial contacts.

The agent has the contacts. Many writers don't know any appropriate editors; even if they do, the typical agent tends to know many more and also knows which editors like to see what material. A dynamic agent achieves the maximum exposure possible for the writer's material, which greatly enhances the odds that the material will get published—and for more favorable terms.

Having an agent gives your material access to the powers-that-be who otherwise might be inaccessible. Publishers assume that material submitted by an agent has been screened and is much more likely to fit their needs than the random material swimming in the slush pile.

If and when a publisher makes an offer to publish the material, the agent acts in the author's behalf and negotiates the advance (the money paid up front), royalties, control of subsidiary rights, and many other important and marginal contractual clauses. The agent acts as the writer's advocate with the publisher for as long as the book remains in print or licensing opportunities exist.

The agent knows the most effective methods for negotiating the best advance and other contract terms and is likely to have more leverage with the publisher than you.

There's more to a book contract than the advance and the royalty schedule. There are several key clauses you may know nothing about but would accept to expedite the deal. Negotiating any deal can be intimidating if you don't know much about the territory; ignorance is a great disadvantage during a negotiation. An agent, however, understands every detail of the contract and knows where and how it should be modified or expanded in your favor.

Where appropriate, an agent acts to sell subsidiary rights after the book is sold to the publisher. These rights can include serial rights, foreign rights, dramatic and movie rights, audio and video rights, and a range of syndication and licensing possibilities. Often, a dynamic agent may be more successful at selling the subsidiary rights than the publisher would be.

No agent succeeds in selling every project she or he represents. Some projects, especially fiction, are marketed for a long time before a publisher is found (if ever). What's important is that you feel sure the agent continues to believe in the project and is actively trying to sell it.

For his or her work, the agent receives a 10 to 15 percent commission against the writer's advance and all subsequent income relevant to the sold project.

Although this is a noticeable chunk of the income from your work, the agent's involvement should net you much more than you would have earned otherwise. The agent's power to round up several publishers to consider your work opens up the possibility that more than one house will make an offer, which means you will be more likely to get a higher advance and have more leverage regarding the contract clauses.

The writer-agent relationship can become a rewarding business partnership. An agent can advise you objectively about the direction your writing career should take. Also, through his contacts, an agent may be able to obtain book-writing assignments you would never have gotten on your own.

There are many ways to get an agent; determination will be one of your most important assets. The best way to gain access to potential agents is by networking with fellow writers. Find out who they use and what's being said about whom. Maybe some of your colleagues can introduce you to their agents or at least allow you to use their names when contacting their agents. Most agents will be receptive to a writer who has been referred by a current and valued client.

Literary Market Place (R.R. Bowker), Writer's Market (Writer's Digest Books), and Literary Agents of North America (Author's Aid Associates) list names, addresses, and specialties of agents. You can also write to the two major agent trade associations, the Independent Literary Agents Association and the Society of Author's Representatives, and request a current copy of their membership lists. Membership in either organization implies that the agent meets specific performance requirements and professional standards.

The universally accepted way to establish contact with an agent is to send a query letter. Agents are less interested in oral presentations. Be sure the letter is personalized; nobody likes generic, photocopies of letters that look like they've been sent to everyone.

Think of the query as a sales pitch. Describe the nature of your project and offer to send additional material (enclose a SASE). Include all relevant information about yourself—a resume if it's applicable. If you're querying about a nonfiction project, many agents won't mind receiving a complete proposal. But you might prefer to wait and see how the agent feels about the concept before sending the proposal.

For queries about fiction projects, most agents prefer to receive story synopses; if they like what they see, they'll request sample chapters. Most agents won't consider incomplete fiction manuscripts, basically because few publishers are willing to.

If you enclose a SASE, most agents will respond, one way or another, within a reasonable period of time. If the agent asks to see your material, submit it promptly with a polite note that you would like to hear back within four weeks on a nonfiction proposal, or eight weeks on fiction material. If you haven't heard from the agent by that time, write or call to determine the status of your submission.

You're entitled to circulate your material to more than one agent at a time, but you're obligated to let each agent know that you are doing so. (Some agents won't consider multiple submissions.) If and when you do sign with an agent, immediately notify other agents still considering your work that it's no longer available.

At least 200 literary agents are active in the United States, and their perceptions of what is and isn't marketable will vary widely, which is why a few or even several rejections should never deter writers who believe in themselves.

Some agents charge a fee simply to evaluate your work (most don't), regardless of whether or not they choose to ultimately represent it. Writer's Market and Literary Agents of North America identify those agents who charge fees.

When an agent eventually agrees to represent your work, it's time for the agent to begin selling herself to you. Just as when you're seeking employment, you don't have to work with an agent simply because she wants to work with you.

Do some checking before agreeing to work with a particular agent. If possible, meet the agent in person. Much can be learned from in-person meetings that can't be acquired from telephone conversations. See what positive or negative information you can obtain about the agent through your writers' network. Ask the agent for a client list and permission to call clients for references. Find out the agent's specialties.

Ask for a copy of the agent's standard contract. Most agents today will want to codify your relationship with a written agreement; this should equally protect both of you. Make sure you are comfortable with everything in the agreement before signing it. Again, talking with fellow writers and reading books on the subject are the best ways to acquire a deeper understanding about industry practices.

When choosing an agent, follow your best instincts. Don't settle for anyone who doesn't seem reputable, or who isn't genuinely enthusiastic about you and your work.

Agents aren't for everyone. In some instances, you may be better off on your own. Perhaps you actually do have sufficient editorial contacts and industry savvy to negotiate good deals by yourself. If so, what incentive do you have to share your income with an agent? Of course, having an agent might provide you the intangible benefits of added prestige, save you the trouble of making submissions and bargaining, or act as a buffer through whom you can indirectly negotiate for tactical reasons.

You might also consider representing yourself if your books are so specialized that only a few publishers are potential buyers. Your contacts at such houses might be much stronger than any agent's could be.

Some entertainment/publishing attorneys can do everything an agent does, though there's no reason to believe that they can necessarily do more. A major difference between the two is that the lawyer may charge a set hourly fee or retainer instead of a commission, or any negotiated combination thereof. In rare instances, writer-publisher disputes might need to be settled in a court of law, and a lawyer familiar with the industry then becomes a necessity.

The plusses and minuses of having an agent should be calculated like any other business service you might retain—it should benefit you more than it costs you. Generally speaking, the only real cost of using an agent is the commission. Of course, using the wrong agent may cause you more deficits than benefits; but then you will have at least learned a valuable lesson for the next time.

Your challenge is to seek and retain an agent who's right for you. You're 100 percent responsible for getting yourself represented, and at least fifty percent responsible for making the author-agent relationship work for both of you.

Extra Bonus Note

Jan Nathan
Executive Director
Publishers Marketing Association

Do your research. Find out if the market is already flooded. If so, perhaps you should not do the book on that subject or you may want to approach it from a different perspective.

Have realistic expectations. Maybe your book will become a best seller or sell 100,000 copies... but it may take ten years to do so.

The prime ingredient is perseverance. Don't give up too soon or too easily.

If one publisher rejects your manuscript, it might mean it just isn't right for them. Publishers often specialize in a particular area so you really shouldn't be shocked if a business publisher declines your manuscript on HOME GARDENING. Research the Writers Market, read everything you can about publishing and network with people who are in the business.

photo by Angela Werner

Michael Hoehne

For most authors the word processor, properly managed, is the best single tool for writing and the design should be handed over to someone who would rather do design. For others, writing and page design are together part of the creative excitement and these new tools are just the ticket to get into the game.

chapter **16**

Can I Publish from My Desktop?

by Michael Hoehne

P eople have been publishing books for hundreds of years, going through all the necessary work to be sure their views or knowledge are made public. Have the developments in computers over the last few years really made it any easier to produce books?

In my capacity as the head of the computer design department of a service bureau/print shop, I have learned that the short answer is a loud and clear "Yes!" But as in any craft or industry there are proper ways to use the tools to gain the most from them and to avoid creating more work than you save. This chapter is intended to expose you to the knowledge I have gained from watching the labors of new and experienced "desktop producers". By that term I simply mean those who use a personal computer and commercially available software to write and design a book. I am avoiding the common term "desktop publishing" because it is misleading in that a large component of publishing—perhaps the largest—is distribution of the product. All the work of writing, design, and manufacturing goes for nothing if there is no publisher with connections to get the books into the stores or at least the mail.

Many of you already use a word processor to write the copy; far fewer of you use a page layout program to set the final type and the appearance of the finished page. But the feasibility of the process should be apparent when I point out that this very book was produced by the methods I am discussing.

Anyone can and should use a word processor to help with the creative work of writing by easing the chores of organizing and revising. It is much more of an open question whether an author should become involved in book design. Nevertheless, the readers of this book are probably interested in design considerations, also known as page layout, so I will touch on that, too.

This chapter is certainly not exhaustive of the considerations in this business. There is too much variety in the software, the programs or applications, as they are called, to teach here how to use them. Its purpose is to let you know of the kinds of things to think about when deciding to put your next project on computer and to tell you about the most common problems in book production with desktop equipment.

The advantages to the author are speed and control. You can get results as fast as you can work, rather than waiting for typesetting to come back as galleys and then get corrected and reset on the typesetter's schedule. And you have complete control over the appearance of your book. If something doesn't fit, you will know and can fix it immediately.

But with these capabilities come greatly increased responsibilities. When you take over the jobs of art director, typesetter, and paste-up artist, you had better learn their skills or your book will shout "amateur desktop publisher!" To do these jobs properly requires that you spend some time learning what it is all about—what really goes into making a book—or deciding to let others do part of the project. It is entirely reasonable to do only the writing—the word processing—on computer and then give the disk to a free-lance designer for layout and production. Indeed, that is often the most practical approach. But even then, there are ways to do it right.

Word Processing

Let's start with the writing. Most people seem to make the transition from typewriter keyboard to computer keyboard easily enough, but actually that is also the beginning of the problems. The two machines are very different; the computer can and should do more of the work for you. As a layout designer, I can say that the most frustrating jobs are those that come in from people who use the computer as a typewriter; I have to undo a great deal of the formatting that they did so that I can make use of the computer's powers to help in the design.

Any modern computer with word processing software should be able to do the following formatting; it will pay you well to take the time to learn how to make your particular machine do it.

✍ real italics instead of underlines to indicate italics.

✍ real quotation marks and apostrophes (" " and ' ') instead of the inch and foot marks (" and ').

✍ real em dashes (—) instead of double hyphens (--).

There are other details to consider, but these three items show up prominently in the printed piece and will scream "Cheap!" if they are neglected. This can affect your credibility; I always wonder what else the book's creator is ignorant of or careless about. When I mentioned that people have been creating books for hundreds of years, I also hoped to imply that the biggest problems of æsthetics and readability have been solved. We would be wise to take advantage of tradition and not introduce jarring details in our printed pieces that distract the readers from our message. Using typewriter-style elements in a piece that otherwise looks like a typeset piece is just such a distraction.

Next are the techniques that really put the computer to use in saving time:

✍ real paragraph indents instead of tabs or (shudder) multiple spaces.

✍ real extra margin settings for special paragraphs such as quoted passages and hanging indents (outdents) rather than carriage returns at the end of each line and multiple tabs at the beginning of the next.

✍ use of a single tab for each column in a table rather than multiple tabs to the preset locations.

✍ and best of all, if your software has the capability, is the sensible use of "style sheets", compact descriptions of each different paragraph appearance, which can be applied to any paragraph at any time to insure that all such similar paragraphs have identical specifications, including typeface, typestyle, margins, and space above and below. Style sheets also greatly simplify changing your mind and reformatting during the layout operation, whether you do the layout yourself or pay someone else to do it.

These four items have a definite effect on the scheduling and costs of the production. Many's the time I spend half the production hours removing extraneous characters to overcome the way the lines of text shift around awkwardly when I change from the author's generic typeface to the specified final ones.

The items listed above will not only make your project look better, but in most cases will make your work easier, too. The paragraph formatting commands ultimately give you less to worry about while you are typing and make it easier to give your piece a uniform look, which gives it a coherence that the reader will appreciate. I cannot describe here exactly how to do that because each program uses different commands.

That the word processor eases fears of typing errors and revisions should be obvious, and you probably also know of the powers of spelling and grammar checkers, programs that mark possible errors so you won't overlook them. Some checkers even "automatically correct" errors or at least offer to. My tip here is not to trust them. I read a book in which the editor proudly announced that this edition was produced with the help of a spelling checker. I didn't see any words spelled wrong but I did notice that most places where the word "globe" was appropriate, I saw "glove". Note that "b" and "v" are adjacent on the keyboard; it is obvious what happened. Computers do not understand concepts like homonyms, context, dialect, and intention. Always have a human proofread your material. See if you can find the typo in this book.

In some cases, the formatting capabilities of a word processor are all you need to make a simple document look good, but most documents will benefit from being arranged by a page layout program. The question is whether you should undertake that yourself.

Page Layout

While word processing is not very different from the writing you do now, page layout is definitely a whole new world to most writers. You are confronted with terms like "kerning", "tracking", "leading", "widows and orphans", "parent box", "font conflict", "page color", "linking", "TIFF files", "DPI", "target printer", "overset", and many more. Maybe not all of these will trip you up but they are an indication of why some people are authors and others are professional production people. There is a lot to know to master real design and production.

Books have been written about design and there are many, sometimes conflicting, theories. This chapter will not attempt to teach design, only to say that it is something that you should be aware of. Your library is a good first place to look and you will find the newest books on the subject in a bookstore that specializes in computer literature, believe it or not. It has become apparent that with so many people using page layout and typographical software, there was a need for explanations of the "whys" in addition to the "hows". A pretty complete choice of good books is available from the mail order house, PRINT, 3200 Tower Oaks Blvd., Rockville, MD, 20852-9789; request their catalog. Another easy introduction is to analyze book designs that you like and try to follow them. After a while you will develop your own theories and then write your own book about them.

Advertising for page layout software stresses how easy it is to design pages with the product. And it *is* easy compared to the traditional methods. But book production done well is basically an exacting craft and "easier" is not the same as "just push a button". The most basic consideration is an awareness of design principles and the resources you have available. It is a consideration that professionals have dedicated their careers to.

After the design is finished, you will probably need the services of—what else?—a service bureau. This is the company that has the printer that you can't afford to buy (about $3,000 [laser printer] to $150,000 [phototypesetter or imagesetter]) to make the crisp masters for the printing press or high-quality photocopying. Basically, you will take your computer disk to the service bureau for "output", that is, the paper or film from which printing plates are made for the presses, and then take that output to your print shop where they will run off thousands of copies for you.

Here is a major tip: when you take your disk to the service bureau, have your name and phone number written on the disk label. This will definitely make a very good impression.

When an author brings in a document for me to print out and I ask "What fonts did you use?", a common reaction is "Huh?" There are hundreds of typefaces, or fonts, available in this business but never before was it something that an author had to consider. Now it is. Not only is it an æsthetic concern, but the service bureau must know before they start to print your document which typefaces you used in it. They probably have on hand the fonts you used but if not, special arrangements must be made.

You should find and consult with the service bureau and the print shop early in the design process so you don't just show up at their door two days before deadline with a difficult- or impossible-to-produce file. Things to watch out for include whether your print shop wants to use computer-produced or traditional tint screens, whether they want holding lines or black boxes for photos and color patches, indeed, whether they want paper ("repro" or "mechanicals") or film ("negs") for the masters. It all makes a difference in time and money. There is an advantage to using a company that is service bureau and print shop in one, as they often solve problems without bothering you; otherwise you can get caught up running back and forth across town as one company blames the other for difficulties.

Although the complexity of page layout programs may seem over-whelming, it is possible to master all this without taking classes, seminars, tutoring, and self-teaching tapes—but be aware of what you are getting into; have realistic expectations. For most authors the word processor, properly managed, is the best single tool for writing and the design should be handed over to someone who would rather do design. For others, writing and page design are together part of the creative excitement and these new tools are just the ticket to get into the game.

Computer production may now seem like too much of a hassle for you. Good. You won't make the mistake of giving up your writing time to learn computer tricks. But while almost anything produced on the computer will look somewhat better than a typewriter production, it is only by arranging to do the job properly that you will gain all the advantages of desktop production—faster, cheaper production and better appearance.

Robin's Play & Learn Book

How To Entertain Children
At Home Or In Preschool

Creative Activities &
Challenging Ideas For Preschoolers

*As seen on Oprah Winfrey, Sally Jessy Raphael,
Hour Magazine, People Are Talking. . .*

- Poems
- Learning Activities
- Simple Crafts
- Games

- No-Bake Cooking Recipes
- Songs
- Fingerplays

Written By: Patricia C. Gallagher

Illustrations By: Susannah H. Thomer

HOW TO HAVE A SUCCESSFUL
CHILD CARE EXPERIENCE

DAY CARE PARENTING

- Choosing a center • What's Available • Handling the Guilt
- Adjustment time • Infant Care • Morning good-byes
- Afternoon hellos • Educational program
- Protection from abuse • Parent/Staff relations

APRIL HUBBARD and CLEMENTINE HAYBURN

April Hubbard

In contrast to the writing of the book, the more difficult part lay ahead with trying to get it published. We had such a time with that, I'm still not sure how we did it. Then again, nothing's ever easy.

chapter **17**

A Different Measure of a Book's Success

by April Hubbard (as told to Paula DuPont-Kidd)

Not long ago, the co-author of my book "Day Care Parenting: How to Have a Successful Child Care Experience" attended a workshop for daycare providers. Imagine her surprise when the material sounded familiar, mainly because it turned out the speakers were using our book as the reference source, touting it as "the complete source; the only book you need."

If you can measure the success of a book by how well it's received by the experts, and not by its financial success, then our book was a success. Still, after spending $8,000 to publish it, not to mention months-worth of hours researching and coordinating it, we're only $3,000 in the hole now.

Writing a book and publishing it was a dream of fame and fortune. I remember sitting at lunch with an outline for the book with Clementine Hayburn, my friend and co-author, talking about how much money we would stand to make. The reality was trying to organize meeting times with a co-author, and sorting publishing professionals from fly-by-night salesmen.

Write what you know

"Day Care Parenting" evolved from a pamphlet Clementine and I wrote for parents whose children attended my Mother Hubbard Child Care Center. We saw problems arise from the way parents interacted with their children at the center. Sometimes parents became so absorbed with their own schedules and stress, they forgot to take time for their children. For example, when one father picked up his child, he would hurry her along barking at her to grab her coat and bag, ignoring her efforts to show him her artwork. A mother greeted her child with questions of how he got so dirty or whether he was a good boy instead of asking the child how he was or if he had a good day.

Guilt, too, is a stumbling block for parents that prevents the daycare situation from being a positive one. I wanted to address this in the book, to let parents know that it's OK for parents to work and that children attending daycare would not know any differently. A child whose parent apologizes repeatedly for having to send him to daycare is eventually going to believe there is something wrong with attending daycare, thus making the situation negative.

On the other hand, I've seen some real positive and innovative approaches parents used to help their children understand why they had to leave and go to work, or give the child something to look forward to when they go home together.

The catalyst to writing the pamphlet was an upset father who did not deal well with leaving his daughter. He was frustrated each day as he dropped her off. I wrote a note to him. It backfired, and he was very angry. This is when Clementine and I thought a pamphlet emphasizing the positive techniques parents could try would be an easier pill to swallow.

But of course, I didn't stop there. The idea dawned on me that certainly the problems we saw were not unique to our little haven in Delaware and that the number of "daycare parents" must certainly be on the rise. I also could not find any other books on the market that dealt specifically with the broader-based role parents play in the daycare experience.

Daycare often has a bad reputation, perceived by some as the blame for future juvenile delinquents and behavioral misfits. There are also the horror stories of child care providers who abuse, neglect or brainwash children. But aside from the rare, abhorrent daycare center, we found that how parents react to their children in a daycare situation often determines the success of the experience. We based the book on the idea that parental responsibility does not stop at the door.

Parents are worried about us, the daycare providers, when in fact, we are worried about them. But we have learned not all these problems can be addressed with parents, directly or even through the pamphlet. The type of parents we reach with our pamphlet and book are those consciously trying to be good parents and don't mind suggestions that would make things easier on them.

Finding the voice and style

It was important for me to understand my audience and know that parents are sensitive when it comes to their own techniques. For this reason, I learned quickly not to expand on all the negative situations but to focus on the parents who were doing it right. It was difficult, because there were many emotions tangled up in it. Deliberately, we wanted the tone to be positive and encouraging.

I also learned from "critics" not to speak in the "you" voice, pointing fingers and placing myself above my readers. Instead, I used the "first-person, I" voice, in order to speak from my own experience.

In writing a book, I think it's important to understand your audience and know how to present your ideas. This is why we also chose to break up our information into short digestible pieces with a little sub-head. Visually, this proved more interesting than large bodies of gray text.

And now, the difficult part ...

In contrast to the writing of the book, the more difficult part lay ahead with trying to get it published. We had such a time with that, I'm still not sure how we did it. Then again, nothing's ever easy.

First, I hired an editor I learned of through a literary agent who was possibly interested in our book. This was a mistake, the editor did a terrible job and we paid a hefty price for that work. We were back to square one.

Then, I approached an editor of "Delaware Today" magazine, who edited one chapter. Then she went on to recommend her good friend to edit our book. This editor not only changed the words, but the concepts as well.

We weren't about to go out and hire another editor and so instead decided to edit it ourselves using the information we learned from the magazine editor.

Finally, we were ready to send it out to the major publishers in New York City. After all the refining we had done, it was a great disappointment that we were rejected by all of them. I was probably almost ready to give up when I realized that I didn't need the New York publishers to get this book done. Off I went to the bookstore to find what I could on self-publishing.

I received my initiation into self-publishing while watching my son's Little League games. There I sat reading self-publishing guides between his "ups at bat." Quickly thereafter, inspired with the idea we could have full creative control by publishing it ourselves, we sought a typesetter and a fancy artist to design our cover.

Once again, disappointment and frustration settled in as the designs he showed us proved completely wrong for our book. We were not about to retrace the unhappy path of looking for an editor by looking for a better artist and so compromised at designing it ourselves.

We knew we were due for a break and thought we'd get it when we'd found this "great" printer who quoted us a cost of $2,000 to print the initial run of the book. He required, however, $1,000 up front. Completing our circle of bad luck, the printer never printed it and what's more, kept our $1,000!

Finally, we found a good printer and we began peddling the book to Delaware bookstores. The bookstores proved pretty receptive to it and money filtered in here and there. However, a good break came for us when a regional distributor took on our book and began selling it through its network of grocery stores. It was through this connection that we came in touch with a small publisher, who published a lot of locally rooted books.

The publisher offered us a contract that struck us as unprofessional in appearance. It was a bad xerox copy of another contract. Because of the way our luck was running, we didn't want to take chances and looked into getting an attorney to draft our own contract. Although my husband is an attorney, we had to find a specialist in this area and to do so cost us $500. (The steep cost, we thought, would pay off later, in keeping us from other expensive mistakes.) Nonetheless, we finally had a contract with the company and were expecting our financial statements, as agreed upon, every October and April.

It was like pulling teeth to get the company to send us the checks. My calls weren't returned. I let it go for a while in calling them, and needless to say, they didn't call me either. Eventually, I learned that the company has been out of business for three years.

It all sounds like a publishing nightmare, and in many ways, it was and is. However, aside from the lack of success with editors, printers, and publishers, those of us in the field of child care consider the book a success. It has become a useful tool to those in the industry—as proven by workshops based on the book—and the number of orders I still receive for my self-published copy.

Motherhood, teaching, running three lucrative child care centers and even a strenuous golf game could not prove more challenging than trying to publish our book. Then again, those other areas of my life probably helped me to handle the rejections and frustrations.

Still, I'm about ready to polish up my armor and try once again.

DO YOU EVER WISH THAT YOUR PARENTS:

- would pay their fees promptly
- read all notices and newsletters
- be understanding, polite and cooperative with the staff
- have their children adequately prepared for the center
- were calm and patient while their children adjust to the center
- would pick up their children immediately when they are ill
- dress their children properly for play
- be loving and enthusiastic when they pick up their children
- would be interested in the educational program
- would not act hyper and guilty about leaving their children

Comments from parents and professionals about Day Care Parenting

"Along with peanut butter, diapers, and car seats, no working parent should be without this book. Practical advice, down-to-earth suggestions from real life practitioners. Excellent!"
Paula M. Breen
Child Care Consultant

"I really enjoyed Day Care Parenting. Being a working mother with two children in day care, this book helped me deal with my guilt feelings of leaving my little ones."
Beth Lochonic
Working Mother

"Day Care Parenting not only addresses but answers in a simple, easy-to-read manner many questions that concerned parents have about day care. More important, it offers practical suggestions to avoid everyday problems that can easily arise between working parents and their day care children."
Marybeth Auld
Montessori Director of
Newark Montessori Preschool

"Dealing with Headstart families for sixteen years, I find the Day Care Parenting booklet a new and exciting training tool to be used for all parents who depend on child care centers. I recommend to parents who have concerns about their role as

HOW TO HAVE A SUCCESSFUL CHILD CARE EXPERIENCE

DAY CARE PARENTING

- Choosing a center ● What's Available ● Handling the Guilt
- Adjustment time ● Infant Care ● Morning good-byes
- Afternoon hellos ● Educational program
- Protection from abuse ● Parent/Staff relations

APRIL HUBBARD and CLEMENTINE HAYBURN

prime educators of their children to read this booklet."
Bonnie VanLier
Headstart Parent Involvement
Social Service Coordinator
Sussex County Community
Action Agency

"As a child care aide teacher and cooperative work experience coordinator, I believe Day Care Parenting is must reading for parents and child care students. It is a complete and practical guide for those using and working in child care."
Marjorie S. Cann
Christina School District
Home Economics Teacher
Newark, Delaware

"Day Care Parenting gives parents valuable tips and information to help with the growth, development and care of their children."
Sally Pannell, Director
Honey Bear Child Care
Newark, Delaware

"Provides a concise, accurate picture of quality day care. Many useful suggestions are given to parents who may be concerned about placing their children in day care. The authors have managed to cover a many-faceted subject in an easy-to-read format. I highly recommend this book for parents, as well as students of early childhood. It will be a required reading in my next college course."
Sandy Hicken, M.S.
College Instructor
Child Development Specialist

ORDER FORM

Day Care Parenting
How To Have A Successful Child Care Experience

Please send me _____ copy (copies) of the above title at $3.95 per copy.

I am enclosing $ _____ which includes the cost plus 75¢ per copy for postage and handling.

Please send check or money order (no cash or C.O.D.) and mail to:
Four Seasons Publications
Box 125, Newark, DE 19715-0125

Name _____

Address _____

City _____ State _____ Zip _____

AMERICAN SOCIETY OF JOURNALISTS AND AUTHORS, INC.
1501 Broadway, Suite 302, New York NY 10036 • (212) 997-0947 • Fax (212) 768-7414

March 6, 1991

Patricia Gallagher
301 Holly Hill Road
Richboro, PA   18954

Dear Speaker:

On behalf of the more than 800 professional free lances nationwide who make up
the membership of the American Society of Journalists and Authors, thank you
for agreeing to speak at ASJA's 20th Annual Writers' Conference at the Grand
Hyatt Hotel, Saturday, May 4, 1991. Only the very top of the profession are
asked to participate and therefore we are very grateful that you have agreed
to take part and give of your knowledge and experience.

The audience usually consists of a mixture of would-be writers, professional
writers, editors, and agents.

Your workshop moderator will contact you with more details but generally, it
is best not to make a formal presentation. The workshops are informal and the
audience primarily wants to ask questions. You can just tell them who you
are, what you do, and what advice you have for writers. "War stories" of
surprising successes and missed opportunities always go over big.

We ask that immediately after your panel, you go to THE INFORMATION EXCHANGE
ROOM for a short while so that the audience can ask you questions on a one-to-
one basis.

We hope you will stay for lunch and enjoy attending other workshops during the
day.

Again, thanks for agreeing to spend your valuable time with us to help the
next generation of writers as well as the current one.

Sincerely,

Ruth Winter
Conference Director

BOARD OF DIRECTORS PRESIDENT Katharine Davis Fishman EXECUTIVE VICE PRESIDENT Florence Isaacs   VICE PRESIDENTS Janice Hopkins Tanne,
Ruth Winter SECRETARY Alice J. Kelvin TREASURER Nona Aguilar EXECUTIVE COUNCIL MEMBERS AT LARGE Thomas Bedell, Murray Teigh Bloom, Sherry Suib Cohen,
Mark L. Fuerst, Judith Kelman, Terry Morris, Chris Welles DIRECTORS AT LARGE Elise Miller Davis, John W. English, Pat McNees, Annie Moldafsky, Ruth Pittman,
Rachel Pollack, Shimon-Craig Van Collie, Barbara Yuncker **EXECUTIVE DIRECTOR** Alexandra S.E. Cantor

REGIONAL CHAPTER CHAIRPERSONS BERKSHIRE HILLS Joan German MIDWEST Sylvia McNair NORTHERN CALIFORNIA Iris Lorenz-Fife
ROCKY MOUNTAIN Rachel Pollack SOUTHERN CALIFORNIA Isobel Silden WASHINGTON DC Beryl Lieff Benderly

Priscilla Y. Huff

My best advice to others in any kind of writing is to be persistent! Never stop trying and never stop learning what you need to know. If you really want to be a writer, you will, if you don't give up!

chapter 18

Work for Hire: A Valuable Learning Experience

by Priscilla Y. Huff

How did I become involved in writing? I began to write six years ago for a local newspaper at four cents a word. I would write assigned features, or follow leads I would hear about. I would also take the photos, because the paper did not have a full-time photographer. I really enjoyed doing the interviews and writing the stories until a new editor came in and said that all free-lance feature writers had to become "stringers." This new position meant I would be spending several evenings a week away from my husband and three young sons.

I couldn't do this, so I quit, but writing for the paper had helped me learn the basics of article writing. "If I could write for a newspaper," I thought, "why not magazines?" I began to write short stories, which were rejected. Then I queried some of the well-known women's magazines, and again, nothing was accepted.

Meanwhile, I began to subscribe to *Writer's Digest* magazine and I read each issue from cover-to-cover. I bought Writer's Digest's annual "Writer's Market" and also joined its book club. I read and studied about writing. This self-education paid off when my first article about my sister-in-law's clowning business was accepted by *Income Opportunities*. From then on, I have written more than thirty articles on women's home-based businesses, and went on to write a book about this subject that will be published by Pilot Books some time in 1991. Presently, I am writing another book about home-based service businesses.

At the same time I began to write for other markets, and wrote feature articles for *Lady's Circle, Quilting Today, Pennsylvania Magazine* and others. Then in June 1990, one of the editors from *Income Opportunities* asked me if I would be willing to write a 30,000-word manual for them under a "work-for-hire" contract to be completed in two months! The title of the manual was to be, "How to Profit From Your Crafts."

When the *Income Opportunities* editor asked me to write this, I knew that under this type of contract, I would be paid for the project, but that I would most likely be forfeiting my rights to future sales. However, I had never worked on as large a project, and I wanted the experience.

Working from an approved outline, during the next ten weeks I worked approximately four hours a day on the manual. During this time I transported two sons to and from work (teaching one of them how to drive—a harrowing experience for any parent!); worked on another major article; went for a week on a family vacation; did various writing assignments for my writing business (resumes, press releases, etc.); and tried to do at least the basic household chores expected of me as a wife and mother!

Despite everything else in my life, I finished the manuscript by the first week in September. I do not know if I would do a similar project in so short a time again. However, what I learned in the process has been invaluable to me as far as other writing projects.

Invaluable lessons

A Good Outline: *Income Opportunities* had given me the word length, and a sample of a similar manual. From there I wrote an outline which the magazine approved. As I came to each step in that outline, I sought out the information I needed, then wrote accordingly. This way, I felt less overwhelmed in approaching such a large project.

Effective Research & Resources: I have made crafts over the years, but I would be the first to say I am not an expert in this field. However, I wrote letters, made phone calls, and tried to get information from every possible source I could on selling crafts. My most valuable resources were the professional crafters themselves. They not only gave me tips based on their own experiences, but happily referred me to their sources of information such as publications they found invaluable and experts in the craft field.

Organization: Everything related to this project went into folders which were all kept in one box. When my oldest son moved out to get married, I had turned his bedroom into my home office. My husband built shelves and more shelves, which hold all my current and completed projects (each writing project has its own folder), reference books, my business files, notebooks, and anything else pertaining to my writing.

If I cannot find needed information in my office in less than a minute—a suggestion I read in *Home Office Computing*—I take a few minutes to re-organize my files or whatever, so I will not be delayed again. This periodic "busy work" enables me to spend more time writing than searching for "lost" papers, etc.

Office Equipment: Without my Radio Shack (IBM compatible) computer and printer, my office telephone (which can handle three-way calling and other basic functions), my heavy-duty Smith Corona typewriter, and other office necessities, my job as a writer would be much more difficult. I took a basic computer course, and also have a computer consultant I hire when needed.

Believe me when I say I am "computer-*ill* iterate," but I learned what I needed to produce my writing, and now I cannot imagine writing using only my typewriter! Several years ago I took out a small business loan to buy my office "basics" and it was money well spent as far as my writing career is concerned.

Write, everyday: With this project I had to write everyday, no matter what! If you are a parent working from your home, you know how difficult at times that can be! I had great support from my husband, and my sons helped by cutting back on their squabbling with one another and even did a few extra chores around the house, (for a fee, of course).

I wrote whenever I had the time and energy. Sometimes I would not start until 9 p.m., because there were less interruptions from my family and phone calls. Actually, my sons and husband are more understanding about my writing (even though my youngest son asked me why I didn't get a "real job" like his friends' mothers) than my parents and grown brothers.

They have a hard time accepting that I am a writer working from my office, and will call or drop in for a visit whenever they want. They're getting better (as I get published more and more), but I realize, too, that to them I'll always be a "good" daughter and sister who will not mind if they call or come for short, unannounced visits.

Despite interruptions, etc., I wrote whenever I could, sometimes for only fifteen minutes at a time, but for at least a *total* of two to four hours a day. At times, I found it very difficult to sit down and write, but having a deadline to meet was a helpful incentive for me. Now, that I am working free-lance, again, I have trouble disciplining myself to work—until I ask myself, "Do you want to substitute teach again?"

When I think of some of those experiences I had as a "sub," I say "No way!" and begin to write as fast as I can. Really, I was a good substitute teacher, and often had fun teaching that way, but writing full-time is my goal and I do not want to give it up!

As I mentioned before, I do not know if I would do a work-for-hire writing project again, but I proved to myself I could start and finish a large project such as this. I have felt much more confident in starting my other books, and am following much of the same steps I did in writing this manual.

My best advice to others in any kind of writing is to be persistent! Never stop trying and never stop learning what you need to know. Set up attainable goals, and those you might only dream about. Work to accomplish the small goals, but never stop working toward those larger ones. If you really want to be a writer, you will, if you don't give up!

April 21, 1991

Rieva Lesonsky
Editor In Chief
ENTREPRENEUR
2392 Morse Avenue
Box 19787
Irvine, California 92714-6234

Dear Ms. Leonsky:

Six years ago, Dale Hersh of Clarks Summit, Pennsylvania, was
tired of being frustrated in trying to find everyday items for
left-handed people. Thinking that other lefties like herself
self must have similar difficulties, Hersh started her own
home-based, mail order business, Lefty's Corner.

Hersh says, "It took me one-and-a-half years just to find
suppliers who made left-handed products. Then I had to convince them to let me purchase smaller wholesale quantities
than they usually sold to retailers."

Today, Hersh's business offers in its catalog over two hundred
articles "...designed with Lefties in mind," with more being
added every week as suppliers are now approaching Hersh to
carry their products.

Would you be interested in having Hersh's business profiled in
your "Business Beats" section of ENTREPRENEUR? I would like to
detail how Hersh found her suppliers and highlight some of her
most effective promotional methods for such a specialty business.

I write about women's home-based businesses (over twenty articles and one book); and I am presently completing a book about
how to start a home-based service business.

Thank you for considering this story idea. I look forward to
your reaction.

Sincerely,

Priscilla Y. Huff

Enc.

Evelyn Kaye

I offer a well researched, well written book to appeal to people who want something unique, original, and different, with information on travel which isn't available elsewhere. And after all, where else can readers call up and chat with the author?

chapter **19**

Self-Publishing Is the Sure Bet in the Gamble of Publishing

by Evelyn Kaye

W hen people ask me why I've turned to self-publishing after having twelve books published by major publishers, I tell them the truth: sheer frustration.

My writing life began as a news reporter, on staff for *The Guardian* in Manchester, England, and Reuters News Agency in Paris. When motherhood struck twice, I became a free-lance writer with articles in *Ladies Home Journal, Glamour, Parents, McCalls,* and other magazines. I was also published in the *Boston Globe, New Jersey Record* and The *New York Times.* The books came along too, sometimes with friends, sometimes on my own. That's how I learned that the glamour, hype, and over-blown statistics of book publishing are just like horse racing: a gamble. You pick your book, you bet your cash, you print the copies, and it's over in a flash.

"Crosscurrents: Children, Families and Religion" published by Clarkson Potter/Crown in 1980 began well with a promotional tour. But, then as now, I have found that no matter how many radio, TV and press interviews I conducted, There Are Never Any Books In The Stores. It was the normal attack of the TANABITS Syndrome (There Are Never Any Books In The Bookstore). Ask any author. The book was remaindered within months despite excellent reviews and full-page articles—because it was completely unavailable. It's in many libraries, is often cited in research, and still inspires orders for copies. But it taught me an important lesson: it's hard to sell a book that's not there.

With my later books, I carried copies to bookstores myself. I wrote press releases and self-interviews. I provided lists of contacts. I made suggestions for the jacket design. I helped select photographs. It was a first-hand education in book publishing and I was sure that I could NOT sell books just as well as most publishers.

So when my agent told me last year that my great idea for "Travel and Learn: The New Guide to Educational Travel," was turned down because several New York publishers said there was nothing else like it on the market, I said I'd publish it myself.

My Bible was Dan Poynter's "The Self-Publishing Manual." His philosophy: "We firmly believe the best way to sell most nonfiction books is with book reviews, news releases and a limited amount of highly targeted direct mail." The yellow stick-ums marching through the pages marked my progress along the way. I budgeted $5,000 for expenses, but no payment for my time.

First, I pinpointed the market. My readers are people who enjoy travel but don't want to laze on the beach. They like to learn something about the places they see, and they don't mind the challenge of the unusual. They travel intelligently.

Next, I spent six months on research and writing, reading lavishly illustrated travel brochures for Tahiti and Tibet in the dreary winter days of February, which was fun. I asked a friend to critique the manuscript, paid a copy editor to spot my errors, and paid an artist to design a cover.

My husband had lived through the joys and traumas of all my previous books. He's a computer freak and was delighted to help me design the book on my machine. He taught me how to use the different typefaces, layout, and typographic features, and worked with me as we prepared the final copy.

I called the printers for quotes, chose a company in New York, and ordered 1,000 copies. A self-publisher thinks of 1,000 books as twenty heavy boxes of fifty books which can be stacked in the kitchen, the livingroom, the bedroom, or the basement, plus the ten boxes of padded envelopes for mailing, plus fifteen boxes of press materials. The idea of 2,000 copies was tempting but then we would have been living in the bathroom.

At the library, I collected names of magazines, newspapers, newsletters, organizations, and groups that might be interested in the book. These were turned into lists of labels using my computer's nifty skills. I wrote a press release, flyer, designed an order form and review page, and sent them out.

During those weeks I developed my super-speed fold-stuff-stamp-seal routine. See me do a mailing of 100 in just over an hour! It takes about ten minutes to stick 100 stamps on 100 envelopes. I divide then into eights, wet them with a sponge, and whip down the line sticking them on. Next I do the peel-off labels, at eight minutes per 100. Last, I fold four pages and stuff them into the envelope and seal it with tape. I've done mailings for a thousand and more, and it's not too bad, apart from the monotony. I'm not sure I could add it to my resume as a creative skill, but I listen to the radio and watch the envelopes pile up and think literary thoughts.

Right from the start, the response to "Travel and Learn" was positive. A travel bookstore in Maryland ordered ten copies. An early review in an Idaho paper said: "For the always-learner and inveterate traveler, this book is perfect." Dozens of media people asked to see review copies. My local post office and I were on first name terms as I bought stamps by the roll and they accepted my bags of padded envelopes with big smiles.

Six months later, I've just reprinted another 1,000 books. It's satisfying to open the mail and find orders, checks, and often, personal notes and comments. One woman said this sounded like the book she'd always wanted and please send two copies. Another tracked down Blue Penguin Publications through the Library of Congress. One would-be reader called a newspaper reporter who had mentioned the book in an article on self-publishing and demanded the publisher's address. A public radio station was inundated with calls and letters for weeks after I was the guest on a talk show. Someone in Michigan asked me to send the book to a friend in Maine and would I enclose a gift card. (I chose a tasteful picture of sailing boats.) Out of the blue, two orders arrived from Finland.

For me, there's a sense of re-establishing a direct link between the writer and reader. In the old days, writers used to hand-carry their books to printers to be printed and bound, and then distribute them. Modern mega-publishing interrupted the relationship. Authors face a mine field of agents, editors, and publishers to negotiate before they can start writing, and readers are bombarded with "hysterical hype" before they get to buy the book. Today, books are created and sold just like brand-name sneakers; buy this from Author X because it's better than that one by Author Y. If the book doesn't sell, dump it quickly and replace it with another model.

I equate self-publishing with running a boutique instead of mass-market stores. I enjoy being a member of a community of self-publishing individuals who do their own thing and I find an ever-increasing number of us out there.

This time, I'm in charge. The orders come in, and books go out immediately. It's no way to become a millionaire but I have the satisfaction of doing what I want. The frustration level is way, way down. I offer a well researched, well written book to appeal to people who want something unique, original, and different, with information on travel which isn't available elsewhere. And after all, where else can readers call up and chat with the author?

Blue Penguin Publications

147 Sylvan Avenue, Leonia, NJ 07605   (201)461-6918
                                                        Press Office

NEWS RELEASE

Winter 1990

SECRETS OF THE BEST WINTER VACATIONS

Vacations in the winter months are cheaper, better and more fun especially in the fastest-growing field of travel today - educational trips offered by museums, colleges, universities and such varied groups as the Smithsonian, Audubon Society and Elderhostel.

You can study Spanish in Mexico, French in Paris, or Japanese while you live with a family in Tokyo. Join a seminar in London and explore Britain's lively theaters. Listen to music in Eastern Europe with concerts and operas in Vienna and Prague. Cruise amid ice floes in the Antarctic, swim with sealions in the Galapagos Islands, or find the true 'aloha' spirit of beautiful Hawaii.

TRAVEL AND LEARN: The New Guide to Educational Travel describes more than a thousand educational vacation programs in the United States and abroad, offered year-round by 162 carefully selected organizations.

Early reviews are enthusiastic: "Perfect for an inveterate traveler," "A refreshing entry into the crowded travel field," "The range of topics is amazing." The book gives names, addresses, phone and fax numbers of the organizations for immediate information.

For a FREE leaflet, write to Blue Penguin Publications, 147 Sylvan Avenue, Leonia NJ 07605. **TRAVEL AND LEARN** is available at independent booksellers, or directly from the publisher ($23.95 + $2.05 shipping) at 1-800-800-8147.

Kate Kelly

While I began selling magazine pieces and doing some ghostwriting here and there, I was troubled by the prospect of how I was going to make a decent living at this profession.

chapter **20**

Publicize Yourself— Who Knows Your Product Better?

by Kate Kelly

If I were to share with you the secret of my publishing success, it would be the information contained in my first self-published book, "The Publicity Manual." It is the resource guide by which I run my business. No one needs to tell me to practice what I preach! I use free publicity all the time to promote my books and my business. Any author or self-publisher will.

One of the major changes in the publishing industry today is that self-publishing is no longer viewed as a refuge of last resort. Those of us who self-publish have chosen to because we know we can make more money by maintaining control of our own product. About a year after I self-published "The Publicity Manual," I started receiving offers from other companies who wanted to take it over. When my agent came through with an offer from a "real" publisher, I was sorely tempted because, as a writer, one of my goals was to be published by a New York publishing house. But after giving it some thought, I was reminded of all the reasons I self-published in the first place. I decided to maintain control myself. Now—ten years since that offer—and eleven years since I first published the book, I'm very glad I did.

Why? Because I spend more time selling and promoting my books than any publisher would. I don't pull it off the shelves after six months because it isn't a blockbuster, and the only books I remainder are about twenty of an old edition which might still be kicking around when an updated edition arrives from the printer. The book is never out of date, even though it was written eleven years ago. It has 1990's advice in it because I'm always willing to pay for new material to be added as the public relations business changes over the years—something large publishers don't do with any regularity.

The same is true for my other title, "How To Set Your Fees and Get Them." I self-published it from the beginning. (It was written in response to customers who successfully gained publicity for their new businesses, and then called to say, "I got the publicity, and I've got some new clients. What am I going to charge them?") It, too, is updated every two years, and I'm always promoting it.

How my business started

Shortly after I moved to New York City, I decided I only wanted to work for someone else for a limited amount of time, so from the base of a full-time job, I set about working to become a free-lance writer. While I began selling magazine pieces and doing some ghostwriting here and there, I was troubled by the prospect of how I was going to make a decent living at this profession. As I continued with a full-time job while freelancing on the side, I became intrigued as I began reading about those who were marketing information by mail. Could I make the equivalent of a salary from a mail-order business while I continued to write? I wanted to try it, but I needed an inspirational idea for a book.

My regular employment at that time was as a public relations consultant, and a friend who ran a seminar business began asking me to come and teach business owners how to get their own publicity. We began having enough interest in the topic that I was teaching a new course every two months, and thereby was born the idea for "The Publicity Manual."

Shortly thereafter, I came across Dan Poynter's "The Self- Publishing Manual," and using it as a guide, my husband and I started our business. Like most other self-publishers, we started out small. We did as much of the work as we could ourselves, I typed the book myself, and, since at that time it was published in a handsome looseleaf-workbook format, we collated the book ourselves, walking round and round our apartment living room putting those books together by hand. (As the business took off, our first indulgence was spending the extra $200 to have the books collated!)

Since that time, I've continued to pursue a writing career. I've been published in many national magazines; I've ghostwritten several books; I'm co-author of "Organize Yourself!," which is published by Macmillan and has sold more than 200,000 copies; and I have just had published a social history book, "Election Day: An American History, An American Holiday." Throughout all my projects, publicity has been vital to making sales.

Despite my success in the conventional publishing world, I know one thing: I will always maintain my publishing business, and I'll add other titles when the time is right. There is no better way to sell certain types of specialized materials. To give it up would be to give up a very important part of my income. What's more, it is ceaselessly interesting and a lot of fun.

What I've learned

When Patricia Gallagher talked about what she would like to have me include in this chapter, she said, "Show the readers something—include something like the letter that got you on "Good Morning America," or "Phil Donahue."

Her comment helped me decide what to show you. But first I'll tell you a secret: I haven't ever been on "Good Morning America" or "Phil Donahue."

Despite that, my business is still very successful. Many of us (perhaps you), are not promoting information that belongs on those programs (in my case, my information is too specialized to be of interest to a program that must serve a mass audience), but there are plenty of other ways to promote your business.

Instead, what follows is a sample of the publicity I generated during my first year of business that aided in selling out my entire first printing. This promotional blurb appeared on the last page of a restaurateur newsletter.

"The Publicity Manual," complete do-it-yourself guide for publicizing your business without paying for the services of a professional. Practical information on techniques and ideas for newspaper/magazine publicity as well as radio/TV. How to write releases, contact media, prepare for interviews. Includes sample press releases, worksheet, planning chart, resource directory of major media outlets and other publicity aids. Tabbed, looseleaf manual outlines step-by-step generic publicity program than can be easily applied to any business...Author, Kate Kelly, public relations instructor and consultant says, "Once armed with fundamentals, entrepreneurs are particularly effective at getting their own publicity because they are their own best spokespeople."

As you can see, there's nothing spectacular in the write-up, nor is the publication one that most people would have heard of, but it was for me, perfect publicity: It was free editorial exposure to an audience that wanted to learn to do its own publicity. I got the mention by mailing a two-page press release to the newsletter's editor, and I mailed her a review copy of the book when she eventually called back. Through little expense (and not a lot of effort), I got the story I needed—it sold books—all of them.

Of course, since that time I've gone on to receive national exposure for my books in publications such as Family Circle, Working Woman, and Writer's Digest, and it's been wonderful, but the type of publicity I seek on a regular basis is the publicity shown above—something simple in a trade publication newsletter or magazine where I can reach the buyer very efficiently and directly when he or she is most likely looking for my type of advice. "The Publicity Manual" has been featured in newsletters and magazines for hair salon owners, alternative energy retailers, funeral directors, lawyers, management consultants, nonprofit association administrators and many other professional specialties.

"How To Set Your Fees and Get Them" has been sold through publicity in publications geared to everyone from accountants to calligraphers.

If the book you're hoping to have published (yes, even with a major publisher you'll have to do most of the publicity yourself) or self-publish needs a mass audience, then you are better off approaching the morning news programs and "Geraldo," but if your audience is a definable segment of the market (knitters, home contractors, gardeners, exterminators, dog lovers, copywriters, etc.), you may be very happy with narrowing the focus of your publicity.

Regardless of who you eventually approach, there is some basic information about publicity that you should know.

Publicity basics

The self-publisher or small business owner is well-prepared to run his or her own publicity program. Who knows the product better than you? Who cares more about it than you? And who better than you to make sure it gets the public exposure it deserves.

1) **Decide the message.** The first step is identifying what about your new book is of interest to an editor (and eventually the reader or viewer)? Is it a first-of-a-kind? Did your research come up with some startling information? Do you have a new system for changing someone's life? Once you identify what your strongest feature is, that will become the "news hook" around which you write your press release.

2) **Prepare proper written material.** This could be a press release, a captioned photograph, or a well-written letter. All press releases should include the following elements:

   ✍ who to contact for more information. This should include the name, address and telephone number of this person (likely you or a staff member) goes at the top of the page.

   ✍ release date, usually for "immediate release."

   ✍ headline. This should be a factual (not a clever) summary of what the release is about.

   ✍ body of the release. The release is written in the "inverted pyramid" style—a term you may recall from English class. All vital details (who, what, when, where, why) are given in a short first paragraph while all other details are provided in descending order of importance. A release should conclude with information about what the public can do if interested (call or send for more information; buy the book and if so, where and at what price).

Press releases should be written simply and clearly. Sentences and paragraphs should be kept short, and glowing descriptions of yourself avoided. Let the reporter add the superlatives.

Once written, the release should be typed (double spaced), and, if it runs more than one page, it should be stapled together.

The following release is one I've used as a basic release describing "How To Set Your Fees and Get Them:"

FOR IMMEDIATE RELEASE
HOW TO SET YOUR FEES AND GET THEM—
NEW EDITION OFFERS UPDATED PRACTICAL ADVICE FOR
SELF-EMPLOYED

"Entrepreneurs who are just starting out are understandably cautious when setting a rate for their services, but more experienced professionals have difficulty with price-setting, too," says Kate Kelly, a business consultant and author of the newly revised edition of her classic "How To Set Your Fees and Get Them." "Surprisingly, many are pricing themselves too low."

Because there was little written information on fee-setting, Ms. Kelly, who teaches and lectures on the topic, wrote "How To Set Your Fees and Get Them." The book shows business owners and professionals the process they need to go through in order to establish a fair rate for their services. It also includes helpful but simple formulas, information on various ways to present one's rates, strategies for successful pricing negotiations, and concrete advice and examples from both clients and the self-employed.

In addition, the new edition provides some additional formulas, expands the section on how to structure one's fee, cites examples of recent successful price negotiations, and updates the advice offered in the original text.

"Fee-setting is something which affects the self-employed every single day, because in order to succeed, they must be paid what they are worth," says Kate Kelly. "This book provides readers with the knowledge and the confidence they need in order to master this very important business skill."

Also discussed are topics such as what to do if the client says 'no;' when to employ retainer and contingency fees; how to prepare a letter of agreement (sample letters included); when to bill for expenses; and speeding up the payment process. The book also tackles the knotty problem of setting a dollar amount on intangible inconveniences such as delivering on a tight deadline, working over holidays, and billing for special expertise.

The new edition of "How To Set Your Fees and Get Them" is available from Visibility Enterprises, 11 Rockwood Drive, Larchmont, NY 10538, $17.50 postpaid.

ABOUT THE AUTHOR: Kate Kelly is a business consultant, writer, and author. She has conducted numerous workshops and seminars on fee-setting for entrepreneurs. She is the author of "The Publicity Manual" and co-author of "Organize Yourself!" (Macmillan). Her articles on business and consumer topics have appeared in Woman's Day and Parents as well as many other publications. She is listed in "Who's Who of American Women" and is featured in "Maverick," a book about successful entrepreneurs.

3) **Select the media to be approached.** This could be one publication or program for a specific feature (such as an interview on "Good Morning America" or for your local newspaper), or it could be fifty-plus publications if you're sending out a general announcement. When deciding which media to approach, think in terms of what magazines, newspapers, radio, or television programs your customers follow.

4) **Get the correct contact information.** Be sure to have the name of a specific person to whom the material should be sent. If you don't

know who is in charge of feature interviews or book reviews, call and ask.

5) **Determine timing.** If you've written about how to have a perfect garden, you're most likely to get publicity in spring and summer. (If, however, you've got tips on fall maintenance, jot a few of them down and encourage your newspaper or a magazine to do a story.) Remember that your material must be sent well in advance of the time you want the publicity. Newspapers would generally work only a few days or perhaps a couple of weeks ahead. National magazines are sometimes thinking four to five months in advance in order to hit the stands on time.

6) **Send your material.**

7) **Follow up with a phone call.** You don't have to phone every time. Set priorities. Follow up with the publications where the story will do you the most good. When you call, don't push. Just confirm that the material arrived, and try to get a general sense of what they thought of it.

8) **Send a thank-you note** for publicity received.

A few additional tips

Know the publication or program you're approaching and try to understand their needs. Editors and program producers are interested in one thing: Will this benefit or be of interest to my readers (or viewers or listeners)? The better you understand how your book will be of value to their audience, the better chance you stand of getting the publicity you want and need.

Respect the time of any member of the media. If you need to phone the press, try: "I'm Kate Kelly, and I would like to discuss an idea with you. Do you have a minute?" If they have some time, they'll likely talk to you then, but if they're working on a deadline, you've given them the opportunity to request that you call back.

Take them at their word. If a reporter or producer asks you to call back at a certain time or to send them a review copy, be sure to do so. You're asking for free media exposure, so do what you can to accommodate them.

As you pursue publicity, you'll likely be surprised at the results. A major radio interview you're looking forward to may bring few sales; other times, a small item can bring astounding results. One point that is indisputable though is that publicity breeds publicity. I sell many books because I am mentioned in the resource lists in many start-your-own-business books. I solicited few of those mentions; I was included because of publicity I had received elsewhere. The same will likely be true with your business. A story about you in your local shopper newspaper may well result in important exposure elsewhere.

In the final analysis, publicity is priceless. If you take the time to master the basic skills and then invest the effort to implement them, publicity will pay off for you, too.

John Kremer

One final piece of advice (the best I can give you): Stick with it. Don't give up too soon. The longer you stay in business, the more you will be noticed. Persistence does pay off. Stand up and be noticed!

chapter **21**

If You Can't Find the Book You're Looking for, Write It

by John Kremer

I started my own publishing company in 1982 because I was tired of waiting for the big New York publishers to make up their minds that my writing was worth publishing. At the time, besides my free-lance writing, I was working as a consultant in the design, development, and marketing of toys and gifts. My background in these special markets convinced me that I could market my books as well as any New York publisher and, as I have found out, I was right.

When I began to research the publishing field, the first thing I discovered was that much of the information I needed was simply lacking. So I created it.

For example, when I was looking for a printer for my first book, I sent out requests for quotations to more than fifty printers because the listings in "Literary Marketplace" were not detailed enough to tell me which printers would be most appropriate for my book. As a result, I wasted a lot of time and postage sending queries to printers who were clearly not equipped or ready to do the job. Moreover, the difference between the low bid and the high bid was $4 a book! To help other new publishers to target the best printers for their books, I published the first edition of my "Directory of Book Printers." Since then, I've distributed more than 29,000 copies of the directory and have just come out with the sixth edition.

One book, of course, led to another...and another. When I attended the American Booksellers Convention in San Francisco, many publishers came up and told me how much they liked my "Directory of Book Printers." But, then, many of them added, "Now can you help me get them out of my garage?" Of course, I could. I knew at least 101 ways to market books.

I left that convention planning to write a short guide outlining 101 ways to market books, but as I did further research and thought more about the subject, I ended up writing a 320-page book called, appropriately enough, "101 Ways to Market Your Books." And, because I couldn't fit everything into one book, I wrote two other books at the same time, "Book Marketing Made Easier," (which I think of as the workbook for "101 Ways"), and "Book Marketing Opportunities: A Directory," (which was a 320-page appendix to "101 Ways").

Selling it before writing it

Even before I wrote a word of any of these books, I sold 300 copies through a special pre-publication offer that promised delivery of all three books within six months. And since I have always placed my customers first, I had to deliver. I wrote 800 pages in six months. Because I couldn't write these books and run a company at the same time, I hired my first employee, Marie Kiefer, who is still my general manager.

Every time I sell out the stock of a book, I revise it. As a result, most of the books have gone through three editions—and often as many title changes. For instance, the "Directory of Short-Run Book Printers" became "Directory of Book, Catalog, and Magazine Printers" (in the hopes, of course, that I could pick up additional sales to businesses). When that idea didn't really work as well as I had hoped, I went back to my basic customer base, book publishers, and re-titled the newest edition, "The Directory of Book Printers."

Because the audience for my books on publishing and book marketing is somewhat limited, I found two marketing techniques that work best for me: 1) direct marketing and 2) targeted publicity, primarily in magazines and newsletters. But, the most important sales tool I have—as is true of most books—is word of mouth. And the only way to generate effective word of mouth is to write good books. That I do.

The wrong bookstore shelf can kill sales

I have published several books that were not in the book publishing and marketing field. "Tinseltowns, U.S.A.," a trivia quiz book about towns and cities in the United States that have starred in movies or TV shows, was a miserable failure. The book got great publicity, hitting the front page of the Life Section of USA Today and attracting the attention of lots of radio talk show hosts (who love trivia). In addition, I sold second serial rights to *Celebrity Plus* magazine and syndication rights to the Entertainment News Syndicate. But the book didn't get good distribution through my distributor because I was never able to convince my sales representatives that the book would take off. As a result, the book wasn't in the bookstores when the publicity hit. I put a lot of promotion into this book well in advance of the publication date (including giving away 1,500 copies at the ABA convention), but without the backing of the sales reps, the book was doomed.

"Tinseltowns, U.S.A." was not the type of book that can be sold via direct-mail; it required bookstore visibility. And it didn't get it. Even when the reps did sell it to bookstores, the book got lost on the shelves. Why? Because it was designed as a trivia book to be placed face out on the shelves like all the cartoon books. But, because the book was about movies, it got shelved with the movie entertainment books, most of which are large hardcover books with lots of photographs. "Tinsletowns" was lost in that crowd. For the record, I lost about $20,000 on that book. And I still have 6,000 copies in the basement. Someday, when I have a few frivolous moments, I might spend some more time trying to market that book, but for now it just isn't worth the effort.

My other general book, "Mail Order Selling Made Easier," has had much better reception. Not only have I sold book club rights to two clubs (Fortune Book Club and The Executive Program), but I also sold first serial rights to *Income Plus* magazine and British Commonwealth rights to McGraw-Hill U.K. in England. Plus I have several larger publishers interested in reprinting the book as a trade paperback. Finally, this was my first book to make Quality Book's best-seller list (for two months!) Meanwhile, the bookstores, media, and mail order catalogs are all devouring the book.

How was this book different from "Tinseltowns, U.S.A.?" First, it was better designed for its market. And, second, I have a much better distributor now with sales representatives who are really behind the book. Both B. Dalton and Waldenbooks have picked up the book, plus all the major wholesalers.

Besides the books, I also publish two newsletters, the thirty-two-page bimonthly "Book Marketing Update" and the four-page weekly, "Book Promotion Hotline." I've also developed a media and marketing database of 18,500 key contacts which I sell as No-Frills Data Files and which I rent as mailing labels. Finally, I have also written four related reports on radio phone interviews shows, the top 250 TV news/talk/magazine shows, selling to mail order catalogs, and selling to premium/incentive buyers.

Re-packaging information

I'm a firm believer in re-packaging information and extending your line. As a result, besides the reports and newsletters, I also do consulting work and speaking engagements. Thus far, I haven't done audio or video, but it is inevitable, I guess, if I ever find the time.

As it has turned out, I have been occupied putting out information to help other publishers so that I still haven't gotten around to publishing the book I originally intended to publish when I first started my company. I will get to that book—I promise you—but it won't be until the fall of 1991. Watch for it! Don't worry. You won't be able to miss it. It'll be in all the papers and magazines—I guarantee it!

P.S.—The Postscript is one of the most read and most effective parts of a direct mail letter, so why shouldn't it work here? One final piece of advice (the best I can give you): Stick with it. Don't give up too soon. The longer you stay in business, the more you will be noticed. Take at least ten minutes every day to do some little bit of promotion for your book. If you make just one or two contacts every day, your book will get noticed. Persistence does pay off. Stand up and be noticed!

As featured in USA Today and other media

Tinseltowns, U.S.A. by John Kremer

- **USA Today** featured *Tinseltowns, U.S.A.* on the front page of the Life Section on Monday, August 22nd (see above).
- **Celebrity Plus** magazine has bought second serial rights and will be excerpting two or three chapters of the book.
- Here are just a few of the other magazines that will be reviewing or excerpting the book as well: **Alaska Airlines, Albuquerque Monthly, Delta Sky, Houston Monthly, Mpls-St. Paul, Travel Holiday, Twilight Zone, Utah Holiday, Weekly World Views**, and others yet to be confirmed.
- And here are just a few of the newspapers that will be featuring the book as well: **Cedar Rapids Gazette, Harrisburg Patriot News, Kansas City Star, Madison State Journal**, and others.
- While in Albuquerque, the author did a live 15-minute interview on **KKOB**. 50 more radio interviews are scheduled for September through November.
- 1500 advanced review copies were distributed at the annual **American Booksellers Association** convention in Anaheim, California, where the book received enthusiastic praise from booksellers. Over 250 copies were autographed by the author during a half-hour session at the convention.
- The author will be attending the following regional bookseller conventions: **Upper Midwest Booksellers Association** in Minneapolis, Minnesota; **Mid-Atlantic / New York Booksellers Association** in Atlantic City, New Jersey, and **Rocky Mountain Booksellers Association** in Denver, Colorado.
- During these conventions he will be available for interviews in these cities as well as Saint Paul, Minnesota; New York, New York; and Boulder, Colorado.
- For bookstores and other retailers, a two-color counter-top display gives the book added exposure.

For more information, call toll-free: (800) 669-0773.
Ad-Lib Publications, 51 N. Fifth Street, P. O. Box 1102, Fairfield IA 52556

Vicki Lansky

In the beginning we promoted our book using our "relative marketing strategy"—that is, I traveled to cities to make media appearances wherever we had relatives as well as B. Dalton stores. The bookstores would stock any city I went to for publicity.

chapter 22

The Difference Between Authors and Publishers: Writing What Sells

by Vicki Lansky

I never planned on being a professional parent or a publisher. I was an art history major in college and afterwards worked as a sportswear buyer in New York City.

When my husband got a job in Minneapolis, I found myself dealing with this transition by becoming active in the Minneapolis Childbirth Education Association, which prepared couples for childbirth. When Dana, our second child, was born I became active on the fund-raising committee where I rather accidentally put together a fund-raising cookbook for them. Rather than everyone's favorite recipe, I wanted to put together a book that would be of interest to new mothers. Five other mothers helped me. We had a total of two meetings (with children in tow) and the only title ever suggested for it was perfect: "Feed Me I'm Yours." I was also responsible for finding the printer, making the budget, copyediting the book and also selling it. I had taken out the copyright in my name because the organization's attitude at the time I proposed it was, "you do it and we'll see." It was much later when I learned I was not only the author but the publisher as well. After all, I had never worked in the print world and had carefully avoided writing classes in school.

In the beginning, Bruce was not exactly thrilled about the time I was putting in on this volunteer project. But the first review of "Feed Me I'm Yours" in a Sunday edition of our Minneapolis paper (which covered the whole state) brought in hundreds of orders. When I told Bruce a few weeks later how we were now getting reorders, his marketing ears perked up. Soon we had the book typeset, and established Meadowbrook Press and I was soon packing and shipping books out of the house as well as making media appearances showing how to make your own baby food. We were never against manufactured baby food but I demonstrated how easy it was to make it yourself and I was always comfortable working with the media.

In the beginning we promoted our book using our "relative marketing strategy"—that is, I traveled to cities to make media appearances wherever we had relatives as well as B. Dalton stores. The bookstores would stock any city I went to for publicity. In 1975 it was easier for a small press to get into the chains than it is now. After selling 100,000 copies out of our home, Bantam picked up the mass market rights, which got me my first "Donahue" appearance, and both versions are still sold today with over two million copies in print.

We also discovered that we could sell to infant clothing stores. Finding special marketing channels, which often require more "lenient" discounts, became an important part of our business. Bookstores are not always the best place to sell books.

Large publishing houses love it when a small press "tests" the market for any book. We had many reactions when the book first came out and we tried to sell it to New York houses. Even B. Dalton, at that time located in Minneapolis, would only place it where we promoted it.

I've now written over twenty books, (and for years I thought my last book was my final book). When I got divorced in 1983, it also meant I got divorced from our publishing company. In 1987, I found myself drifting back into publishing—after a few years as a literary agent—by putting back into print some of my titles whose rights had reverted back to me through my Book Peddlers company. I also mail order all my own titles through a small "Practical Parenting Catalog" because no bookstore ever carries all my titles.

So I have books that I have written (and write) for other publishers because I don't always have access to channels of distribution some of them have. Others I now publish myself. These are distributed to the book trade by Publishers Group West for a deep discount, and I go after those "other" markets myself. I keep my overhead low by staffing only two regular employees and work at keeping my lifestyle intact. I am able to do this in part through our growing use of desktop publishing. My office is three blocks from my house. I travel a fair amount for both business and pleasure.

My book credentials have opened many venues for me. I write a column for both *Sesame Street's Parent Guide* section as well as for *Family Circle*. Over the years, I have written newspaper columns, recorded regular radio-taped parenting segments and traveled all around the country making media appearances both large and small. I'm often asked to speak, but I try not to because it inevitably becomes a time-commitment problem.

I've always considered myself more of a publisher than an author though I know most people don't perceive me that way. I don't publish what I don't think will sell. That's a different attitude than wanting to "say" something and hoping it will sell.

KOKO BEAR'S BIG EARACHE
By Vicki Lansky

Please send me _____ copies (6 bk min) at the special discount rate for health professionals of $2.77 a copy (44% discount from $4.95 retail). If prepaid by check or charged, no additional postage charge will be added.

Name _____

Group _____

Address _____

City/St/Zip _____

Phone _____

Visa [ ] MC [ ] Exp. Date _____

Acct. #_____ Signature_____

KOKO BEAR'S
BIG EARACHE

Preparing Your Child for Ear Tube Surgery
by VICKI LANSKY

The Book Peddlers, 18326 Minnetonka Blvd., Deephaven, MN 55391
Call 1-800-255-3379 or 612-475-3527

The Book Peddlers

For immediate release:
For more information,
contact: Dorothy Skelly

18326 Minnetonka Boulevard
Deephaven, Minnesota 55391
612-475-3527

ANOTHER USE FOR...101 COMMON HOUSEHOLD ITEMS

BY VICKI LANSKY

* An A-to-Z guide to multiple uses for everyday items
* Vicki Lansky's popular column in *Family Circle*
  magazine features an "Another Use For..." section

Both trivia buffs and devotees of household hints will have a
field day with this handy little book. It brings together a store-
house of practical tips and hints on multiple uses for
everything from address stickers (put them on books and
tapes you lend out), alcohol, and aluminum foil to wading
pools (use to store toys, clothes, etc. under the bed) and wax
paper. Under each alphabetically listed common house-
house item are five to ten additional--and in many cases,
surprising--uses for that item. For example:

Another Use For...TOOTHPICKS
* To help keep birthday candles upright, push a toothpick into
  the bottom of each candle before placing it on a cake.
* Before repainting or wallpapering your walls, insert tooth
  picks in the holes left by the nails or picture hooks that
  you've removed.
* Use a toothpick to push lace and other hard to handle
  materials in place under the pressure foot on your sewing
  machine.
* When frying sausage links, put toothpicks through two at a
  time. It will keep them from rolling around and they will
  need to be turned only once.
* If you lose a screw out of your eyeglass frames, a wooden
  tooth pick tip will hold your glasses together until you
  can get them fixed.

trade paperback ISBN 916773-30-2
15 line drawings, 150 pages, 7" x7"
March 1991 pub date
$6.95 retail

Vicki Lansky has collected and shared her practical hints and tips for years through her numerous parenting books, media appearances and feature columns. Her *HELP* hints column has appeared monthly in *Family Circle*
Magazine for over 3 years. She also writes a *Practical Parenting* column for *Sesame Street* Magazine's Parent's Guide Magazine. Vicki lives and offices in Deephaven, MN, a suburb of Minneapolis.

Another Use For...101 Common Household Items is available in bookstores or by mail for $6.95
plus $2.25 postage and handling by calling 1-800-255-3379.

Extra Bonus Note

Marguerite Kelly
Author of The Mother's Almanac

I thought that you might be amused at the way The Mother's Almanac was born. My neighbor and I started researching and writing the book in 1969, taking a year to produce 15,000 words before sending it to an editor we had heard of at Doubleday. We even included sample art although we knew that authors were not supposed to choose their own illustrations. We continued to write, with increasingly faint hearts, for the next nine months and then the editor called and said, "Sorry, we can't publish your book because your co-author only has a degree in English and you haven't even been to college. Doubleday can only publish hardcover books by experts."

With tears in my eyes, I looked at THE WHOLE EARTH CATALOG and Newsweek on my coffee table and said, "I think there is a misunderstanding. We had something more informal in mind like THE WHOLE EARTH CATALOG, about the size of Newsweek—in soft cover." And she said, "Oh, that's okay. You don't have to be experts to write a soft-cover book for Doubleday."

We were given a joint advance of $10,000. and told to bring back the camera-ready mechanical, which we were delighted to do and to pay for it, which was not as wonderful, but acceptable. (That is no longer necessary with Doubleday to produce your own camera ready material.) We were told what typeface to use for the text and heads and told to use clay-coated paper. By the time we went into production, we had accumulated the following totals: Total time: 6 ½ years; Total cost: $10,500 out of $10,000 advance; Total promo and advertising: 0

Karen Van Westering was our editor who would check and oversee our progress but we did the rest: hired the illustrator, the designer, the design consultant, typists, proofreader, and supervised it all. We dragooned our friends to help us index the book.

The book was however chosen by the sales reps to be one of three books that they pushed to the stores which was an enormous help. It was serialized, excerpted by Woman's Day, chosen by a couple of book clubs and translated into French, Portuguese, anthologized in England and quoted all over the country. It has gone into thirty five printings, sold more than 700,000 copies and been completely revised and updated for release in May of 1992. Its sequel, The Mother's Almanac II, about children from ages six to twelve, came out in 1989, has sold 60,000 copies, including BOMC, and gone into its second printing. Doubleday printed some copies in hardcover, by the way.

Just to amuse you, Trisha, so you'll realize your book will be much appreciated by prospective authors. In case you get faint-hearted, good luck.

202

Dr. Jeffrey Lant

If you're talking on the subject of your book—and if not, why not—you will thus have the opportunity to promote it at least a month before your talk, at your talk, and, through either a review of your talk and/or a review of your book, after your talk.

chapter **23**

Marketing Your Book Before It's Published

by Dr. Jeffrey Lant

Even before your book is published you should be marketing it. There are three major reasons for this:

First, most publishers get lousy credit terms from their printers because most printers want a substantial fraction of their money in advance of printing (from one-third to one-half the total cost). They usually want the remainder within thirty days. Thus, there's a real economic incentive to start getting money in as fast as possible.

Secondly, from a marketing standpoint, it makes good sense to connect with your prospective buyers as many times as possible. We know that most buyers need to hear about a book as many as seven times within eighteen months before they actually buy it—even when they like the topic! With a mass market book, the prospect may get these seven nudges within a single week. But most of us have to be much more creative about how we get our books to our prospective buyers' attention.

Finally, there are certain marketing techniques you can only use before a book is published. After it's out, these marketing alternatives cannot be used. Since no publisher wastes a chance to promote his books, to lose this opportunity approaches criminal.

When to start marketing

Book marketing begins the moment you've selected a subject and, more importantly, a title. One mistake too many publishers make is to wait to begin marketing until they have their product in hand. Don't be one of them!

As soon as you've got a title, begin to both create a sense of excitement and anticipation about your book, and to sell it.

Send a pre-publication announcement to the book trade publications and any professional associations to which you belong. But don't just announce your book. Sell it. Don't send this announcement personally, use the name of your publishing company, even if you are the publishing company. Thus, "JLA Publications announces the forthcoming publication of Dr. Jeffrey Lant's latest book 'Money Making Marketing: Finding the People Who Need What You're Selling and Making Sure They Buy It.' Special pre-publication offer $22.50 (postpaid) until June 1. $34 thereafter."

To make this announcement work, you've got to know the ultimate retail price of your book, your pre-publication price (all books should have them), and the cut-off date for pre-publication orders.

If you've published books before, use this opportunity to promote both your previous work and your forthcoming title. Thus, "JLA Publications announces the forthcoming publication of Dr. Jeffrey Lant's new book 'Money Making Marketing' in June 1987. This is the fifth volume in his 'Get Ahead' series, which also includes 'The Consultant's Kit: Establishing and Operating Your Successful Consulting Business' ($34 postpaid)." This announcement should include complete purchase details for both your forthcoming and your current title, including your name, address and telephone number.

Many publishers feel squeamish about including this information. Don't feel that way. If a publication doesn't want to print it all, it won't. Ordinarily, however, if they've got the information readily at hand in a form they can easily use, they will. Don't be the one withholding information from your buyers. At the very least, put print publishers in the position of doing so!

Look for excerpt possibilities

All publishers know about excerpts, but few have an excerpt strategy. Excerpts from books should be printed both before and after publication. Excerpts should begin to appear about sixty days before publication and should continue to be offered to publications as long as your topic is interesting. What I am saying differs significantly from prevailing ideas, that dictate running excerpts only at publication time.

Other specific marketing ideas

Since publications work far in advance, the minute you've got your book's title and a short 150 to 200-word synopsis and, of course, the publication date, it's time to start lining up excerpt possibilities. To make your excerpt strategy a success, you must:

✍ Keep a list of all the publications which might be interested in running articles. So that you know what to give them, you need samples of these publications. You cannot offer a 2,000-word article to a newsletter whose articles are never longer than 500 words.

✍ Get the names, addresses and telephone numbers of the editors of these publications. As soon as you're sure you've got an article for them, offer them excerpt rights. Remember, these excerpts should not appear more than sixty days before the book itself. But make sure that they do begin then.

✍ Contact these publishers and offer them articles. Find out whether they're interested and when their deadline is. If they like your material, make sure you get compensated by being given either a resource box at the conclusion of the article or an ad. The following are ideas to keep in mind about both these marketing vehicles.

The resource box

If you want to see a good example of a resource box, you need look no farther than the conclusion of this article. You must do the same thing. Your resource box should list the complete title and postpaid-price of your book, the author, name of publisher, address, and telephone number. If you take MasterCard or Visa (and if not, why not?), include this information. No, you won't always be able to have it included, but don't be the one to edit this information out. You include what you want to have in the resource box. And before someone else edits anything out, fight for this material. It's critical from a marketing standpoint. Also, if you have a catalog listing your other titles, make sure you tell people where they can write or call to get it.

An advertisement

You won't be surprised to learn I attempt to get both a resource box and ad. Why not? I'm not being directly compensated by the publication for my super material. Thus, I ask for, and usually receive, both. If you do, make sure your ad doesn't run in the same issue of the publication as your article and resource box. The reason is obvious: If you can connect with your buyers with complete follow-up details on two separate occasions instead of just one, you'd be mad not to do it.

If, however, you can't get the resource box at the conclusion of your article, then you'll have to use your ad in the same issue. That's unfortunate, but it does happen.

Don't forget to clearly indicate that your book is available for a pre-publication discount and the date at which the discount expires. Not surprisingly, Americans love a bargain. As your deadline approaches, your sales will increase. Be aware that once these bargain conditions have been publicized, people will use them long after the deadline has passed. People send me money for books at the pre-publication price for books which have been out several years! In this case, send them a polite note and ask for the balance.

Properly using a flyer about your book

Each book you produce should have an individual eight-and-a-half-inch by eleven-inch flyer with information on its contents, benefits, and complete order information. Develop this flyer as soon as you can. In some cases, this flyer cannot be used until your book is paginated. Since this is one of the last tasks to be accomplished before actual printing, you'll only have about four to six weeks to send your flyer out before your book is published. Thus, planning is crucial.

Gather a list of media sources to which you want to send review copies. Develop a cover letter and response coupon and send these, along with your flyer, to book reviewers. Send this as soon as you can. Ask them to let you know whether they'd like a review copy. If they do, as soon as your book is available, you can send it, along with a note telling them you are sending them the book as they asked you to do. This system gives you more control over the generally wasteful process of book-reviewing that most publishers have.

Send this flyer to all publications that don't need to see your book to promote it. These include publications put out by alumni, fraternal and sororal organizations, civic, religious and other groups. Most of these organizations publish magazines and newsletters that don't need to see your book, but can nonetheless publish complete order information. This being the case, why do so many authors, and publishers, content themselves with the barest mention of their books (ordinarily just the title)? After years of reading my alma mater's *Harvard Magazine*, I've discovered I'm probably the only author/publisher who provides complete order details. Astonishing!

Selling the unpublished book to your house mailing list

As I've written in other articles, there are certain prerequisites for profiting as a publisher. The first prerequisite is developing a series, that is not publishing single, non-related book titles. Secondly, work assiduously to build up a house mailing list of buyers. If you meet these two conditions, you make it easier to sell copies of forthcoming books. Thus, sell your as yet unpublished book in the following ways:

As soon as you have a title, contents description, publication date and pre-publication price, begin to tell your former buyers about it. If you are certain you will meet your publication date—only you know your own habits and your authors' habits, then you can begin to sell it. Remember, you are allowed a grace period of thirty days after your announced publication date in which to fulfill orders. After thirty days, you must alert your buyers if there is going to be a delay in shipping. You are then allowed an additional thirty days in which to fulfill their order. If you still cannot do so, you must refund their money. Therefore, be liberal about your publication date. And meet the date you eventually announce.

Incorporate information about forthcoming books in all your marketing documents, and make sure each forthcoming book has its own flyer. Even when you don't know the number of pages, estimate. You can easily make a persuasive marketing flyer from a book proposal, for what else is a proposal but a marketing document? Use this flyer as a package stuffer, in your outgoing mail and invoices, etc.

Arranging speaking engagements to promote your book

As a rough rule of thumb, allow six months of lead time to arrange any speaking engagement. This means that if your book is coming out June 1, you should start lining up engagements in January. As I've written in my book "Money Talks: The Complete Guide to Creating a Profitable Workshop or Seminar in any Field" ($32.50 postpaid), each talk you give should be preceded by an article you wrote and should be followed by a review of what you've said. If you are not being paid directly for your talk, you should also ask for ad space so that you can promote your book through the organization's publication. Lant Rule of Thumb: ask for twice the dollar value in ad space of what you should have been paid for the talk.

If you're talking on the subject of your book—and if not, why not—you will thus have the opportunity to promote it at least a month before your talk, at your talk, and, through either a review of your talk and/or a review of your book, after your talk. Each of these opportunities should be accompanied by complete order details about your book. All this should be arranged at the time you book your talk, which, remember, may be six months in advance of the date itself. Yes, planning is crucial.

Marketing goes hand-in-hand with writing and book production

What should now be clear is that marketing is not an activity that you, as an author or publisher, can afford to leave until your product is actually ready. That's foolish. Marketing begins the moment you have a title and gains speed as the book moves towards actual publication.

People continually ask how I, despite not having a single employee, get so much attention for my books. The answer is plain: at any given time, I am promoting books that have long been out. This promotion is based on either the fact that they have been updated, and are thus in a sense new, as well as the fact that they continue to solve the problems of designated publics.

I am also promoting books which are newly published and therefore benefit from our general obsession with the new, as opposed to the worthwhile. Finally, and importantly, I am promoting books that are not yet published and may, indeed, not even be written. In this way, the amount of marketing attention any single title can get is far, far greater than most publishers realize or utilize.

Knowing how expensive the publishing process is, knowing how quickly printers want their money, I quite prefer financing as much of my operation as possible by marketing and selling my books as soon as I can, right from the moment of their inception, than by waiting until the time they—and the printing bill—arrive together. At that moment, it is time not to start marketing but to move into another phase of marketing. That, however, is another story.

Example of a Resource Box

This resource box was written by Jeffrey Lant.

Dr. Jeffrey Lant's latest book is "Money Making Marketing: Finding the People Who Need What You're Selling and Making Sure They Buy It." He is also the author of "The Unabashed Self-Promoter's Guide: What Every Man, Woman, Child and Organization in America Needs to Know About Getting Ahead by Exploiting the Media." Each is $34 postpaid from JLA Publications, 50 Follen St., Suite 507, Cambridge, MA 02138 or (with your MasterCard or Visa) by calling (617) 547-6372. Don't forget to ask for your free copy of my Sure-Fire Business Success Catalog and details on how I can improve the profitability of every marketing document you're using.

Judy Lawrence

*When I followed up, which I soon learned was the real
key to any success, the reporter wondered what she could
write about "a bunch of blank charts." "Blank charts!
Let me tell you how this book has changed people's lives,"
I said.*

chapter **24**

"Common Cent$" Began With Jars on the Dresser

by Judy Lawrence

L ittle did I foresee publishing in my future when I grew up in Wisconsin living above and working in a cheese factory my whole childhood. I was fortunate enough to earn good money, so I saved it in jars on my dresser labeled "clothes," "college," "car," "savings," and "fun." My older brother used to laugh at my jars and tell me to put my money in the bank so I could earn interest. Not me. I was thirteen-years-old and couldn't care less about interest, I wanted to visually see my money "grow" in my jars.

Those jars were truly the forerunner to my budget book, "Common Cent$: The Complete Money Management Workbook" published nearly twenty years later.

Graduating from college with a bachelors degree in physical education and a masters degree in guidance and counseling, working as a school counselor, later as a counselor on a Navajo Indian reservation, then at an adult technical vocational institute and finally as a real estate agent gave me no clue that I would someday be writing and self-publishing a book.

Those experiences unknowingly actually prepared me for my future budget book. Often I would give fellow workers, students, and real estate clients suggestions for handling their money and would draw up different individualized workcharts to help them see their whole financial picture. Many times people would say "You ought to write a book." Fool that I was, I believed them.

Since I knew absolutely nothing about this industry, I pretty much reinvented the wheel and learned everything the hard way. I thought all books were done in New York, but I had no contacts there. I assumed I needed a finished copy before I could contact publishers so I took the printing class at the vocational-technical institute where I asked to do the typesetting and printing of the book for a class project. I'm embarrassed every time I see that crude, comb-bound, inconsistent inside color book in my file. But it did get me the typesetting still used in the book ten years later.

Without realizing it, I had become a self-publisher which had put me in company with people like Wayne Dwyer, Bolles etc. and in competition with the 45,000 titles published each year and 300 new publishers each month.

Back in 1981, I was totally unaware of any of those facts or of books like Dan Poynter's self-publishing book which would have made my life a little easier. I set off to sell my book. With my new book in hand, I went to three local bookstores and asked about the demand for books on this topic. Since 1981 was recession time the answer was, "Yes, we need a book like that." That was the extent of my sophisticated market research. It was time to sell "Common Cent$."

I went back to Milwaukee that summer "schlepping" canvas bags of books from store to store including bookstores and stationery stores. Somehow I managed to get on a TV show and was interviewed by a newspaper. Two important lessons I learned on that trip were to ignore what people said and watch what people did. At one store the manager said, "Lady, budget books don't sell in the summer." I couldn't accept that. I had bags of books in the trunk and more in my garage at home so I ignored his advice and proceeded to sell hundreds of books. At another store, I was blocked off from personally speaking to the manager and pointing out the many wonderful features, but I watched as he whipped through the pages, looked at the blank back cover and said "no." I realized then I needed a message on the back cover to quickly tell readers why they want to buy this workbook.

When I returned to New Mexico, I had sold out of my 400 books and needed to go for the "big run:" 1,000 copies. Again people tried to discourage me "Lady, you can't do a two-color inside and three-color cover for under $10,000." I had no business or math background but I had enough sense to know that $10,000 for 1,000 books does not compute when the retail price is $5.95. Undaunted, I eventually found a sympathetic printer, and a hard-working free-lancer to do the collating and binding for thirty cents each and was able to print 1,000 books and make a profit.

Books in a detergent box

The real test of determination came with my first big order in 1982 of 4,000 copies to an office supply distributor. My new printer, Delta Lithograph (great printer for me and introduced the more professional looking spiral binding to the book) in California shipped off the order directly until I found a goof on one page. All truckloads of books were immediately called back to the printer for repair, but in the meantime there I was with a deadline to meet. Over the weekend my husband and I salvaged the order by shipping out 2,000 to fill half an order from books I had in stock. This meant assembling a display box, packing a dozen in each, and finding boxes and packing material. Now, there was the catch. To this day I wonder what the warehouse people thought as they unpacked "Common Cent$" books from Charmin and Tide boxes—the only salvageable boxes available from dumpsters on a Saturday and Sunday. Then the big question: Is this what I really want to be doing? Somehow I decided it was.

What about marketing? After a few miserable attempts at placing advertisements I found most letters were coming from the other "vultures" trying to sell me something, rather than any customers, it became very clear that advertising just didn't work for my purposes. Free publicity did. I also learned I immediately was put in a "catch twenty-two." Stores would not stock the book without publicity and the media didn't want to interview me if the book was not available in the stores. It was a tricky maneuver, but I learned to stretch the truth and time everything so books were available and interviews took place.

In the beginning I was so naive. My grand plan was to market the book by getting publicity city by city in New Mexico and then branching to surrounding states. One day a friend told me Houston alone had a population the same size as all of New Mexico (two million). The light bulb went on and I sent off the book to the *Houston Chronicle*. When I followed up, which I soon learned was the real key to any success, the reporter wondered what she could write about "a bunch of blank charts." "Blank charts! Let me tell you how this book has changed people's lives," I said.

Squeaky wheels get the grease

By the time I finished, the reporter agreed there was a story to write and told me I was clearly the squeaky wheel that got the grease, because in her two-foot-pile of books there was no way she ever would have selected mine to review. With $1,000-worth of orders later, I knew what I needed to do and proceeded to seek publicity in *Changing Times, Working Woman, Woman's World, Chicago Sun Times* and numerous other publications along with radio and TV nationwide.

I had my share of good and bad experiences with distributors who carried the book, but the story was always the same when publicity hit—the books were not in the stores (a problem that has remained, with and without a major publisher). Eventually Dow Jones-Irwin approached me, asking to publish "Common Cent$." I had already sold over 30,000 copies on my own, but decided to let go of my "baby." That arrangement brought more credibility, and stabilized the book with all the major distributors, which I still benefit from as a self-publisher again. Overall, however, the marketing end of it was disappointing. In the beginning, 200 books were mailed out to reviewers and I called to ask what response they were receiving. There hadn't been any response because there was no follow-up. I soon realized the publisher didn't handle marketing the same way I did. They generally worked with more sophisticated books and buyers and had a different approach to marketing, which was not as effective with my type of consumer-oriented book.

"Common Cent$" was a different story. There was no question about it's salability. Anyone I talked to in the company always knew about "Common Cent$" and either owned one or gave one to relatives. But marketing this book wasn't cost effective for the publisher. By this time there were also many changes happening editorially. After some time, it became apparent that "Common Cent$" was slowly becoming an orphan in this publishing house. I soon started taking on the marketing end again myself and after three years, mutually agreed with the company to buy back the rights.

Would I do it all over again? Well, I certainly wouldn't give up any of the incredible lessons I learned, people I met, confidence I gained, or gratitude of knowing my project has met the many individual needs I had intended for it as a counselor. But I will say after ten years it has been a long haul and I know what burnout is all about. Currently, the business and sales just seem to keep on going and sales continue year after year with minimal marketing input or energy on my part since my energy level is still at a low ebb. I'm learning to trust, however, that what is meant to happen will happen now that I have done all the footwork. There are thousands of "Common Cent$" users out there "hooked" on buying a new workbook every year to use for controlling their finances. In the meantime, I am teaching more budget workshops (which includes the sale of "Common Cent$") and one-on-one budget counseling. I'm now waiting to see what the nineties will bring for my own direction and the life of "Common Cent$."

LAWRENCE and CO. PUBLISHERS (dba Common Cents Inc.)   Post Office Box 13167   Albuquerque, New Mexico 87192   Telephone (505) 821-7103

COMMON CENT$ Consulting and Workshops

INFORMATION SHEET

BOOK CATEGORY:	Personal Finance, How To Business
TITLE:	COMMON CENT$: THE COMPLETE MONEY MANAGMENT WORKBOOK
AUTHOR:	Judy Lawrence
ISBN:	0-9607096-6-5, Lawrence & Co.Publishers 0-87094-694-3 (Dow Jones-Irwin) (1986-1988)
PRICE:	$10.95
NO. OF PAGES:	84 pages (includes 56 fill in worksheets) 4 pockets
PUBLISHING CO:	Lawrence & Co. Publishers - current Dow Jones-Irwin - former
PRINTINGS:	13th - January 1991
ADDRESS:	P.O. Box 13167 Albuquerque, NM 87192 (add $2.00 for postage & handling)
PHONE:	505/296-8792
CONTACT PERSON:	Judy Lawrence
DISTRIBUTERS:	Bookstores: Ingram, Baker and Taylor, Gordons, Buying Clubs: Advanced Marketing Services

CHILD CARE AND YOU!

A Comprehensive Guide To Organizing A Profitable Home-Based Business

A Basic How To Do It Guide

. . . Including hundreds of creative play and educational ideas for parents, grandparents, teachers, aides, volunteers and college students

Patricia C. Gallagher

Dorie Lenz

Producers receive many letters and calls daily. It's not always easy to remember every contact. So when you make your follow-up call, it is important to give your name, title, organization and the reason you're calling.

chapter **25**

How to Get on Television

by Dorie Lenz

Note from Editor: *For those of us who work in public relations or who work for non-profit organizations, Dorie Lenz, Public Affairs Director of WPHL-TV in Philadelphia, offers great advice on tips for appearing on TV. "How to Get on TV, A Guide for Non-profits," is a booklet she compiled as a public service for non-profit organizations in the tri-state Pennsylvania, Delaware and New Jersey.*

Reprinted here, Dorie offers constructive information for writers representing non-profit organizations or causes and for those whose books qualify for discussion on public affairs programs. Public affairs programs are generally geared to serious issues that concern society in general and are not intended for commercial or promotional purposes.

• • •

The competition for money and for volunteers has greatly increased in the last few years. We know that you are aware of this and of the need to make your organization known to as large an audience as possible. Let free public service time, offered by your local TV stations, help you by airing your message to area viewers.

Each station receives hundreds of calls and letters asking, "How do we get an announcement on TV?" or "How can we appear on a program?" The purpose of this chapter is to show you the best way to prepare your requests so that you can increase your chances for getting on the air.

Television is the most powerful means of communication. More people receive their information from it than any other source. Use it so that the communities you serve so well will learn about your goals, programs, and events.

What is a PSA?

A PSA is a public service announcement. It is a "no charge" message that acts like a commercial. It promotes events and services of non-profit organizations and groups that serve the community. PSAs run from ten to sixty seconds in length.

This is your opportunity to let viewers know what's important about your group in your own words. Concentrate on a single idea or event. Don't try to say everything in one PSA. You can send others in the future.

To have the greatest impact, your PSAs should go to all the stations at the same time. The more a message is aired, the more likely it is to be remembered.

There are two kinds of PSAs. One is created at no cost by the station from your copy. An announcer reads the edited copy while the information about your organization or event is seen on the TV screen.

The other kind of PSA is produced outside the station by a professional production company for a fee.

If your organization is new or not well known, it is helpful to send a cover letter with background information and a copy of your 501 C3 form. You can get this by calling the Internal Revenue Service. Ask them how to obtain a tax exempt application. They can tell you which form you need, how to order it, and answer your questions about how to complete it. There is a filing fee. If your application is approved, you will then receive a 501 C3 form. This is your proof of your non-profit status.

Most stations will not air PSAs that are controversial or mention a personality from another station. Commercial sponsors or products usually are not accepted.

Most commercial TV stations are committed to air many PSAs throughout the broadcast day. It is their contribution to the community.

How to get your PSA copy on air

Many PSAs are sent to stations daily. The more help you give a station, the better the chance that you will get your message on the air. Don't send a one- or two-page news release which gives detailed information about your organization or event. This format will seldom be edited to a PSA. Your copy should be simple and to the point, highlighting the essentials. If there is a telephone number for viewers to call for more information, include it at the end of the copy.

It is very important that you note the copy requirements mentioned later in this chapter. Many PSAs are never used because they don't get to the stations in enough time to edit and produce them.

When submitting a PSA include:

✍ Organization name and address,

✍ Name of publicity contact and phone number,

✍ Start and stop dates for PSA to air,

✍ Length in seconds. Time the copy, reading at a normal speed. It's better to be a few seconds longer, than too short. This will give the station more copy to use if needed.

✍ Type and double space copy to allow for easy reading and editing.

✍ If a word is difficult to pronounce, include the phonetic spelling.

When do these PSAs air? Policies differ. Some stations will air your PSA only once while others will air it several times over a period of days, weeks or months.

There is a great deal of competition for these spots. If your PSA is not selected, don't be discouraged. Keep sending them. Eventually yours may be chosen. Note that fewer PSAs are received over the summer. If you can send yours then, you may have a better chance of getting on the air.

Sample copy for your PSA

```
     Haven House
     442 Ivy Road
     Philadelphia, PA 19131
     (215) 123-4567
     CONTACT: Arlene May
      Foster Care Coordinator
      (215) 123-4568
     START: Immediately
     STOP: November 15, 1990
     PUBLIC SERVICE ANNOUNCEMENT :30 seconds
     Haven House provides temporary shelter and
services to Philadelphia's dependent and
neglected children. To make it in today's
world, these troubled and abused youngsters
need love, caring, and direction. Foster
parents can give these kids the chance they
deserve. Learn how you can make a difference
in a child's life. Become a foster parent.
Training sessions begin November 15. For more
information, call Haven House at area code
(215) 123-4567.
```

The pre-produced video PSA

Increasingly, local organizations are having their PSAs professionally produced by video production companies. It is an investment worth considering because it almost always guarantees that a station will accept your PSA for airing. You might ask a Public Service Director at a station for the names of production companies and then inquire about their services and costs.

A PSA can be produced in several ways. You can use a series of slides, video shots on location or an effective spokesperson. Perhaps you have a clever idea that you would like to try. All can get your message across. The producer will supply the special effects, work with you on the script and music and arrange for the off-camera voice, if needed. The production company creates a "master" tape of your PSA. They make copies for you to distribute to TV stations.

Remember, your PSA doesn't need to be elaborate to be effective. It will be judged on content and technical quality.

Don't use your home video equipment to produce a PSA. It will look amateurish and not meet broadcast standards.

More on pre-produced videos

Although a thirty- or sixty-second PSA gives you more time to deliver your message, consider sending a shorter version. Often a ten-, fifteen-, or twenty-second PSA can fit into an available time slot when a longer one will not. Or you may want to send a thirty second and a ten second of the same PSA.

When the tape is ready, make sure the label on the box identifies the name of the organization and lists each cut and length in the order that they appear on the tape. Your accompanying letter should include information about your organization or event as well as the start and stop dates for your PSA to air.

If your PSA is promoting a dated event, make sure that stations receive your videotape a few months in advance.

You will be contacted if there are technical problems with a videotape.

Usually your tape will air for several months in rotation with other PSAs.

Most stations prefer not to return tapes after they've aired. If you want to submit your PSA again a year later, necessary changes and new copies can be made by the production company for a fee.

Public Affairs programs

One of the most effective ways to get your message across to a wide audience is to have a member or members of your group appear on a talk program. Generally these programs are not shown in prime time. You will be seen, regardless of the hour, by many thousands of viewers. What you say may be quoted at a breakfast table. You may even hear from friends you haven't seen in years. More importantly, your audience will have learned about a problem, concern or event that should receive public attention.

To get the producer's attention

Here are some ideas:

✍ Watch the program. This will make you familiar with the format of the show and the host's style.

✍ Write to the producer on your organization letterhead if you have one. A typed letter is easier to read.

✍ Include a short summary of your organization's history and aims.

✍ What is new, innovative or special that people should know about?

✍ Will viewers learn something helpful?

✍ Does it interest a wide audience?

Send the following material if possible:

✍ Names of potential guests, with titles and addresses

✍ Suggested list of questions for the host.

✍ Copies of any newspaper articles and brochures about your organization or subject.

✍ Telephone number and/or address to appear during the program

✍ Television is a visual medium. Any horizontal 35mm slides, videotapes, film clips, photos, objects, free brochures, etc...will add interest to the program. Let the producer know you have them, but don't send them unless requested.

In your cover letter to the producer include, "I will call you in a few days."

Producers receive many letters and calls daily. It's not always easy to remember every contact. So when you make your follow-up call, it is important to give your name, title, organization and the reason you're calling.

You've been booked for a program

Almost everyone feels somewhat nervous and apprehensive before appearing on TV. Relax. It's almost never noticed by the viewers. They don't expect a performer, so enjoy yourself. You're the expert!

1) The highest ranking member of your organization may not necessarily be your most articulate or lively spokesperson. If possible, send someone who speaks easily and well before groups.

2) Be prepared to discuss your organization in general terms, even though you may represent only one area of its total program.

3) The interview will be more effective if you decide ahead of time the most important things you want to say and how to say them in the clearest way.

4) If you will be using terms that may not be readily understood outside your field, be sure to explain them in everyday language.

5) Don't overuse statistics. A human interest story will be remembered long after percentages are forgotten.

6) Don't wear white shirts or jackets, very pale suits or dresses, glossy fabrics, or busy patterns. Red doesn't reproduce well. Use it sparingly. Large shiny necklaces and earrings glare on camera.

7) The makeup you wear for daytime is all you need for TV.

...during the interview...

1) Use your natural speaking voice.

2) Don't look at the cameras or monitors. Look only at the interviewer or the person speaking.

3) The host of the program is addressed by first name.

4) Answer questions fully, but don't make your answer a monologue.

5) If the interviewer appears to be searching for a question, don't hesitate to jump in with a statement, information, etc.

6) If you're seated with another guest, you may want to turn to him/her on occasion with a comment or question.

7) If you've forgotten to make a specific point and your time is running out, just interject, "Perhaps the most important service viewers should know about is..." or something similar.

...after the interview.

When you leave the station, don't forget to take your visual materials along with you.

Don't be concerned if you think that you've forgotten to mention certain facts. It's not possible to say it all within a limited time frame. What is important is that you've brought your organization to the attention of thousands of viewers in your area.

How to get news coverage

Here are some ways to try to get news coverage:

✍ Two weeks in advance, send a typed news advisory that is short and to the point to the assignment editor and the news producer.

✍ The information should answer the five W's...Who? What? When? Where? Why? Add basic details. Include the name as well as daytime, night-time and weekend phone numbers of a contact person. If needed, you can attach a second page with more background information.

✍ Organized and well-planned material is more likely to be noticed and considered for coverage.

✍ The material is filed with other news events that will occur that day.

✍ A day or two in advance of the event, call the assignment editor to make sure your news advisory was received. If not, be prepared to give all the details.

✍ Most stations will not object to your call. Consider phoning after, not before their newscasts. Mid-morning or early afternoon is the best time.

✍ Remember that TV is visual. News needs pictures to show while the story is being told. Be prepared to present your event in as interesting a way as possible. For example, the subject is education. An event built around the parents and their kids has more impact than two spokespersons sitting at a conference table talking about a problem.

✍ When the station's news crew arrives, give them a copy of the news advisory and help them identify those who are being taped. Sometimes the news crew will want to make a short "on the spot" interview with a key person. Choose someone who is well-informed and able to speak in a clear, concise manner.

Following the above format does not guarantee coverage, but it will head you in the right direction. News departments make decisions about what will be covered on a daily basis. Their final selections depend on many considerations. For example, they may plan to cover an event, but a fast-breaking important story will take priority. Each station has a limited amount of on-air news time. Your request may be one of many. So, don't be too disappointed if a crew doesn't show up. Try again for another event.

Sample news advisory

CONTACT: Jill Paris
 Public Relations
 215 196-4840 (day)
 215 406-1565 (night/weekend)
TO: Assignment editor and news producer
NEWS ADVISORY
 YOUTH MOTION DANCES FOR KIDS
 DRUG PREVENTION PROGRAM
WHO: Youth Motion group
WHAT: Benefit Performance
WHEN: Tuesday, September 19, 7:30 P.M.
WHERE: Wilson Community Center
988 Front Lane
Philadelphia, PA 19131
WHY: Proceeds to benefit the No Drugs
         Youth Education Program which is
         under the direction of the
         Philadelphia Council for Drug
         Prevention.
DETAILS: YOUTH MOTION GROUP is a modern
         dance ensemble, founded in 1980,
         whose members are from 10 to 17
         years of age. The performers are
         multi-racial and live in
         neighborhoods throughout the city.
         Delaware Valley Dance Magazine
         calls them "unusually talented and
         disciplined." They have performed
         in schools, churches, synagogues
         and senior citizen centers in
         Philadelphia. John Boyer, the
         director of YOUTH MOTION, says, "
         Our dancers are concerned about
         kids on drugs and want to help
         bring the No Drugs Youth Education
         Program to as many young people as
         possible."

Carol J. Manna

But ultimately I always believed in the "rightness" of what I was doing. I felt I could help a lot of people. And that someone, somewhere would believe in this project too.

chapter **26**

Believe in Yourself and "Something" Will Happen

by Carol J. Manna

I founded Organization Unlimited in 1981 as a service business designed to help corporate, small business, and residential clients to organize their filing systems, desktop/paperwork clutter, closets, kitchens, garages, basements, and other storage areas. Organization Unlimited is currently based in Skokie, Illinois, but offers its services nationally. In 1988, I received a special award for excellence in Paper Management.

In 1985, I had an idea to produce a video that would demonstrate to the consumer space-saving procedures and tips on how to organize their homes for greater efficiency and peace of mind. Since organizing is such a visual task, a video seemed like the best medium for the message. After years of helping people get organized, I realized that a great many of my clients were lacking the visual ability to organize their belongings into logical, space-efficient patterns. A long time believer in the "learn by doing" approach, I felt that a video would help many people learn the basics of organizing principles in a fast, easy-to-assimilate format.

After writing the script, I read twenty books on film and video production, talked to many professionals in the video business, wrote a business plan, and proceeded to contact any and every person, organization, or company who might have an interest in my idea.

The four-year search to find the right combination of "players" was not without frustration, delay, and disappointment. More than once, it seemed like my project was finally ready to move ahead, only to dissolve because some previously unmentioned, but major ingredient was missing. Each time required that I start all over again, learning more about sales and marketing as I developed the project. Considering that my liberal arts degree never included a course in marketing, or even a business class, each step was a new and difficult one.

At one of the many conventions I attended to learn more about the new home organizer products, I was introduced to the Stanley Hardware Steel Plank Closet Organizer. I was so impressed with the superiority of that product, I talked to the person in charge of marketing it. Many months, phone calls, and letters later, Stanley Hardware agreed to help promote my video idea. Simultaneously, I was also talking to Rubbermaid for their support. Rubbermaid was also interested. Finally, after five years of working on this project, the video was produced with the help of the best, most quality-minded, consumer-oriented sponsors I was fortunate enough to attract.

The video is available through a coupon enclosed in Stanley Hardware's Steel Plank Closet Organizer line and through Rubbermaid's Space Organizer line of consumer products.

Throughout the entire duration of this project, I was fortunate enough to have two friends who believed in me. Their love and support was critical to my well-being and success. Many times you will need to turn to someone when things get rough. And they will get rough. It is imperative to have at least one person to whom you can talk. I will never forget, during my first of many disappointments with this project, my friend Marlene said, "Carol, if you don't do this, someone else will." That was all I needed. Sometimes, you just need someone in your corner to spur you on.

Another friend, who is "in the business," told me, "Carol, you don't have any money, you don't know anyone, you will never make it. I just don't want to see you get hurt." Three quarters of that statement was correct. But the bottom line is, I *did* make it. After an agonizing five years, I did see my dream come true. Basically, I just refused to give up, no matter what happened. And there were many times when I came very close to giving up. But ultimately I always believed in the "rightness" of what I was doing. I felt I could help a lot of people. And that someone, somewhere would believe in this project too.

The best advice I could give to first time authors is:

1) Be the best you can be.
2) Create a tremendous product or service that in some way will help people.
3) Be the first to market it.
4) Read "Think and Grow Rich" by Napolean Hill. This book is the granddaddy of all the self-help books and for good reason. It is an invaluable resource for helping to guide you along your path.
5) BELIEVE IN YOURSELF!
6) Realize when one door closes, it is because another and more promising door will open somewhere else. So, "Knock on every door. Ring every bell. And your prayers will be answered."
7) The process will take much longer than you realize. It will also cost more money and take more time and energy than you can possibly imagine. Do not let that stop you, however.
8) Feel the fear, but do it anyway.
9) Realize things usually get worse before something wonderful happens.
10) Read inspirational stories by successful people you admire. Recalling the early years, Paul McCartney once said, "We'd be lost in the rain on the way to a gig and our car would break down. But we always knew something would happen."

I often think how much poorer the world would be if the Beatles hadn't possessed the courage, stamina, and drive to carry on. Everyone has a special gift to offer the world. But you must first discover it, then offer it, and at all times have the courage, strength, patience, and faith to realize, "Something will happen." It did for me. And if you believe strongly enough in yourself and in your dream, it will happen for you, too. However, be prepared for bitter disappointment and heartbreaks. I am just beginning to realize, recovering from my own heartbreaks, that maybe that is part of the process, as well.

ORGANIZATION UNLIMITED

FILING SYSTEMS   TIME MANAGEMENT
LIBRARY SYSTEMS   SPACE MANAGEMENT

Post Office Box 3301 • Skokie, Illinois 60076 • 312/677-0555

Contact: Carole J. Manna   FOR IMMEDIATE RELEASE

(708) 677-0555

Chicago----ORGANIZATION UNLIMITED, is a unique time/space management service dedicated to easing the panic and frenzy of disorganization and replacing it with manageable environments and money-saving systems. Created by efficiency consultant, Carole J. Manna, the company's clients range from huge commercial/plant operations to small businesses and even personal residential properties. The Skokie based ORGANIZATION UNLIMITED, is now serving all of Chicago and neighboring areas.

"Sometimes it takes a long time for someone to realize that their surroundings have overwhelmed them," says Manna, "and once you lose control over your business or your personal life, you lose your peace of mind." For that reason, no project is too big or too small for Manna to accept. Corporate executives call because they can't find the top of their desk for all the accumulated paperwork. Young professionals hire her to design and set up their filing systems. Some clients, unable to organize their at-home drawers, closets, and living area ask for Manna's assistance in simplifying and organizing their day-to-day environment to make the best use of available space.

ORGANIZATION UNLIMITED, establishes the groundwork and foundation for good management, "I advise and counsel people in the focus, discipline, and concentration necessary to get organized and stay that way," says Manna.

DEE DUNHEIM
Communications/Public Relations

MOTHER
TERESA's
SOMEDAY

by
Claire Jordan Mohan

illustrated by
Susannah Thomer

Claire Mohan

*Writing books is easy—selling books is just the opposite.
Like most other first-time publishers, I thought the world
would come swarming to my door, begging for more and
more copies. The reality was I had to go out into the
world!*

chapter **27**

Providing Spiritual Role Models for Children

an Interview with Claire Mohan

Q: How did you get involved in writing?

A: How I got involved in writing is a long story and goes back many years. How I got involved in writing a book is a shorter one and more to the point. Since I am a teacher, I am always looking for new and better ways to reach my students. Since I am a teacher in a Christian school, I look for ways to inspire the children to do good, to lead moral lives, and to serve the Lord in their own way.

A few years ago while teaching second grade, I was searching for the life story of Kateri Tekewitha, an Indian saint. Though I looked diligently, I could not find a book I felt would interest my class. So I did a little research, wrote a story, and read it to my class! They enjoyed it—I found out I was a writer of children's stories.

Although I already knew I could write and I continued to do so in other areas, it was a couple of years before I attempted to write another story for young people. While I was teaching fifth grade, I gave an English assignment I felt would help me better know the students in my class while giving them a chance to express themselves. The topic was "My Hero" and I explained to them just what a hero was. As I read over the completed papers, I was disappointed in finding compositions about musicians, rock stars, and the like. Finally, I came to one entitled "Madonna." It did my heart good to read those words. At last, one of these Christian children had chosen the mother of God as a role model. You can imagine my horror when I found I was totally mistaken—Madonna was a lingerie-clad rock singer!

I decided it was time to write another book. This one was about a girl named *Gonxha*, whom we all know today as Mother Teresa of Calcutta. Spurred on by this, I then wrote another story on a saint with whom they were all familiar, Mother Mary of Jesus the Good Shepherd, who started life as a girl named *Frania*.

Q: Did you self-publish initially?

A: No, in the early days it never occurred to me to self-publish. For a long time I traveled the route of sending the stories to the many Christian publishers. In return, I received encouragement but no firm offers to buy. Once I had the confidence that they were good enough, self-publishing came to mind. Still the projected cost deterred me for a while until finally my husband urged me to look into this.

Q: What advice do you have about this option?

A: My best advice would be to have a daughter who had already done this! (I did.) In lieu of that, read the many books available. Think about it carefully. Then, go ahead—try it. For me, the first step was finding a good short-run publisher. I made several phone calls and found a book manufacturer forty-five minutes from my home. I gathered my materials together and paid him a visit.

One thing I learned is that there is much contact between writer and book manufacturer and it is very important that you be available to each other. When my publisher quoted me a price, it seemed higher than I had expected. Should I go with him or try a publisher whose rate was lower but was located far from me? I decided to go with him and feel it was one of the wisest decisions I made. There are so many consultations involved and so much repartee that it would be difficult to take care of this by mail or long distance phone calls. Although the printer was not always easy to work with in some areas, which I will not go into, I respected his superior knowledge and the result was a beautiful book.

Since my books are for children, I needed an illustrator. I was fortunate in locating the perfect one not far from my home. This, too, is an important decision and not to be entered into lightly. You must find someone with whom you have rapport—someone who can read your mind and is not sensitive should you wish to make changes. This time Susannah Thomer, an illustrator, filled the bill!

Q: How many books have you written?

A: I have written three books and am working on a fourth but so far have only published two. Since self-publishing requires a large investment, I did not wish to get in too deep.

Q: Was your family supportive?

A: I don't know how anyone could do this without support. I was very fortunate in my choice of husband, and the fact that my daughter knew all the ins and outs of self-publishing. Her help in publicity, promotion, and distribution has made my burden light. As a teacher, my time and energies during the school year are totally devoted to my school work, leaving little time to devote to the time-consuming work involved in distribution.

Q: By what means did you sell the most books?

A: Writing books is easy—selling books is just the opposite. Like most other first-time publishers, I thought the world would come swarming to my door, begging for more and more copies. The reality was I had to go out into the world! Because my book had turned out so professional, I believed in it and overcame my fear of approaching bookstores. Though all those I visited took copies of the books—I realize now this is not the way to do it. You don't achieve success by dribs and drabs—ten copies here, and twenty copies there.

So, my next step was to mail a copy to all the Catholic dioceses in the country so they could recommend them to their school libraries. This generated some interest but the response was not overwhelming. Too late, I learned that libraries want library bindings. Since I had been given poor advice in the beginning, I am now paying $3.50 to have each book re-bound as orders come in.

Newspaper feature articles brought a quick response but it was not a continuing one. As for newspaper ads, they were expensive and the results poor. The same goes for TV shows. I have been on three national shows,

"The 700 Club," "Mother Angelica Live," and CNBC. These give you exposure, build up your confidence, are interesting and enjoyable, but they do not bring in orders if books are not in stores or if your address and phone number are not given on the show.

Footwork and perseverance seem to be the things that bring results. Armed with my book, "Mother Teresa's Someday" and a rough draft of a new one, I approached the superior of a convent with an idea for a children's book about the foundress of her order. Sister loved the idea, wished me luck, and was about to dismiss me. I couldn't let this happen, so I took the plunge. I told her unless she could purchase 1,000 copies, I couldn't go to press. Believe it or not, though her decision took two weeks, she did order the copies! Since then she has ordered an additional 250 copies.

In my particular case, it seemed a good way to go. Before I invest any money in my next book, I plan to do the same. This time, however, I'll have two successful books to show.

I think the only way to sell books is to "live" books and never stop pushing and finding new ways. Since my schedule is so tight, it is only thanks to my daughter's efforts in publicizing them and keeping the phone lines busy that my book boxes are emptying.

As most of us already know, you could write the most wonderful book in the world, but if nobody knows about it—it goes nowhere.

Young Sparrow Press

P.O. Box 265
Worcester, PA 19490
(215) 361-7139

For More Information:
Claire Jordan Mohan
(215) 361-7139
Patricia Gallagher, publicist
(215) 364-1945

FOR IMMEDIATE RELEASE

Catholic school teacher Claire Jordan Mohan was touched when she learned that at least one of her fifth grade students chose Madonna as her heroine. But it didn't take long to figure out that the student was not so much inspired by the blessed Mary, the Madonna, as by the performer who provocatively dances in scanty lingerie.

With that inspiration and the lack of children's saints books in the library, Mohan has recently published the first two books in her Children's Heroes Series, **"Mother Teresa's Someday"** and **"A Red Rose for Frania."** Both books are published by Young Sparrow Press of Worcester, Pa.

Thoughtfully researched and crafted for 6- to 12-year-old readers, **"Mother Teresa's Someday"** focuses on the young life of Mother Teresa of Calcutta, with uplifting prose and cheerful illustrations by Susannah Thomer.

In **"A Red Rose for Frania,"** Mohan tells a heart-warming story of the young Polish girl, Frances Siedliska, who later became Blessed Mary of Jesus the Good Shepherd. Beatified in April 1989, she was the foundress of the Sisters of the Holy Family of Nazareth.

"When you tell a child a story about an adult, it's nice to describe what their lives were like as children. Children relate to children," says Mohan whose experience with children started with raising five of her own. She then ran a successful daycare center with one of her daughters and attended Villanova University. After graduating summa cum laude, she went on to teach elementary school. When she's not teaching or writing, she spends time with her 11 grandchildren.

The high praise and acclaim her books have earned from educators and the Archdiocese of Philadelphia have led to TV appearances on Eternal Word Television Network's (EWTN) **"Mother Angelica Live"** and the 700 Club's **"Straight Talk with Scott Ross."**

-more-

Evelyn Clarke Mott

Read books, magazines, and newsletters about writing and selling manuscripts. To make a sale, it's important to learn how to write and submit professionally.

chapter **28**

Child's Fascination Builds Steam to Publish Book

by Evelyn Clarke Mott

I have just received one of the most difficult things for which I have ever worked—my first book contract! I spent more than a year writing and photographing "Steam Train Ride," a picture book for three- to seven-year-olds. A year later, I have a contract in hand.

The idea to photograph and write "Steam Train Ride" came about through my son Christopher's passion for trains. As a toddler, his desire for train books was insatiable. Soon, words like "tender" and "semaphore" had become part of his everyday vocabulary. After reading so many steam train picture books, I was surprised and disappointed to find none included photographs of steam trains. Christopher's desire to "see pictures of a real steam train" provided my inspiration to create one.

The one question fellow writers keep asking is, "How can a newcomer without an agent break into children's books?" I don't pretend to have all the answers, but I've compiled a list of tactics that worked for me.

1) Tell everybody. If you don't know anybody in publishing, chances are someone you know does. A great source of publishing contacts is through your local librarian. My local librarians liked "Steam Train Ride" and took it to the county's Childrens' Book coordinator. The coordinator wrote me a wonderful note and said she knew a retired children's book editor who might give me advice. It turned out the editor was semi-retired, working part-time

as a field editor. She told me, "I'm not making any promises, but I'll take a look at your manuscript." That was a year ago, and she was the editor who sold "Steam Train Ride" to my publisher, Walker & Company.

2) Read books, magazines, and newsletters about writing and selling manuscripts. To make a sale, it's important to learn how to write and submit professionally.

3) Research your book's market and make sure that your book has something different setting it apart from its competition. "Subject Guide to Books in Print" and "Subject Guide to Children's Books in Print" are great starting points, especially for nonfiction writers. Publishing is a business and publishers only buy books that they think will sell. When I came up with the idea for "Steam Train Ride," I looked through "Children's Books in Print" and couldn't find any photo essays about steam trains for three- to seven-year-olds. Finding my niche helped me persevere with my project and helped to make the sale.

4) Join a manuscript critique group. If you can't find one, start one! I couldn't find a children's critique group in my area, so I started my own group, Lakeside Writers for Young People. We now have eight loyal, supportive, and committed members.

5) Attend writer's conferences. Conferences are wonderful places that provide inspiration, information, and a chance to make contacts.

6) Write or call for publishers' catalogs. You can save a lot of time and money by researching publisher's catalogs before sending out manuscripts. Every publisher's list has its own style, and you will have the most success submitting a manuscript that complements a publisher's list.

7) Read! Reading is fun, and it's also a great way to check out different publishers and your competition. I take out so many children's books from my library that the librarians joke, "You're great for circulation!"

8) Join the Society of Children's Book Writers. The SCBW's guides, newsletters, and conferences are great sources for help, the latest information and inspiration. Write to SCBW for membership

information and an application: Society of Children's Book Writers, P.O. Box 66296, Mar Vista Station, Los Angeles, CA 90066.

9)   Persevere! I'm embarrassed to admit that there were many times when I was ready to give up. Book publishing is such a competitive field with so many wonderful and talented and experienced authors that it is often difficult to see where you fit in. But, if you have a great manuscript that you believe in and are willing to work hard, your chances of getting published are excellent. Perseverance does pay off. With my head in the clouds anxiously anticipating the release of my first book, "Steam Train Ride," I just signed a contract for my second book, which is about hot-air balloons.

45 West Afton Avenue
Yardley, Pennsylvania 19067
March 27, 1990

Ms. Amy C. Shields
Editor-in-Chief
Walker & Co.
720 Fifth Avenue
New York, NY 10019

Dear Ms. Shields,

    I had the pleasure of working with Barbara Bates on <u>Steam Train Ride</u>. She requested that I send it directly to you. I hope that you enjoy it.

    I believe that <u>Steam Train Ride</u> would be most effective as part of a series of transportation photoessays. My ideas include a modern train, racing car, cable car, subway, hot air balloon, boat, helicopter, and zoo monorail story. I have some ideas for marketing the series and would enjoy participating with that aspect of publishing, too. With the attention to quality that Walker & Co. has shown in Ron Hirschi's and Linda Quartman Younker's work, I feel that this series would prove to be visually appealing, entertaining, and successful.

    My background includes a bachelor of science in business administration (marketing major) along with professional training in photography. As a mother and lover of children's books, I have tried to combine my talents with my interests.

    A librarian from my local branch showed <u>Steam Train Ride</u> to the Bucks County Free Library's Children's Book Coordinator, Ms. Marianne Gilmour. I was pleased to receive a note from Ms. Gilmour stating, "Beautiful photographs, very readable text, and popular subject. As a children's librarian, I think it would be popular."

    I look forward to hearing from you. If you have any suggestions, I would be most appreciative to listen to them. Please feel free to call me anytime at (215) 493-0920. I am willing to do whatever work is necessary to make <u>Steam Train Ride</u> more attractive, enjoyable, and informative to children. Thank you for your time and attention.

                        Sincerely,

                        Evelyn Clarke Mott

                        Evelyn Clarke Mott

So You Want To Open A Profitable Day Care Center...

A Basic "How To Do It" Guide For:

- Teachers
- Nurses
- Parents
- Corporate Personnel
- Hospital Staff
- College Students

Patricia C. Gallagher

Doris Patterson

You don't have to make your own mistakes; you can profit greatly by others! That is why it is such a good idea to belong to a writers' group with active professionals among its members, and share with them.

chapter **29**

How to Profit From Mistakes

by Doris Patterson

When on our family's first camping trip, I forgot the coffee pot, made an ice chest out of a bread box, panicked when a thunderstorm hit, and raced home with the kids. I had enough other goofs to fill a book. An editor of a publishing company loved my story and bought it, laughing. Soon after, I got a call from New York. This publisher now had a book division and wanted me to write a book on family camping. "Why on earth—I've made just about every mistake," I wondered.

I learned lesson one: "That's what makes you an expert," they said. "You made mistakes, you can tell how to avoid them." Then the editor I worked with made a mistake and was fired and my book was fired along with him. I sent it out on my own, and it was snapped up by Abingdon Press, a religious publisher who wanted a camping book to help families play together.

"Your Family Goes Camping" paid royalties for fifteen years, in spite of the bookstores mistakenly placing my book on the shelf with the religious books like the kind Abingdon usually published.

Lesson Two: Publishers and bookstores can make mistakes, too. You can help them and yourself as well if you alert them to inconsistencies and poor placement.

Lesson Three: Work actively to promote your book; do not leave it to the publisher. You can send flyers to bookstores, give talks, get your own publicity (see Trisha Gallagher's tips) so people will know to ask for the book and stores will have to keep their fingers on it.

Lesson Four: Time tells whether the title is a mistake. Association for

Research and Enlightenment (A.R.E.) Press published my second book, changing the title to "The Unfettered Mind," listing early prophecies of Edgar Cayce and discoveries that confirmed them (from personal research). But when the book did not sell well they changed the title back to mine, "ESP in the Edgar Cayce Readings." It paid royalties for ten years.

Lesson Five: You can profit from helping others avoid mistakes. My third book, "Be Your Own Psychic," was written because many people made the mistake of thinking Edgar Cayce was alive, and even more made the mistake of thinking they had to have a psychic for guidance in their affairs. The same press, A.R.E. Press, agreed to publish this book based on Cayce material on how to find your own inner guidance.

Lesson Six: Sometimes too much help is a mistake. A publishing "committee" decided to add more material, so the editor decided to help me by rewriting several chapters herself. In doing this, she made them far different from mine, and was listed as co-author. By accepting her help I had given her half the book. The book is still in print, has paid royalties for fifteen years, but it does not feel like my book. Also, because it was published and promoted by A.R.E., the company had the co-author with them to speak at conferences, and controlled the publication outlets.

Lesson Seven: Be extra careful if dealing with a subsidy publisher. Have a literary or legal specialist go over your contract. Talk to more than one other author who has used that publisher. Take neither ads nor promises at face value. I wanted my book, "The Light in the Mirror," the biography of my uncle, Albert E. Turner, to be published in a timely fashion. I had dedicated the book to his widow, Gladys Davis Turner—also former secretary of psychic Edgar Cayce—who was suffering with leukemia. I took it to a subsidy publisher because they promised to have it out in four months if I gave them the manuscript on computer disks. But it turned out the publisher's computer was not as powerful as mine, they had typesetting code problems, they redid the chapters adding so many typos I didn't quite find them all in the galley proofs. Their printers had labor problems, adding another month of delay. The publication took eight months, not four. Still Gladys did get to see a copy.

Lesson Eight: You don't have to make your own mistakes; you can profit greatly by others! That is why it is such a good idea to belong to a writers' group with active professionals among its members, and share with them.

Lesson Nine: Remember, the one who never made a mistake never made anything else either. If you make one, get some good out of it!

YOUR FAMILY GOES CAMPING

A complete guide to where to go, what to take, and what to do

DORIS T. PATTERSON

If you plan to be among the millions of camping vacationers in this country, this practical manual should be your first step—whether you have never camped before or are an experienced camper wanting more fun and comfort on your next trip.

Writing specifically for the *family* that wants to camp, Mrs. Patterson begins with you in the planning stage. Stressing simple, inexpensive equipment, she tells what to take, how to take it, and what to do with it upon arrival. There are recipes, illustrations, maps, games, crafts—and an entire chapter devoted to taking baby to camp in comfort and safety. Here is *everything* a family needs to know for an average camping trip.

In addition there is an appendix with six suggested tent tours and another which tells where to write for information on state and national parks in the United States—including Alaska—and Canada.

Mrs. Patterson writes with such enthusiasm that you will be anxious to get started on the trip that will bring you and your family closer to nature—and to each other.

About the author . . .

DORIS PATTERSON'S interest in the out-of-doors dates "from the time I was knee-high to my daddy." Now, with four children, she and her husband have found that camping is the only practical way to have an all-family vacation. So the six of them—two of the children were taken along while still babies—have been enjoying nature together. The experiences of these trips, with those of her childhood, have supplied the material for her book for family campers.

ABINGDON PRESS

Jean Ross Peterson

And every contact who responds in any way to my promotion receives a personal thank-you letter!! Friends, colleagues, hosts, producers, writers, strangers—lots of letters, weeks of work, but I love every minute of it.

chapter **30**

Nonfiction Authors Can Be Their Own Agents

by Jean Ross Peterson

Ten years ago I decided to write a book because I was angry. From my experience with friends who asked me for advice about their financial dilemmas, and from all I read in magazines and newspapers, I realized that most people feel insecure about managing their money. This lack of confidence in financial matters frequently turns an investor into a victim of self-serving or unscrupulous advisors. Thievery, intentional or not, impels a witness into action. I read a book on how to write one. Because I live alone, I have no domestic distractions; I finished my manuscript in four months. Next I read a book titled, "How to Get Happily Published." I did exactly what the author told me to do, and thirty days later I signed a contract with a small publishing firm.

I was convinced then, as I am today, that a non-fiction writer does not need an agent in order to become an author. What is needed is a credible work submitted with proof to the publisher that this is a book that will sell. Before I spend five minutes on research or write one word, I give considerable thought to the potential market for the book. I identify the consumers. Where do they live? What are their ages, jobs, incomes? Why would they need my book? I write down a complete description of the potential book buyers, and refer to it as I write the manuscript. Obviously, the larger the market, the greater the sales. Publishers like to see dollar signs when they evaluate manuscripts. Not only do I provide a publisher with proof of the sales potential for a book, I also present my promotion plans when I submit a manuscript.

These plans, too, begin before I write a book. A pre-determined plan allows the writer to use pertinent examples as the chapters unfold. I could, for instance, use a quote from an interview with either Smith or Jones when illustrating a point I'm trying to make for the reader. Jones lives in my area. Smith lives on the East Coast. I will quote Smith because that gives my book a wider geographic interest; this works to my advantage when I am plugging my book on national talk shows.

The actual promotion work, however, is what I do after the manuscript is accepted and while I wait for published books to reach the bookstores. Never, never believe that anyone involved in the publication of your book will do anything to promote or sell it. (Unless, that is, you really did go to Mars, or you discover how a chocolate cake diet and a suntan improve your health.) No matter what you hear from a publisher on this matter, smile, and get to work at once.

I dedicate six months of solid promotion and marketing to each book I write. After that, it has to make it on its own. I try to think of my book as a widget entering the marketplace, competing for shelf space, media attention, and the consumer's spending money. My first project is to design and print two flyers that describe the book, provide my credentials as an author, and provide a photo, and an order form. One flyer is designed for the public—a generic flyer. The other one is focused on the media and includes an invitation to receive a review copy of the book. (Clear with the publisher first.) Second, I write a letter to friends announcing the book and soliciting their help in "getting the word out" about publication. A copy of this letter and twenty generic flyers are prepared for mailing, but held until I know books are available. Friends are happy to distribute flyers for me, and in this way I can reach hundreds of people in all geographic areas. My next mailing goes to clubs, associations, organizations—all the impersonal contacts that will receive notice of the book. These pieces are folded, stuffed, sealed, stamped, addressed and also held for the publication date. By now, I have boxes of mail ready for the post office.

My third project involves the print media. I pay little or no attention to book reviewers, focusing instead on feature writers, columnists, and magazine editors. I believe more people read feature pages and magazines than book reviews. Also, the possibilities of syndication are better. This third project requires time and creativity. I do not send out a form letter to anyone. Each letter I send to a writer is carefully tailored to meet the interests of the recipient. Once the announcements to the press are ready for mailing, I tackle the radio/TV resources. In addition to my letters and flyers, I place a full page ad to run for six months in *Radio/TV Interview Report*. This exposure, plus my individual contacts, has averaged about eighty interviews per book. Most are "radio phoners"—I like these since only my voice leaves home, and I can talk wearing anything, blue jeans or a bathrobe. I always offer a "free" something to listeners who send me their S.A.S.E. This is another way to get a generic flyer into the hands of thousands of potential book buyers nationwide. In addition to the free offer, I use Book Call and their 1-800-ALL-BOOK number so listeners can phone in an order right after an interview. Every letter and piece of correspondence that leaves my house includes at least one line of humor! And every contact who responds in any way to my promotion receives a personal thank-you letter!! Friends, colleagues, hosts, producers, writers, strangers—lots of letters, weeks of work, but I love every minute of it.

Extensive correspondence and desk work needs a balance. For physical activity, I pile flyers in my car and head to all the spots around town where I can leave them in stores, post them on public bulletin boards, or distribute them to strangers while I shop and walk from place to place. For additional balance to the sedentary labor, and as a way to stay in touch with consumers (it's easy to lose sight of why you wrote a book and to get caught up in the media hype) I give lectures, workshops, seminars for community colleges, professional organizations, clubs, and corporate employee groups. And everywhere I go, my books go with me. The people I meet and the conversations we have are two of the greatest rewards from the writing process. Often I feel it is I who benefit the most from these verbal presentations of my current book's topic.

Before I describe the final phase in the process I follow, from conceiving the idea for a book to the selling of that book, I want to elaborate on my mention of the dangers a writer can encounter when favored with media attention. It is exhilarating to answer the phone and find that a reporter from *USA Today* wants to interview you. It is printed proof of a successful endeavor when you hold in your hand a front page article based upon your comments and those in your book. And when a producer from the "The Today Show" calls to invite you to be a guest on the program, the reasonable reaction of exhilaration can make a subtle shift into hubris. By this I mean that a writer can lose perspective about his written words. He or she can, in fact, substitute the importance of self for the value of the information supplied to a reader. I say this from experience and from discussing this potentially dangerous trap with other writers. My concern for writers who do receive more than ordinary attention from the media may appear exaggerated. It is of such concern to me, however, that I have never regretted saying "no thank-you" when I received my invitation from "The Today Show."

My final effort for the success of a book turns me from author into vendor. How can I reach the consumers who do not go to bookstores? When I wrote a book for parents, I placed books in children's toy and clothing stores. When I wrote a book for those who wanted to take control of their own finances, I placed books in office supply stores. Naturally, the businesses that contract for my books—the widgets—get part of the profit. Sales in non-bookstores are extremely successful, and my muscle tone improves as I load my wares into back room storage facilities. A vendor's business license serves also as convincing evidence to the IRS should they question the deductions on my tax returns. Is all the work to write, promote, and market a book worth the effort? Absolutely it is. If I measure the rewards solely in cash, the benefits are modest. But if I evaluate the friendships, challenges, mental gymnastics—even the doubts and disappointments (never a best seller!) —then I know the benefits are extraordinary.

If there is one aspect of the writing/publishing experience that drives me crazy, it is distribution. My books are published by a mid-size company. Their catalogs and independent sales force are as good as any, I suppose. However, in considering whether or not their size is a handicap when Ingram, for example, decides to place an order or to re-stock their inventory, I believe it is. However, I have heard similar frustrations about lack of distribution from authors published by the big name companies. Frankly, I think it is the distribution system itself that is at fault. (System for distribution is an oxymoron.)

There is a trade-off, in my opinion, that still makes me prefer a smaller publisher to a New York giant. I have some control or influence over my titles, cover copy, editing and illustrations. Some battles I win; some I lose. With each book I write, I become more resigned to the stupidity of the established publishing business.

You would think, I assume, that I would self-publish since I have so little confidence in the "establishment." Well, I would prefer to do that, but I must choose between writing another book or spending my time in production and distribution. I compromise to write.

JEAN ROSS PETERSON
(415) 854-1562

1259 EL CAMINO
SUITE 221
MENLO PARK. CA 94025

May 10

Dear Trishia:

Help! I need your help.

Would you be a clipping service for me? I have decided to write the
book on moving - moving for singles, families, retirees.

If you see any articles in your paper on the topic, please clip and
send. I figure to spend the next five months on research. then
start the writing.

For some reason, I'm still a bit unsure about the idea. I talked to
several in the book business; all said it is a good idea. ONe book
store owner, who's judgment I trust, asked, "Where will it fit on the
store shelf?" Well..... He said it goes in the real estate section.

If a book buyer asks the rep where the book fits, and the rep isn't
sure, the book is not purchased. I don't see it in real estate, but
then I don't know where else it should be. Maybe he is right.

Which title (or none of the below) do you like?

HOW TO MOVE AND RELOCATE
MOVING MATTERS
MOVING RIGHT ALONG
HOW TO MAKE ALL THE BEST MOVES
HOW TO MAKE ALL THE RIGHT MOVES
HOW TO MOVE AND RELOCATE: A Guide For Families, Singles, Retirees
HOW TO CUT THE COSTS AND STRESS WHEN MOVING
IS THERE A MOVE IN YOUR FUTURE?
DON"T MOVE WITHOUT IT

Your idea on a title?

Maybe I feel unsure, still, aobut the project because I can't find
my title. Maybe I am lazy and hate the work ahead. Maybe it _is_
a dumb idea.

Be honest. Tell me what you think.

Thank you.

Lou.

Jea

HAVE YOU EVER SAID? . . . **MY FINANCES ARE A MESS!!**

Do you want to . . .

- always know every fact and figure about your finances?
- find a fast and easy way to keep lifetime records?
- have peace of mind about your financial future?
- spend only 20 minutes a week at your desk?
- increase your capital and investments?
- be your own expert money manager?

Sex, age, education, occupation—there are no requirements for success. "Personal financial freedom is a reality for everyone," says Jean Ross Peterson, author of TURN CHAOS INTO CASH: A Complete Guide to Organizing and Managing Your Personal Finances.

Peterson gives you the same effective plan she teaches in her lectures and to her clients. Now you can take control of your finances and increase your wealth.

- Can record keeping actually earn you extra money?
- Why is an ATM hazardous to your financial health?
- Who is your "financial buddy"?
- Where and how can you find some "free" money?
- How can you control impulse spending?
- Are credit cards your friend or your enemy?
- Are there errors in your social security records?
- Is a budget a waste of time and effort? (Yes!)
- Which records should you keep—and how long should you keep them?

Editors of Sylvia Porter's Personal Finance *declare Peterson "one of the best-organized financial authorities we know."*

Peterson answers these questions . . . and many more. A graduate of Stanford University and a specialist in economic education, she is regularly quoted in national publications on topics related to family and personal finances. Some examples are: *USA TODAY, Los Angeles Times, US Air, Good Housekeeping,* and *Sylvia Porter's Personal Finance.* Her talk show interviews number well over 250—many hosts request repeat appearances. Among her popular books is the highly regarded IT DOESN'T GROW ON TREES.

TURN CHAOS INTO CASH is available in bookstores and from *Betterway Publications, Inc.,* Box 219, Crozet, VA 22932. For a review copy call Bob Hostage, (804) 823-5661.

Jean Ross Peterson

For further information please contact:
Jean Ross Peterson, (415) 854-1562
1259 El Camino Real, Suite 221, Menlo Park, CA 94025.

Diane Pfeifer

I was getting married for the first time at age thirty-seven to a professional comedian. Just for fun, we strung the altar with fifty yards of popcorn, had the guests throw popcorn, and of course, I made a huge three-tiered popcorn wedding cake from my book recipe. Our "corny" wedding made national magazine coverage in Star *and* Weekly World News.

chapter **31**

Recipe for Success: Self-Publishing Your Cookbook

by Diane Pfeifer

Writing and publishing my cookbook, "For Popcorn Lovers Only," seemed a natural step after my former careers in chemistry and songwriting/music publishing. I had once signed a music contract with a large company, but realized I was doing all the work so I formed my own publishing company, Strawberry Patch. I got over forty of my songs recorded by such artists as Debby Boone and Paul Anka. I still run my company out of our house and now use it for our book publishing as well.

When I was inspired to write my popcorn cookbook, I jumped in with typically confident and unresearched abandon. As I proceeded with seventy-five-pound bags of popcorn and seasonings stacked to the ceiling, a confusing computer and no typing ability, I discovered that this was no three-minute song.

I continued concocting recipes when I happened to read about a local woman who had published a country music stars' cookbook and I contacted her. She loved my idea and hoped to get a larger publisher or premium offer to finance it. She was basically a consultant, teaching me how to write my recipes correctly and finding me an affordable design team and printer. But no offers came through, and I was faced with postponing the book or paying for it myself.

By chance I found a wonderful publishing book that convinced me to self-publish and taught me how to do it step-by-step. I worked out a percentage for the consultant, since an hourly fee would have been enormous, and also allowed her to list her company as co-publisher on the first printing of 5,000. The book was indeed expensive after food supplies, design and cartoonist fees, four-color cover, photography and separations, props, airbrush, make-up artist, food stylist, recipe and text editors and attorney fees—not to mention seven months of work with no pay!

My first mistake was pricing the 160-page book at $11.95 to recoup my investment faster; it sold much better at $9.95 on later printings. Also, the size (eight-inch square) didn't fit standard cookbook racks and the worst was having the printer deliver all 5,000 books to my house instead of my warehouse.

I began leaving books at cooking, video and gift shops on consignment— a bookkeeping nightmare which was totally impossible to monitor, even if the book was now in stores to buy. In the meantime, I contacted popcorn, spice, and popcorn popper companies for possible premiums and incentives. After getting a positive response from the local division of a major popcorn company, I presented the book and coupon ideas myself. They had already made me an offer when out of fear (and greed) I called in another consultant. I lost the deal by asking for more money and by bringing in someone business-like instead of the friendly family approach they had with me. They confided this to me two years later after I approached them again by myself. I finally got a coupon redemption offer for my book in 500,000 popcorn packages with terms not as good as their original offer.

As far as bookstores, I had a few good-sized distributors, but with no publicity there was no interest and no sales. Then two events happened: I contacted the Iowa Department of Agriculture and found out the popcorn capital of the world was Vinton, Iowa. I called Vinton's Chamber of Commerce and not only got myself invited to their annual Iowa Popcorn Festival, but was crowned Popcorn Princess as well. With local TV coverage and newspaper articles, you can imagine how much fun publicity I got as "Popcorn's Princess Di!"

The second thing was more personal; I was getting married for the first time at age thirty-seven to a professional comedian. Just for fun, we strung the altar with fifty yards of popcorn, had the guests throw popcorn, and of course, I made a huge three-tiered popcorn wedding cake from my book recipe. Our "corny" wedding made national magazine coverage in *Star* and *Weekly World News*.

From there I hired a public relations service to send my book to 500 newspaper reviewers and also arranged much more reasonable co-op mailings through PMA (Publishers Marketing Association). I got some nice features in major newspapers to use for press and also began demonstrating my popcorn recipes on local TV talk shows to get a good video demonstration.

Since we planned a New York trip, I called Macy's special events' department and offered to do popcorn demonstrations in the store. They accepted but said they only promote through a tiny newspaper ad, so I had their public relations head send me their New York TV/radio newspaper contacts. After sending out press kits and videos, I got booked on "Regis and Kathie Lee," plus I got a half-page feature in the food section of New York's *Daily News*.

Before the show, I called B. Dalton's cookbook buyer who was interested in carrying my book but couldn't place an order unless I was with Ingram or Baker and Taylor. Needless to say, I called both companies with the promise of a national B. Dalton's buy and became an instant vendor. After that show, I sold my second printing of 5,000 books mostly through bookstores and by direct-mail from their 900-number. I have since appeared on "Everyday with Joan Lunden," "Attitudes," and my book was plugged on "The Home Show" with Gary Collins. I've also appeared on many local talk shows with baby in tow when my husband is performing in that town so we could be together to write it off.

My biggest disappointment was finding how difficult it was to list my book in catalogs. Still, I stayed doggedly persistent submitting my book, sending press releases and finally, as musical chairs would have it, some of the book buyers changed to my advantage. My book is now featured in an upcoming Publisher's Clearing House video catalog and new Christmas catalogs for both Spiegel and The Popcorn Factory. For Spiegel, I also have a gourmet blend of popcorn spices that I'm now beginning to market. To find catalogs, I used a couple of direct-mail books that told which ones carried books or gourmet items.

As far as other titles, my husband Jeff Justice wrote his first book, "The

Pregnant Husband's Handbook" before and after our baby daughter was born. His subject was more accessible and we sold 10,000 in the first six months, some of it through direct-mail. We have a gift shop list of 3,000 that we acquired from a self-publisher who sells books at gift shows. Using four-color glossy flyers with a postage-free return card, we regularly send out co-op mailings with other small publishers and have gotten great returns and reorders. We rent our list and welcome co-op publishers. Other good mailing lists are available through Para Publishing and Ad-Lib Publications.

Self-publishing definitely isn't for everyone and not all phases of the business are appropriate for everyone either. But as you can tell from my story, I ended up doing things better myself mostly out of enthusiasm and persistence. My husband and I now split up the publishing chores. I basically do all the promoting, publicity, shipping and order-taking but anything to do with negotiating catalogs, printers, chain stores, etc. is Jeff's area. Our house gets pretty crazy with a baby toddling, popcorn popping, books scattered, computers computing, phones ringing and UPS waiting at the door, but we really love it. We have just released our latest collaboration, "You Know You're a New Parent When...," and yes, I'd certainly do it all over again.

New Arrivals From Strawberry Patch!

The Pregnant Husband's Handbook. *"Crawl-Away"* Bestseller! This funny quiz book is perfect for baby showers and pregnancy gifts. Moms-to-be love it, too! (*$5.95 Retail*) AND
You Know You're A New Parent When. *After baby arrives. . . .and stays.* Laugh those baby blues away with hilarious cartoons and comments about those first years. Ideal gift for parents of newborns to toddlers. (*$5.95 Retail*)

For Popcorn Lovers Only. *Popcorn Lover's Paradise!* Popcorn cookbook has 160 pages of recipes, trivia and cartoons as seen on "Regis and Kathie Lee", "The Home Show" and "Joan Lunden". (*$9.95 Retail*) PLUS **Popcorn Lover's Gourmet Spices** in Taco, Cajun and Pizza blends. (*$8.95 Retail*)

Order Toll-free: Strawberry Patch / 1-800-875-7242 / P.O. Box 52404, Atlanta, GA 30355-0404 / Visa/MC Accepted

Dan Poynter

I began by submitting articles to "Parachutist Magazine" in 1963. While they didn't pay, the articles helped me to develop my writing style, established me as an expert in the subject, and provided me with a reservoir of material which could later be strung together for a book.

chapter **32**

Expert Advice from a Self-Publishing Expert

an Interview with Dan Poynter

Q: Why are nonfiction book publishers so helpful and friendly?

A: They like their work. Nonfiction books do not compete with each other—each book is unique. So publishers do not feel threatened by another book. Remember that most publishers specialize in certain lines. This is why you may hear a publisher say, "It is a good manuscript, it is not for us but why not show it to . . . "

Q: Why do you self-publish?

A: I self-publish to save time, make more money and to keep control of the product. I don't have the time to wait to see if some big publisher likes my material. Why ship your manuscript off to New York when you can give it to a printer and have it on the shelves in a month or two? Reader/buyers deserve new material, not two-year-old information. Timing is important and you may miss your market or someone else may beat you to it. Another important consideration is why settle for a 10 percent royalty when you can have it all? And remember, the publisher will usually change your book to fit a niche in his product line. The text, cover, and title may be changed.

Q: What are the economics of self-publishing?

A: A regular publisher will give an author a royalty of 6 to 10 percent of the cover price and a little more if the book goes back to press. If you invest your own money, you should get about 40 percent. So, the economic question to ask yourself is: Can the publisher with all his connections and distribution system, sell four times as many books as you can?

Q: To what do you attribute your success as a self-publisher?

A: Mostly it is because I came from marketing and mail order, not from the library or academic worlds. I write and publish information people want and need. It is packaged nicely (if you want it to sell like a book, it has to look like a book) and I market the product properly. I am selling valuable information to a small well-targeted group at a good price. This realistic pricing allows me to spend more on promotion—which sells more books.

Q: Is self-publishing for everyone?

A: No, some people should self-publish and others should not. Would-be entrepreneurs should remember that writing is an art, while publishing is a business. Many people are unable to do both well. If you are a lovely creative flower who is repelled by the crass commercialism of selling one's own product, you should stick to the creative side and let someone else handle the business side. Consider where you will be happier and you will make more money.

Q: I understand you have sold some of your books in unusual places?

A: Several hundred copies of "The Self-Publishing Manual" were sold back to the printer McNaughton & Gunn. They use the book as a premium and give a copy to new publishers/prospective customers. The largest dealer for the "Frisbee Players Handbook" was Wham-O the Frisbee disc manufacturer. Wham-O sold the books to members of its International Frisbee Association. After designing the cover and printing "Business Letters for Publishers," Delta Lithograph bought several hundred copies to give to new publishers. Their edition has *Compliments of Delta* on the cover. Xerox set the type for "Word Processors & Information Processing" to demonstrate their laser printer as a typesetter, bought 1,000 copies to be used as examples of their work and gave me thousands of dollars worth of computer gear for the privilege.

Q: How does your approach to book marketing differ from that of the major publishers?

A: New York markets books the way Hollywood sells films. They test a new product for audience reaction and if the results are positive, they invest heavily in promotion. If the initial reaction is negative, they withhold the promotion money and let the product die an early death. When the film or book has about run its course, they yank it off the market and replace it with a new product—and start all over again. In the case of books, the balance of the stock is remaindered or pulped.

I market my books like breakfast food or toothpaste: I bring out the new product with a lot of promotion and establish a market share. Then I proceed with modest promotion and continue to sell the book to increasing markets year after year. After all, it is easier to promote the same book twice than to write a new book.

Q: Do you recommend co-authorship arrangements?

A: Normally I do not recommend collaborations as they have all the problems of any partnership. Co-authorship is the same as the traditional author-publisher relationship with all its problems. Going-it-alone avoids royalty payments, extra accounting, splitting of revenue and author hand-holding.

Q: Do you recommend operating a publishing business out of one's home?

A: For many people, it is the ideal set up. The commute is short; the hours are flexible and the tax breaks are better. You can get a snack when hungry, take a nap if you become tired, lie in the sun at noon and work in the evening. It takes organization, discipline and a little imagination but working like this provides a no-stress atmosphere.

Q: How can a one-book, one-subject author-publisher maximize return?

A: Spin off is an important concept: Repackaging the same information for various markets—such as magazine articles resulting from book chapters or book chapters used as the basis for conference workshops or a series of magazine articles packaged into a book. Another way is to rewrite the book aiming it at a different audience.

One-book, one-subject author-publishers often carry books on the same subject by other publishers. While they don't make as much on these books, the inventory is smaller. The additional titles not only help to flesh out their brochure, they become known as an information center on their subject. My monograph titled "Bookshelf" shows how to set up this new profit center.

I am considered to be an expert in parachutes and skydiving—probably because of all my writing in those areas. Expert witness work in legal cases pays more than $150 per hour. There are many ways to capitalize on your expertise.

Q: You have a lot of books. Are all sold to bookstores?

A: Yes, but there are many places to sell books besides bookstores. Some 90 percent of my books are marketed within their own activity areas. For example, my parachuting books and courses are sold through parachute lofts (shops), skydiving catalog houses and through the U.S. Parachute Association. These people buy several hundred at a time, feel a 40 percent discount is very good, pay in thirty days and never heard of returns. By contrast, bookstores complain about 40 percent, order one book at a time, pay in sixty to ninety days if you are lucky and then return the book after several months— damaged. Bookstores are a lousy place to market books.

Q: How does a publisher know where customers can be found?

A: Look in the mirror. Most smaller and newer publishers today are also the author of their books. As author-publishers, they write and publish what they know. They are "participants" in their activity. They know what magazines their potential customers read, what associations they join and what conventions they go to—because, as participants, they read, join and go to the same. Large publishers are like a department store with something for everyone. Small publishers are like a boutique with a narrow line for a highly-targeted market (which is easier to reach.)

Q: What did you learn about marketing from the Frisbee book?

A: Because of the unique design and packaging, the "Frisbee Players Handbook" moved better in gift shops, sporting goods outlets, and toy stores than in bookstores. A while back, I made a mailing to gift and novelty catalogs and several of them picked up the book. Catalogs are nice because they move a lot of product while the company is committed to you for the life of the catalog, usually a year. This just further proves that bookstores aren't the only place to sell books. They aren't even the best place to sell books.

Q: All of your books seem to follow a similar format though they are on different subjects.

A: Once you find a winning combination, stick with it. I use quotes at the bottom of the pages to add variety to the reading and to lend credibility to what I am saying. I print extensive resource lists in the appendix because I feel that readers want and use them. Information like this helps to justify the price of the book as it makes it a manual, a reference source which will be read over and over. Most books have a four-color cover and all have an order blank on the last page—facing out. I don't normally include introductions because I doubt people read them. If there is something important to say, I put it in chapter one.

Q: I note you have order blanks in the back of your books. Why would someone with a copy of your book order another one?

A: That order blank sells a lot of books. In fact, it pulls better than my brochure. Some copies are bought by readers for friends and sometimes friends see the book and want a copy for themselves. The order blank makes the book easy to get; customers send money instead of a letter asking how they may order the book. Note that the order blank is always on the last page facing out.

Q: We note that you are no longer publishing in both hard cover and soft. What precipitated this decision?

A: I used to run about 10 percent in hardcover to make the libraries happy but hardcover in quantities under 1,000 are expensive. The big problem came at the reprint. The hardcover and softcover editions never ran out at the same time. On one book, I found I was shipping the softcover in the tenth edition and the hardcover in the ninth. Some libraries were specifying the hardcover in the tenth edition. I had to write a lot of explanatory letters. Libraries will buy softcover if the hardcover is not available; in doing so they are able to buy more (less expensive) books and service more customers for the same price.

Q: Where do you get all your information?

A: For the most part, I get my information from the library. Of course, I write only about those subjects in which I have extensive personal background. The public, college, and technical libraries in even the smallest towns will have most of the information you need. Use the directories to find addresses of organizations which can supply more information and write to them. Write every firm, individual, and association in the activity to obtain information. Find every book and magazine article on the subject. I maintain lengthy, specialized mailing lists of manufacturers, magazines, associations, etc. My computer allows me to issue a pile of letters requesting information and photographs very quickly. Be a detective. One lead will produce another. I have rather extensive technical aviation and book publishing libraries of my own which help in those subjects.

I also use the communications feature on my computer to collect data from remote data banks. For example, I recently made a patent search in a matter of minutes. A physical search would have taken me days of digging in a patent library and I think the nearest one is two hours away in Los Angeles.

Q: How did you get into publishing?

A: I began by submitting articles to "Parachutist Magazine" in 1963. While they didn't pay, the articles helped me to develop my writing style, established me as an expert in the subject, and provided me with a reservoir of material which could later be strung together for a book. "The Parachute Manual," a 600-page, 2,000-illustration, eight and a half by eleven-inch, technical treatise took eight years to research; this is where I developed the ability to assemble a manuscript. The $45-tome has become an industry standard and can be found in every parachute loft, military and civilian, in the world. I sell over 1,000 copies each year. Now in its third revised edition, there are 16,000 in print.

I became interested in hang gliding in 1973 and finding there weren't any books on the subject, I wrote one. I didn't have any competition at all for a year and a half and now it is in its tenth revised printing for a total of 130,000 in print. More recently, I have been averaging two new books each year in addition to revising those going back to press.

Q: How often do you revise your books? How large is your press run?

A: The initial press run is usually a small 5,000. As long as the book is 98 percent complete and 100 percent correct, I like to hurry it to press. To delay for one more photo or piece of information may mean missing the market. Timing is often important. Then I make the small corrections and additions and return to press for a larger *revised* printing; the size of the print run depends upon the public acceptance of the first printing. Thereafter, I like to revise and reprint the books every one-and-a-half to two years in order to keep them current.

Q: Do you recommend book fairs?

A: Yes, book publishers must attend book fairs, especially the two big ones hosted by the American Booksellers Association and the American Library Association. Whether you should exhibit is another question. If you have decided to pursue the regular book trade, book fair exhibits may be worth your while. A lot depends upon the book's subject matter (and audience), the number of titles in your line, etc. But every author and every publisher should *attend* book fairs because besides being fun, there is so much to learn there. You do not need to display to make contacts, sell subsidiary rights or learn about the book trade. While somewhat less effective than having your own booth, it is simpler and much cheaper to place your books in an exhibiting service. After visiting a fair the first time, you can make an educated decision on whether exhibiting with your own booth is for you.

Q: What is the best way to approach bookstore distribution?

A: The best way to waste money is to make mailings directly to the bookstores. They receive so much beautifully-illustrated sales material, it is difficult to capture their attention.

First, concentrate on making your book *available* to the ultimate consumer. Do whatever may be necessary to get it into the Baker & Taylor and Ingram microfiche systems. All stores can't stock every book but all can get yours in a few days through these systems.

Next go after the distributors such as Publishers Group West, Bookpeople, Inland Book, Pacific Pipeline, etc. They will make your books available to the stores. Some of them have microfiche systems and most have catalogs. Publishers Group West and some others will approach and pitch Waldenbooks and B. Dalton for you.

Then you must build customer demand with news releases, book reviews, interviews, autograph parties, etc. It is up to you to get buyers into the stores.

Q: What is the best way to approach libraries?

A: Your initial attack on libraries should concentrate in three basic areas: try to get a review in *Library Journal* and similar review magazines, approach Baker & Taylor and Quality Books for distribution and make the Publisher Marketing Association library mailing.

In addition to *Library Journal,* there are other valuable pre-publication reviewers such as *Booklist, Kirkus Reviews* and *Choice.* Baker and Taylor is the largest wholesaler to libraries. Quality Books is unique in that they send sales representatives to libraries. Quality asks for a higher discount but they buy books by the carton and they pay on time. Four times a year, the Publishers Marketing Association makes a mailing to 2,500 public libraries across the United States with purchasing budgets of $25,000 or more. For just $95 you can have your brochure included and you do not have to rent the list or do the licking and sticking. For most books, these three things are all you should do in the library market.

Libraries pay on time and they do showcase your book but they usually buy just one copy. Do not spend too much money pursuing libraries.

Q: Is it wise to sell to libraries? Since they make books available to so many people, doesn't this hurt sales?

A: It might hurt sales of fiction but it won't hurt nonfiction if the book is any good. I get at least five orders per week from people who say *I borrowed your book from the library and I have to have a copy for myself.* The library is providing a valuable service by showcasing the book and they even paid for it. The order blank on the last page makes ordering by library patrons easy.

I always include a lengthy resource section in the appendix of my books. This section usually has a list of other books on the subject, the magazines, films, associations, newsletters, and pamphlets, etc. This helps to make the book a reference and, therefore, more than just a quick read.

Q: What is the single greatest mistake made by new publishers?

A: There are many but one of the most tragic is the failure to price the book properly. Books are expensive to manufacture; inventory costs are high because you have to print and store a large number; promotion is costly; wholesalers/retailers take (and need) 40 to 60 percent right off the top. Without a sufficient price, there is not enough money for promotion and without promotion, a book won't sell. If the book fails to sell, there is no money for promotion or even to pay the print bill. You must assume that 90 percent of your books will be sold at wholesale prices and this is why you must price your book at eight times production cost.

Q: What is New York publishing doing wrong?

A: In many publishing firms, the editorial and marketing departments don't communicate. Editorial selects manuscripts, develops them, and then turns over the finished product to marketing to sell. Often editorial produces books they like without great regard for salability. Publishing would be far more profitable if editorial departments worked for the marketing people who are closer to the buying public.

Q: Does New York do anything right?

A: The big New York publishers are very good at selling hardcover fiction and celebrity nonfiction through bookstores. They have the reps and a direct line to the stores. The only way they are going to remain in business or increase their business is to push more books into the pipe. They look for the best books they can find for this method of distribution.

The problem is that the people who frequent bookstores are recreational readers, those people accustomed to plunking down $18.95 for hardcover fiction. Skydivers do not frequent bookstores, they go to parachute shops. Doesn't it make more sense to sell skydiving books in parachute shops? The secret to selling books is to sell them where you find a high concentration of potential customers.

Smaller author-publisher firms do better at non-fiction because they are closer to their markets. As participants, they know where to find buyers. For example, I am a skydiver. I have written several books on parachutes and skydiving. I go to the meetings, visit the national championship, and know the editors of the two magazines. Surely I know better how to reach parachutists than some distant publisher.

Q: How do you know a book is going to sell before you write it?

A: If you don't have confidence that the book will move, you shouldn't write it, much less publish it. Frankly, in starting to produce some of my books, I've felt there wasn't a terribly great market. I wrote the books because they should be written to fill a small, deserving market. In times like these, I know the book will sell but I may suspect the market is not going to be fantastic. So far, I've always been surprised with the results; I've underestimated sales.

On the other hand, I have written a couple of books and chickened out. Due to changing conditions, I decided the markets were not large enough to justify the investment in printing and promotion.

Q: Why are the covers of your books so glossy?

A: That is a plastic coating. It costs a little more but it is a great help in protecting the book. If just a few books are saved from damage in shipping, the whole plastic coating job is paid for. Remember, a book returned damaged, costs more than one more book. There is more paperwork, postage and an unhappy customer.

Q: Do you place a lot of advertising?

A: Never spend money on advertising when you can get publicity free. Put your advertising money into your cover. Put your time and effort into review copies and news releases. Use the free publicity to find which magazines are right for your book. Then spend your advertising money there. Always test before you spend money. Too many publishers start with big ads and blow their promotion budget in the wrong places.

I make up a list of reviewers for each book from the periodical directories. The list is broken down into *perfect matches* and *possibilities*. Books are sent to the first group while the second gets only a brochure or news release and a reply card. Typically, I send out 300 to 400 review copies. Book reviews are the least expensive form of promotion. See my Special Report: *Book Reviews*.

Q: Isn't there a co-op book review program?

A: Yes, one is PMA's *Books For Review* program. A brochure offering 34 books is sent to 2,500 metropolitan daily newspapers. The cost is just $100 per book. Publishers are able to approach reviewers inexpensively while not wasting books or materials on reviewers who aren't interested. The *Books For Review* program is a good example of how publishers can band together to keep their promotion costs down while exploiting free publicity. *Cooperative Book Promotion is* the title of our Special Report on the subject.

Q: How can I tell in advance what it will cost to produce my book?

A: One good way is to write to Delta Lithograph for their "Publishers Planning Kit" (28210-P North Avenue Stanford, Valencia, CA 91355.) If you use this address with the "P code," they will send you the $6.95 kit free. This is a complete book printing planning guide with paper samples, signature dummies, ink samples, paste-up sheets and cost comparison charts.

You don't have to print with Delta, and I suggest you get several comparative quotes, but they have printed several books for me.

Q: How about some of your promotion secrets?

A: Initially, I use book reviews. Then, I send news releases out to many magazines and newspapers. Later I spend most of my energy and money on small mailings directly to potential customers. I am always looking for specialized lists and I tailor my pitch to those on the list. I feel this is the least expensive and most effective approach.

Q: What is PMA?

A: The Publishers Marketing Association is a professional trade group which was formed to promote books. PMA engages in numerous promotional programs on a co-op basis such as book fairs, direct mailings, and buying advertising space by the page for resale to members in smaller blocks at the lower page rate. There are many promotional programs which are cheaper and easier to do on a co-op basis. Members who live outside Southern California cannot make all the meetings, but they are eligible for the promotional programs. For a brochure, write PMA, 2401 Pacific Coast Highway #109-A, Hermosa Beach, CA 90254.

Q: Any words of wisdom for the one-or two-book publisher who is wondering where to expand next?

A: Stay in your field. You have built up an expertise and validated it with a book. Concentrate on your field and expand within it. If the field is not large enough for another book on a different aspect of it, consider carrying other books or products related to that field. Whether your subject area is skydiving, waste water treatment or raising llamas, you can become *the* information center on the subject. While it is nice to have your eggs in more than one basket, never expand beyond two fields. You just cannot keep up with the literature and developments.

Q: How do you know what you write is correct?

A: I send chapters to various experts for *peer review*. As an author, you have a great responsibility to be accurate. Other authors will be using your book later in their research so be very careful before you *commit history*. Peer review finds your errors and makes sure you are not leaving anything out.

Ken Blanchard, co-author of the "One Minute Manager," says he does not write his books—his friends do. He roughs out his thoughts and sends them off for peer review.

Q: How do you typeset your books?

A: I use a Compaq 386 with Microsoft Word, Ventura Publisher and an Apple LaserWriter printer. It is wonderful to have complete control over your product from writing, through editing to typesetting.

Q: Which printer is the least expensive?

A: Each book printer is set up differently. Each specializes in different bindings, print runs, paper types, etc. No one printer will always give the lowest quote. The only way to find the best price is to make up a *request for quotation*. I have used four different printers in the last two years for four different types of books. I go with the lowest bidder by totaling both production and trucking costs.

As long as you deal with a recognized book printer, you shouldn't have to worry about production quality. They know what a book should look like and they want to maintain a good reputation in the book industry. Books are their only product.

Q: Should I copyright my manuscript?

A: Normally, manuscript copyright is not recommended because it is unnecessary. As the creator of the text, you have a Common Law copyright in it. Most authors simply wait until the book is published to register their work. Just fill out copyright Form TX and enclose a check for $10.

Q: Should authors print a table of contents in their brochure?

A: No, most experts agree you should "sell the sizzle, not the steak." Do not give too much detail or the potential buyer may find too many things he or she does not need.

On Bar Coding Books

Soon, without bar codes, your books will not be accepted by the chains and some independent bookstores. So, without bar codes, you will have trouble attracting wholesalers. But, even more important, without bar codes, your books will not appear to be mainstream. They look like they were produced with loving hands at home—definitely small press. In book publishing, different means odd, and odd does not sell. Yes, if you want your books to sell like books, they have to look like books and since the beginning of 1989, that means they need bar codes.

Book bar coding is not all that new. The Bookland EAN was officially adopted as an industry code and symbol in November 1985. Since January 1989, Walden and B. Dalton bookstores have requested that all books have bar codes. Soon, the chains will require that bar codes be on all shipping cartons too.

The U.S. Postal Service is running a pilot program using the bar codes to identify and return loose-in-the-mail books. If the test is successful, it will be expanded to all twenty-one bulk mail centers.

Many library systems sticker books with their own circulation bar codes. If you have Bookland bar codes on your books, libraries can place their stickers over them—rather than hide part of your cover art.

How the bar code works

The bar code speeds the distribution of books. The first three digits (978) tells the scanning computer that this is a Bookland EAN bar code rather than a UPC supermarket-type or other code. The next nine digits are the same as the first nine digits of the ISBN with the hyphens deleted. The last number is a check digit. These vertical lines printed on a book identify the ISBN which in turn identifies the publisher, title, author and edition (hard cover, etc.).

Use the ISBN on invoices, catalogs, order forms, packing lists and the book itself. Use the bar code on the back cover of the book.

How and where

Bar code film masters (negatives) cost $10-$30 and are available from the following suppliers: Landy & Associates, Marc Landy, 5311 North

Highland, Tacoma, WA 98407, telephone (206) 752-5099; GGX Associates, George Goldberg, 11 Middle Neck Road, Great Neck, NY 11021, telephone (516) 487-6370; Precision Photography, Inc., 1150 North Tustin Avenue, Anaheim, CA 92807, telephone (714) 632-9000. For a list of more bar code film master suppliers, contact the ISBN Agency, 245 West 17th Street, New York, NY 10011, telephone (212) 337-6975. Since I live in Santa Barbara, I have used Precision Photography. A quick call to them with the ISBN, price and name of the book (specifying the Bookland bar code) and the bar code film master shows up the next day on UPS for $21., COD. The process could not be easier or faster.

If you need a bar code for a book that has already been printed, just have the bar code printed on 1.5 x 2.5 die-cut pressure sensitive labels and stick them on. 1,000 stickers should run around $25. but may be higher if you only make occasional purchases. Contact Labels Unlimited for a catalog P.O. Drawer 709, New Albany, IN 47150. Telephone (800) 457-2400. Have a film master made as discussed above and then send it to Labels Unlimited for printing onto labels.

Bar codes are not coming sometime in the future, they are here now. Your books are not being printed just for today, they will be sold tomorrow too. Do not shut your books out of the market. Start adding bar codes now.

Tom and Marilyn Ross

With assertive marketing, we secured reviews in the establishment strongholds of Publishers Weekly, Booklist and the Los Angeles Times. These were augmented by plugs in dozens of other magazines, newsletters, and newspapers.

chapter **33**

Sculpting a Book... and a Career

by Marilyn and Tom Ross

B enjamin Franklin said, "If you would not be forgotten as soon as you are dead, either write things worth reading or do things worth writing." We've taken his advice in spades! We did this not to be immortalized—but to be fed and clothed.

Back in 1978, Marilyn wrote a book called "Creative Loafing" and we decided to self-publish it. So much, so good. But with 5,000 hardcover copies clogging our garage, and four hungry teenagers clamoring for food, it quickly became apparent we had to do something dramatic to sell books. Since we had a general interest title by an author who has never been accused of being a shrinking violet, a nationwide author tour was planned. Wonderful concept. But how do we fund it? We hit on the idea of sponsoring writing and publishing seminars along the way to bankroll the tour.

And so we did our *schtick* from Phoenix to Philadelphia, New York to Houston—and several points in between. It was crazy! But we did learn a lot about merchandising a product. Tom pre-sold many books via phone after booking TV, radio, and print interviews. In one place, he had a portable radio with him when calling on bookstore buyers. He pitched them on taking the books as I gave my *spiel* on the radio. In another city, Marilyn had *seven* interviews in one day. By the time number seven rolled around, she couldn't remember if she was repeating herself on the *same show*. Of course, amidst all this we were giving our writing and publishing seminars...There are easier ways to sell books.

But one momentous discovery came out of this whirlwind experience: People hungered for more information on how to publish their books. We were asked over and over again for written material and to consult. The latter we foolishly turned down, feeling we were too busy selling our own book.

Written material was something different. We could come up with that. After all, we'd chosen to drive this author tour and there was Marilyn sitting carefree and complacent while Tom labored behind the wheel. So she began writing chapters on her knee for what was to become "The Encyclopedia of Self-Publishing." With those steps, we cast in bronze what has developed into one of the most fascinating careers a couple could have.

Tom wrote alternate chapters and our "Encyclopedia of Self-Publishing" debuted in 1979 with a rich, leather-like binding and gold lettering. We purposely priced it high. We'd gotten a little smarter by now and were counseling people when they approached us. It was our belief the book could help our consulting business prosper. But if folks weren't willing to spend $29.95 for information that told them all they needed to know to publish their book, they certainly wouldn't be willing to pay us to help them.

With assertive marketing, we secured reviews in the establishment strongholds of *Publishers Weekly, Booklist* and the *Los Angeles Times.* These were augmented by plugs in dozens of other magazines, newsletters, and newspapers.

By 1982 we had a proven winner...and a new agenda. We knew do-it-yourself publishing (not to be confused with vanity/subsidy publishing) was viable for many authors, business people, and professionals with specialized knowledge to sell. It became our mission to legitimize this approach to getting into print. We also wanted to penetrate the bookstore market more effectively than we were able to do ourselves. So we set out to have the first book on the subject published by a respected trade publisher.

On March 2, 1984—after wooing them for what seemed like decades and negotiating like a Christian about to be thrown to the lions—we signed a contract with Writer's Digest Books. It was for a healthy five-figure advance, the largest they had ever given.

A year later, our book—renamed, revised, and repackaged—was on bookstore shelves. What an exciting day when we received notice that "The Complete Guide to Self-Publishing" had soared to the number two spot on their writing best-seller list! It was a main selection of the Writer's Digest Book Club, excerpted in magazines, and again praised by *Publishers Weekly*.

Meanwhile, we moved. You might know anyone who pioneers in self-publishing is a maverick at heart. We relocated our publishing consulting service from a suite of offices in La Jolla overlooking the Pacific Ocean to a remote 320-acre horse ranch nestled in the Rocky Mountains. Operating a business from the boonies has its challenges, however. Our primary mode of communication with the world was one cellular car telephone that worked intermittently and good ol' UPS, which goes *anywhere*.

After clients became disgruntled because they couldn't reach us, and Tom found he was spending the majority of time fixing our self-sufficient power plant, we moved the offices of About Books, Inc., again. This time we chiseled out the ideal location. We bought a church in a tree-studded community of 2,000 people, just two and a half hours south-west of Denver. We now have *six* phone lines, a staff of five full-time and two-part time associates, a fax machine and, of course, trusty UPS.

A typical day? There is no such thing. We do everything from manuscript critiquing to editing, ghostwriting to design, typesetting to print brokering. And people often come in for a few hours or a day of individualized consulting, or they make an appointment for a phone session. Unfortunately, some author/publishers only learn of us after they have a finished book, so developing marketing plans plays a large role in our services too. We specialize in penetrating unorthodox sources—such as syndicated newspaper columnists, newsletter editors, and catalogs—for exposure and sales.

We only go on-site occasionally when there is a major problem or a start-up publishing company needs guidance. Most of our business is done at a distance. As we write this, About Books has clients in California, New York, Colorado, Illinois, New Mexico, both North and South Carolina, Michigan, Ohio, and Texas. What a wonderful bounty from one book!

Alas, as any successful self-publisher knows, it's impossible to stop with one book. (And we have to practice what we preach anyway. Right?) So to complement our guide we've published "How to Make Big Profits Publishing City and Regional Books" and more recently "Marketing Your Books: A Collection of Profit Making Ideas for Authors and Publishers." More are on the drawing board, but client work keeps pushing them to a back burner.

The "Complete Guide to Self-Publishing" did so well in hardcover that Writer's Digest Books brought out a revised and expanded paperback edition in 1989. And it has already gone back to press. Of course, one of the secrets of its success is that we work hand in hand with the publisher. We know they have a new list of books each spring and fall and that they must devote their time to publicizing these fresh titles. So we constantly stoke the fire on our backlist book.

Our publisher cooperates with us in providing extra complimentary copies because they know we'll use them to promote the book. We're always looking for new review opportunities or places to get the book mentioned. In fact, we've written our own news release and created a typeset mock-up review to make it easy for potential reviewers. And we often include a black and white photograph.

This ongoing promotion pays big dividends—and not just in book sales. If you also speak or consult on a topic related to your title, publicity gives you new visibility and credibility. Our book was discussed, we were quoted as the authorities, and one of our clients was interviewed by *Changing Times* magazine in early 1990 for a story titled, "You Wrote the Book...Now What?" As the recognized experts in our mini-industry, we've also been the subject of recent interviews in *The Los Angeles Times, Denver Business, The Spokane, Washington Spokesman-Review,* and *The Rocky Mountain News.*

So you see, we not only sculpted a book, we sculpted a career. One that allows us to meet wonderful people, receive hundreds of fan letters, and help deserving folks make their dreams come true. Ben Franklin—who, by the way, was the father of self-publishing—led the way for us to both write things worth reading and do things worth writing about.

COMMUNICATION CREATIVITY

a colorado corporation

Marketing Your Books
A Collection of Profit-Making Ideas
For Authors & Publishers
by Marilyn and Tom Ross
$9.95 * 140-page paperback, Indexed
ISBN 0-918880-21-1 * LCCN 89-7259

FOR IMMEDIATE RELEASE
Contact: Ann Markham
(719) 395-8659

NEW MARKETING BOOK HELPS AUTHORS, PUBLISHERS BOOST SALES

With over 53,000 books published every year, it's no wonder the majority get lost in the shuffle. A superbly-written manuscript doesn't guarantee media attention or strong sales. Now authors and smaller publishers can find the help needed to rectify this dilemma in a new release from Communication Creativity due out January 29, 1990. Marketing Your Books: A Collection of Profit-Making Ideas for Authors & Publishers shows how anyone can generate greater sales through creative, proven marketing and promotional strategies.

Authors Marilyn and Tom Ross provide in-depth treatment of 13 dynamic book marketing ideas. The Rosses, who previously wrote the bestselling Complete Guide to Self-Publishing, offer readers unique insights drawn from over a decade in this field. They share the secrets of success learned through self-publishing and promoting their own books, as well as consulting with hundreds of publishing clients through their marketing/public relations firm, About Books, Inc.

The Rosses stress marketing considerations even as the author first begins the project. At each stage of a book's creation, they give innovative, yet practical advice. Included in the meaty chapters are editorial tactics to increase sales and ingenious ways to capitalize on free book promotion and media opportunities. The Rosses show how to get a title accepted by book clubs, sell serial rights, and open profitable distribution channels in non-bookstore special sales outlets. Featured are such publicity tools as appearing on radio talk shows and writing newspaper op-ed pieces. The anthology concludes with "The Ross Idea Generator: 44 Winning Strategies."

Marketing Your Books: A Collection of Profit-Making Ideas for Authors and Publishers will appeal to anyone interested in easy-to-implement, resourceful tactics to increase book sales. It is available for only $9.95, plus $2 shipping and handling, from Communication Creativity, Box 909-NR, Buena Vista, CO 81211. Credit card orders may be called to (719) 395-8659.

286

Marcia Routburg

The second submission gave me a positive response! I was shocked, but thrilled. Then, waiting for a contract, I received the humbling note of apology that they couldn't use the book just then, that I should probably continue searching.

chapter **34**

Special Child Spawns a Special Publishing Business

by Marcia Routburg

I wrote my first "story" when I was eight years old. It was supposed to be a mystery-thriller (I used to read a lot of Alfred Hitchcock), and my sister, who was all of ten years old, loved it and thought I should send it to a magazine for publication. I didn't, it wasn't, and it's gone forever.

In college, I took a fiction-writing course, and my professor was very critical. She often repeated, "You must *know* your subject matter very well." She gave me a "C" in the course, which was not very encouraging.

When my daughter, Esther, was born with severe brain damage, my life took on a new course in many ways. Besides all of the demands of a special child, routine living, and challenges, I wrote a few articles related to raising Esther. One was published, and that gave me a sense of accomplishment. For the next few years, I helped dozens of other parents who had "special" children. I began to feel that there was a great need for a short, easy-to-read handbook to help parents through the initial stages. It took approximately a full year of researching, compiling, editing, and re-editing before it was ready for submission to publishers.

I started submitting the manuscript to publishing companies I had looked up in the LMP—"Literary Market Place." This guide includes a listing of publishers according to subject matter. The second submission gave me a positive response! I was shocked, but thrilled. Then, waiting for a contract, I received the humbling note of apology that they couldn't use the book just then, that I should probably continue searching. This was to be the first of many disappointments. But, like I always think, this is also for the best. (The editor did give me a few constructive suggestions that enhanced my book greatly.)

After two long years of more rejections, I had enough. I had enough money, enough stamina and enough desire for all the royalties, so I self-published. Even with all the hard work and mistakes, it is definitely worthwhile to self-publish. Anyone who is determined can learn the ropes of publicity and be just as successful as a publisher (if not more!) Working from my home (I had 5,000 copies stacked in my basement), I sent out publicity releases to newspapers, journals, and organization newsletters. I even included a suggested blurb, in case the publications would be too lazy to come up with their own (it was used many, many times). I decided to approach my publicity program in levels. First would be newsletters and journals, then newspapers and magazines, and finally radio and television. It was a very good plan, but there was a lot of territory I didn't know about, even though I had read most of Richard Holt's book "How To Publish and Promote Your Own Book" (which I highly recommend for beginners).

The first year I was lucky. Besides reviews in organizational newsletters, there was a great article in the *Chicago Tribune*. (It helped that I knew the author and that she was a freelance writer for the *Tribune*.) This brought in a great response. The next big break was getting reviewed in the American Library Association's *Booklist* magazine. This pulled in orders from libraries throughout the country. I had researched other magazines of this caliber, but my subject was not appropriate for them. Concurrent to sending releases and advanced review copies (ARCs)—I got on the phone and tracked down editors who would be in charge of my subject matter, so as not to waste time and having to sending ARCs twice. Then I would call a week or so later for follow-up. I managed also to have the book displayed at relevant conferences, paying for some, some free.

There is a service called the American Book Conference out of Alexandria, Virginia, that sets up a huge display at dozens of conferences throughout the country. Each author should consider the costs and outcome. For other conferences, I would call up the organizer and ask if he or she was having a "combined books booth." Almost all of them said yes, only a few charged a nominal fee. The response was not overwhelming, but I could see a response.

My next level was radio and TV. I had already practiced on local shows and was ready for bigger and better things. I took out a quarter-page ad in Bradley Communications *Radio and Television Interview Report*, which cost approximately $350 for three times). At the outset I got a few calls from small radio talk shows. Then a producer from CNN in Atlanta called and asked me to be on "Sonia Live from LA." I thought, wow! Now I'll get thousands of orders! What a surprise I had—there was hardly any response! Why? Probably because I was not allowed to "plug" the book, they would not flash on the screen how to order (it is not in the chain bookstores, which is another story), and I couldn't find an opening to sneak in a plug. So, if nothing else, I consoled myself by the fact that at least I could use this for a video file to send to other programs. Then, out of the blue, an angel named Patricia Gallagher calls me up (she had seen my ad in Bradley) and wants to exchange some long-distance networking. One of the most useful tips (they were all great!) she gave me was the use of an 800-number for small publishers and self-publishers from Book Call in Connecticut. If they approve, they allow you to use their number, 1-800-ALL-BOOK on radio and TV interviews.

I called right away, got approved after I sent in the book and other promotional pieces, and started using the number. It's too bad I didn't have it for CNN!

Speaking of the media, I'd like to remind you, that *all* interviewers are human. You should not feel intimidated, imposed upon, degraded or any other emotional upset. You are the authority on your book, and you have the control as to what information you'd like to give out or not give out. I've found that interviewers feel free to ask whatever they desire, no matter how personal. Freedom of speech does not allow for freedom in imposition. I've done many interviews on radio and television, which is important for getting your name known (and selling the book). But all these interviews did not come to me. I had to research and find them, also.

To save time and aggravation, it is wise to call the station and ask who the appropriate producer is, to first find out if she would be interested in doing your topic, and then to send your material to that name. You must allow at least seven working days until you call back to check if they received the information. This is important, since they may never call you, simply because the information was either not received, or misplaced, or just tossed aside.

The more they hear your name, the better results you'll get. A case in point: an initial call to the ALA's *Booklist* resulted in their saying that they don't review books such as "On Becoming a Special Parent." I let that go for awhile. A few months later, I decided to send it in, because my chances are just as good as any, right? A few weeks later, they called to ask me a few technical questions, and said it was up for possible review. Then, I didn't hear anything for weeks. I decided to call and see what happened. Speaking to the appropriate reviewer, he said he didn't know anything about "On Becoming a Special Parent." He asked me to send another copy. I did. I called a week later. He said yes, he'd received it and they would be doing a review in the next issue. All because I called back! (It brought in hundreds of orders.)

I then began my speaking engagements. Some were to small support groups, some to conferences. I was very comfortable in the small groups, sold a few books, but it did not pay very much. My conference debut bombed, because I "read" practically my whole speech and people don't like to hear someone reading to them. But, the questions and answers after the speech redeemed me, and I was relieved. There haven't been too many sales from conferences, but my name gets known. Since then, I prepare a list of what direction I want to take, and I just get up and start speaking. My advice to someone courageous enough to begin the adventure of creating a book, go for it! It is rewarding, both monetarily and emotionally, and an achievement that will be forever accredited to you.

BOOKLIST

JUNE 15, 1988
P. 1689–1752 V. 84 NO. 20
ISSN 0006-7385

INCLUDING
REFERENCE BOOKS BULLETIN
AMERICAN LIBRARY ASSOCIATION

Adult Nonfiction

Routburg, Marcia. On becoming a special parent: a mini-support group in a book. 1988. 131p. Parent/Professional Publications, P.O. Box 59730, Chicago, IL 60645, paper, $7 (0-9619347-0-0).

Through her own trying personal experience, Routburg has become especially sensitive to the demands placed on parents of special (i.e., disabled) children. This brief, unassuming yet useful guide offers scores of practical suggestions for the special parent—coping with the child's bodily needs, handling behavioral problems, dealing with doctors and hospitals, fulfilling special educational needs, administering medicine, paying the bills, and confronting certain legal issues. Routburg also offers a commonsensical regimen for the parents on how to maintain a sense of humor and tips on the role and dynamics of the immediate family. Handy terms are listed and described throughout. A bibliography concludes the presentation. No index. MAB.

1649.15 Exceptional children | Handicapped children—Care and treatment | Parenting

Catherine Thomas Skwara

I recommend writers expand their skills and try new markets. This has been a big plus throughout the several long distance moves I have had to make. As my portfolio grows with not only quantity, but also with diversity, I find it easier to reinstate my consulting business in each location.

chapter **35**

Breaking Ground—An Agronomist's Journey to Journalism

by Catherine Thomas Skwara

During undergraduate school I became acutely aware of how easy it was for me to write, and how much I enjoyed it. Well-meaning professors embarrassed me frequently by sharing my essay question answers and I was called upon for publicity and correspondence assignments. But that didn't dim my writing zest.

In graduate school, although I continued my major in agronomy, I was drawn to the technical journalism department. (Agronomy is the study of soils and plant sciences.) After much searching, I found graduate faculty in both disciplines who were supportive of my plans to combine the two fields and I embarked on my formal journalism education. (Times have changed, and now one needn't be a "maverick" to pursue such a degree program.) With an eye for agricultural photography, an understanding of scientific research, course work in technical journalism and a calling to write, the groundwork for an agricultural/scientific journalism career was set.

After graduation, I was employed in several government and private industry positions, that I attained primarily because of my science background. I was, however, able to suggest and develop projects that utilized my communications skills. Some of these projects probably led to the start of my free-lance career, although I wasn't aware of it at the time. For example, I was responsible for encouraging conservation tillage practices among farmers and ranchers in the San Luis Valley, a five-county area in southern Colorado. To facilitate this, I developed a questionnaire, interviewed key operators, and then followed through with newspaper and magazine articles, posters, slide shows, presentations, and radio programs to publicize the results. This endeavor really got me started, for soon after I received my first free-lance assignment!

By working closely with other agricultural professionals in promoting conservation tillage, I let them know I was informed and could communicate well. This paid off when an editor from a regional farming magazine needed someone to investigate and write about a new organization the hay producers were forming within the San Luis Valley. My name was mentioned and the result was "Quality Hay from the Land of Cool Sunshine," a three-page article with my byline, my photographs, and my check! Delivering quality work on time helped open the doors to some sister publications of this magazine and several other articles followed. Each time, I queried the editor before getting deeply involved with the research.

Could you use your specific writing skills in other areas?

I discovered that my skills were transferrable and crossed over to some business writing, such as company brochures and case histories (a type of marketing tool that describes how a company successfully handled a client's request). In most of these assignments, my clients are involved in agriculturally related services or products, and my background in these areas is important. My writing skills speak for themselves in my clips and I assure the clients of my ability to meet their needs.

In dealing with clients who request a product (brochure, etc.) with which I am not experienced, my communications skills are most important because I always show a willingness to learn new skills and use correct terminology. I always convey that willingness to the client.

I recommend writers expand their skills and try new markets. This has been a big plus throughout the several long distance moves I have had to make. As my portfolio grows with not only quantity, but also with diversity, I find it easier to reinstate my consulting business in each location.

Another opportunity for free-lancing articles and other communication skills (researching, photography, etc.) is relaying information from the

"Ivory Towers" of universities and colleges to "everyday people." There is a wealth of new and often useful information "stored" on many college campuses because their "authors" lack the time, talent, or desire to publish. These sources are excellent opportunities for articles, and very often, graphics and photos are available.

Is your family supportive of your efforts?

I have a supportive and proud family. My husband is also involved in agriculture and that gives us the ability to bounce ideas off of each other. As time goes by, his contacts become even more valuable. But don't let your partner's lack of similar interest deter you. I also get involved in community and personal writing projects that interest me alone.

Do you work from home or an office?

I primarily work from home, although certain assignments are better handled in the clients' work place, especially if I need to interact with their employees or use their equipment. But I still prefer to do my creative thinking at home. And when I'm involved in layout and graphics, being able to spread out and leave it spread out until the next day is a big plus.

What should others know about writing an article?

The number one item about writing an article (which, in my case, is naturally nonfiction) is GET THE FACTS CORRECT!! I have spoken to many scientists and other professionals who are leery of being interviewed since they did not have the opportunity to preview the article prior to publication or submission. They have been misunderstood or quoted out of context, or simply tire of explaining over and over basic concepts that a good writer should have researched prior to the interview. A phone call to verify a fact is usually welcomed by the interviewee. Another important DO is to put the most important information in your article in the beginning of the piece—you never know when the editor may cut due to space restrictions, etc., and they normally cut an article from the bottom up.

Some additional advice on article writing and submission includes: Know the magazine to whom you're submitting or querying. Read some sample copies to determine the audience (who as well as what level, i.e., the backyard gardener or a commercial vegetable grower), the writing style, and the subject material (was my story idea recently covered? If so, can I use a different approach?). Send for writer's guidelines. If you plan on submitting photos or graphics, find out if they prefer black and white or color negatives or prints (what size), or color transparencies (slides). Always send duplicates of irreplaceable items. In nonfiction writing especially, time is of the essence. Follow through on your assignments, keep your contacts apprised of your activities. I have found many good leads and received referrals through satisfied clients. If you pay attention to detail, accuracy, and knowing your subject matter, you will find your ability to communicate a sought-after skill.

The best advice that you would give others is...

Find the subject area or type of writing you enjoy the most (nonfiction articles or books, technical writing, promotional/business literature such as ads or brochures, fiction, or whatever), then read whatever you can find on it, take a class or two (courses that critique work in class are wonderful). Do your homework on the subject matter so you can write intelligently and when you're done, SUBMIT IT!! Don't leave your writing in a pile for "someday submission." How often have you picked up a future issue of that magazine you were going to send your article to only to find someone else beat you to it? And don't wait for your article to "be perfect." I haven't met a writer yet who doesn't find something to rewrite every time they reread their work.

If you had to do it over again, you would...

Write more, submit more, ask more questions and follow up on those leads that I didn't think were worth it at the time.

I'd like to add one thing that I've found very helpful. I try to put a few days, even a week or longer sometimes (for lengthy projects if I have the luxury of that much time), between the writing of an article and the editing. It gives me a fresh perspective on my work and I'm amazed sometimes how an area I may have struggled with for hours is suddenly a breeze to edit. Try it!

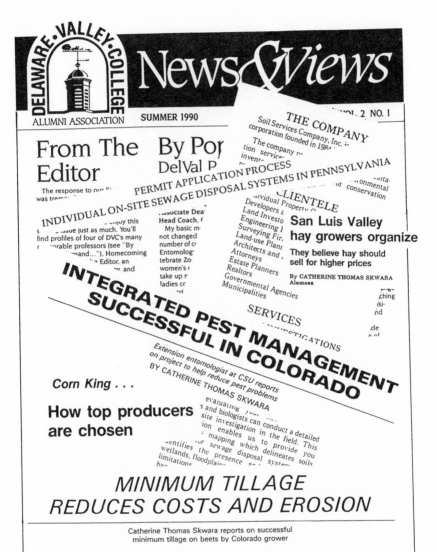

News&Views

ALUMNI ASSOCIATION   SUMMER 1990   VOL. 2 NO. 1

From The Editor

The response to our fi-
was trem-

_ ...joy this
issue just as much. You'll
find profiles of four of DVC's many
favorable professors (see "By
...mand..."). Homecoming
... Editor, an
...v, and

By Por
DelVal P
PERMIT APPLICATION

Associate Dea'
Head Coach, (
My basic m-
not changed
number of c-
Entomolog'
tebrate Zo
women's (
take up r
ladies co
...vi

THE COMPANY
Soil Services Company, Inc. i-
corporation founded in 198-
The company n-
tion servic-
invent-

PROCESS
SYSTEMS IN PENNSYLVANIA
INDIVIDUAL ON-SITE SEWAGE DISPOSAL
...onmental
...ulta.
or conservation

CLIENTELE
Developers z
Land Investo
Engineering I
Surveying Fir.
Land-use Plant
Architects and ,
Attorneys
Estate Planners
Realtors
Governmental Agencies
Municipalities

San Luis Valley hay growers organize
They believe hay should sell for higher prices
By CATHERINE THOMAS SKWARA
Alamosa

...ching
isi-
nd
.de
n of

SERVICES
...TIGATIONS

INTEGRATED PEST MANAGEMENT SUCCESSFUL IN COLORADO
Extension entomologist at CSU reports
on project to help reduce pest problems
BY CATHERINE THOMAS SKWARA

Corn King . . .

How top producers are chosen

evaluating you.
s and biologists can conduct a detailed
site investigation in the field. This
ion enables us to provide you
mapping which delineates soils
...entifies or sewage disposal syste-
wetlands, floodplain-
limitations h--

MINIMUM TILLAGE REDUCES COSTS AND EROSION

Catherine Thomas Skwara reports on successful
minimum tillage on beets by Colorado grower

Rita Tarmin

My original goal of helping parents understand and cope with their situation, I feel, has been achieved. Every parent across the country who has had the opportunity to read my booklet has thanked me for helping them.

chapter **36**

Writing What's "Behind Closed Doors"

by Rita Tarmin

As a freshman in high school, I had a wonderful English teacher, Mr. Michael E. Herron, who had quite an imagination with creative writing. Therefore, he made our assignments just as exciting. My first English paper assignment was on the topic, "Did you ever sit in a bus and watch the noses go by?" It was the first essay I had ever written and received an"A+," as well as impressed the class with my humor. The assignment showed me I had talent I was not aware of; unfortunately no one else was aware of it either, except Mr. Herron.

After graduation, I married and had four children. Through the years, the only thing I ever wrote was an occasional poem which ended up in a drawer somewhere and was never shown to anyone.

In 1983, as my children were starting to get older, I took a correspondence course with the Institute of Children's Literature in Redding Ridge, Connecticut. It was a basic writing course, but I had passed their entrance test and they believed I was capable of being a writer someday.

If anyone would have told me that someday I would write a book, I would have laughed. But in 1989, after going through a difficult struggle with our daughter suffering from bulimia, I decided to write a book to help other parents. While searching the library and bookstores for information to help me understand what my family was dealing with, I found books concerning the medical and psychological points of view on eating disorders. I also found books written by women who had struggled with anorexia and/or bulimia. What I couldn't find were any books telling me, as a mother, how to cope with this problem twenty-four hours a day, seven days a week.

"Behind Closed Doors: A Family's Battle with Bulimia" is a mother's personal experience of living with a teenager suffering from bulimia and/or anorexia.

I wrote "Behind Closed Doors" to help other parents become aware of the signs and symptoms of eating disorders because many of the symptoms can be easily mistaken for normal adolescent behavior. I also wrote it as a means to help family members understand the emotional feelings, the financial strain, and the importance of family and individual therapy. My objective also was to help educate the public and heighten awareness of the severity of eating disorders.

I have self-published the book and am marketing it myself. To date, I have appeared on a number of TV shows and have appeared on radio interview talk shows. I also speak publicly for any organization, or school who is interested in learning more about anorexia and/or bulimia from a personal point of view.

The most important thing I've found from self-publishing is the time needed to promote yourself. If you have the time, and the money, I believe you should attempt self-publishing first. It has been a real growing experience for me personally. For the limited amount of time I have to dedicate to the promotion of my booklet, I am proud of the accomplishments I've made to date.

My original goal of helping parents understand and cope with their situation, I feel, has been achieved. Every parent across the country who has had the opportunity to read my booklet has thanked me for helping them.

I have not ruled out the possibility of a publisher, but until I am comfortable with a publisher who has the same goals as me, I will be very cautious in signing away any rights to my work. Personally, I don't want to make a million dollars, but I would like to see a million families benefit from what we have experienced.

The number of victims suffering from eating disorders has increased from more than one million in 1985 to more than seven million women and more than one million men as of October 1990. The age range has dropped from college level to the high schools, and now has filtered into the elementary schools. Eighty percent of children between the ages of eight and ten are dieting, and the number of male cases is on the rise.

At the present time, I am a correspondent writer for a weekly newspaper. Currently, I am taking the advanced writer's course through the Institute of Children's Literature. As a new writer, it is important to establish yourself in the profession. It takes time, and a lot of rejection notices to build a portfolio as a writer. It's a matter of overcoming the rejection, having the patience and belief that the time will come for your subject matter.

You don't have to become a world famous writer, although I think we would all like to be, to know that your work is appreciated. It helps when people begin to comment on your work, enjoy what you write and look forward to your next article, poem, etc. Everything you write will touch someone, somewhere, at just the "write" time they need to hear what you have to say.

BEHIND CLOSED DOORS
A FAMILY'S BATTLE WITH BULIMIA

BY
RITA TARMIN

Charlotte E. Thompson, M.D.

I have just completed a twelve-city tour and was, indeed, sad to see that the distribution had fallen down somehow and that books were not in the stores. This really is important, and no matter how hard you push publishers, it often just doesn't happen.

chapter **37**

Pediatrician Discovers Treasure in Writing

by Charlotte E. Thompson, M.D.

My first book, "Raising a Handicapped Child," was written to meet the needs of special parents in my pediatric consulting practice. They desperately needed such a guide, and it has been very well received.

So much joy came from the writing and publication of this book that I quickly realized I had discovered a rich treasure. Thus I have a second book just coming into the bookstores, "Single Solutions: An Essential Guide for the Single Career Woman." This was the book I would have liked so desperately twenty years ago when I was newly divorced, had two children, a new pediatric practice and little money.

I have just completed a twelve-city tour and was, indeed, sad to see that the distribution had fallen down somehow and that books were not in the stores. This really is important, and no matter how hard you push publishers, it often just doesn't happen. Thus, you have to create a demand, and that is what hopefully will happen with "Single Solutions." It has been very well received by the women who have read it, and since there are four million single career women, I am hoping it will take off very soon.

Getting the word out about a book is difficult if you are working with a limited budget, or if the publisher will not invest much money into public relations (PR) and marketing. Most publishers don't, (most publishers invest money just in the best-sellers, like Danielle Steele or Sidney Sheldon). Marketing and distribution are the key factors in the sale of a book today, and every author and his or her agent must make the maximum effort to see that adequate marketing and distribution occur. Otherwise the book will quickly die. (The usual shelf life of a new book is three months.)

I have found bookmarks to be the most effective tool for PR on an individual basis. Be sure to always carry some with you and give them to any interested individuals. You do have to be your best sales person, and this does take a little while to learn.

The best advice that I can give other authors is:

1) Don't be discouraged...rejection is just part of writing.

2) Market—market—market.

3) Check every detail.

4) Don't believe that a publisher or PR people have done something unless you see or hear it yourself. Many mistakes are made along the way that can be really major.

5) Placing an ad in the Bradley Publication ((215) 259-1071) for radio interviews is a very cost-effective way to reach a large audience. I have had many interviews because of this publication and enjoyed them very much.

6) Sell books yourself whenever possible, and keep some in your trunk or suitcase at all times.

7) Network with other authors.

8) "The Book Marketing Update" publication is filled with a wealth of information. Call 1-800-669-0773. This is published several times a year and has been an excellent resource for me.

9) If I had to do it again, I would not have a lawyer go over a book contract. An agent should be able to do this adequately and will save you LOTS of money. (I found that it doesn't make much difference what is in your contract because the cost of a lawsuit and the problems it would cause probably are going to outweigh anything else.)

10) Don't be intimidated by editors, agents, or publishers. Value your writing and *keep plugging.* If you love to write, then that's what you must do.

Raising A Handicapped Child:

A HELPFUL GUIDE FOR PARENTS OF THE PHYSICALLY DISABLED

Charlotte Thompson, M.D.

An indispensable guide for anyone who cares for or works with handicapped children.

Comprehensive appendixes provide needed names, addresses, and telephone numbers of important agencies as well as a glossary of medical terms and listings of sources for information.

William Morrow & Co. (Hard Cover)
Ballantine Books (Paperback)
Books on Tape (Audio)

Raising A Handicapped Child:

A HELPFUL GUIDE FOR PARENTS OF THE PHYSICALLY DISABLED

A practical and easy-to-read handbook by a highly respected and compassionate pediatrician, a recognized authority in her field.

Dr. Charlotte Thompson anticipates and addresses all the questions and difficulties parents of a handicapped child have to face from the initial diagnosis to adulthood. Dr. Thompson answers parents' questions on how to cope with a devastating diagnosis, with well-meaning friends and relatives, and with the costs of raising a handicapped child. She also tells parents how to find and encourage a handicapped child's greatest potential, how to find the best educational programs for a child, how to stay informed about new treatments, medications, and research, and how to handle a progressive or fatal disease. The approach is both practical and inspirational throughout, with helpful appendixes listing government agencies, educational programs, recreational facilities, and services for the whole family.

Dr. Charlotte Thompson

has worked with handicapped children and their families for over thirty years. A mother of two, she lives in San Francisco where she is director of the Center for Handicapped Children and Teenagers.

THE CENTER FOR HANDICAPPED
CHILDREN & TEENAGERS
2351 Clay St. #512
San Francisco, CA 94115
415-923-3549

Frances Weaver

One or two hosts around the country have such a loyal following, your books will sell like hotcakes just because Jim Bosley said so in Portland, or Dick Woolfsie gave you the big plug in Indianapolis. Don't sell yourself short when not many orders come in, your host didn't have the confidence of his listeners to begin with.

chapter **38**

How "Kites and Old Ladies" Launched a Widow's Writing Career

by Frances Weaver

Creativity. Say that secret word and collect $200, or some such thing. Creativity we recognize as the key to the finest of self-expression. So what makes up creativity? Where can I get some? What shall I do with it after I have it in my clutches?

John Updike answered those questions for me several years ago speaking to students at the New York State University at Albany. Quite simply, Updike says creativity consists of three parts: (1) the wealth of material stored in your own head, (2) identifying your own genre, your own medium of expression and (3) an audience. We are discussing here that third item: an audience. The vitality of our creativity depends upon the responses we receive from others whether we recognize that fact or not. Without some feedback to our work, we wither. This is true for artists, musicians, dancers, stand-up comics, politicians and other creative types. This applies even more so to writers. One step at a time, let's examine this process of acquiring an audience from the viewpoint of the writer.

What makes a good writer? A successful writer? Something which MUST be said. That's what it takes. Until one compelling all-consuming subject takes over the life of any one of us, we are not writers. We might consider ourselves to have talent in placing words in some semblance of order. We probably have an "If they can do it, I can do it" attitude. We can take the courses and fiddle around with haiku. We can keep journals; mystify ourselves with right brain exercises and searches for our true self, or some such elevation of the spirit. But until we ourselves believe we have something to say important enough to us to let nothing stand in our way, we had better concentrate on learning and living. Writing will follow in its time. Don't misunderstand me, please. Not all of us are out to save the world or lead the quest for the Holy Grail. We must, however, believe we have more of a reason to write than to see our own names on a printed page. For me, it was kites.

Kites and old ladies

You read that right. Kites...actually, kites and old ladies. From my first attempt at writing for publication (an article about fifty-ish women in Colorado who had found a new dimension in our own lives by flying kites instead of running committees or bidding three, no trump) which was eventually published in *Vogue*, I have concentrated on more and more of the options and opportunities open to older women. That's what I care about. That's what I know. That's what I write.

In some extraordinary way, that important subject then branches into seemingly unlimited sub-topics (my word) but your original passion has set you on your way. This holds true, I find, for fiction or non-fiction. We each write from our own base, or our writing loses strength or clarity.

Extensions from my main concern have led to a world wider than I would have fantasized in my wildest imagination. Starting with those kites in the Beulah Valley of Colorado, I now recognize myself as a writer, columnist, lecturer, TV personality, radio guest, publisher, business woman, and world traveler. My son Ross says I'm making my way from being Widow Weaver the Housewife to Frances Weaver, the Household Word. An exaggeration, of course, but typical of the sentiments and support of my family.

Widowhood rearranged my life when I was fifty-five, after my first four articles, all published in *Vogue*. Making a writer of myself, knowing what I wanted to tell whatever part of the world I could reach, involved honing skills and learning more about the craft. Even more important, I had to learn to think of myself as a writer before family and friends would see me in that light. That is why I moved 2,000 miles from home for my second go at a college career.

At this point you see what I was doing: I was involving myself in exactly what I would advocate to the girls my age. I was making a role model of myself. "If you have so many swell ideas, let's see YOU do it." Then my readers could believe me.

For writers of any age or stage of aspiration, I cannot rave enough about community colleges. Without my two years at Adirondack Community College, I would still be floundering around talking about what I might write next week. The assignments, the contact with others interested in writing, the dedication of so many classmates makes the difference.

Finding a genre

College writing courses identified my own genre for me: non-fiction, preferably short non-fiction. Next step: get a column going. That suggestion came from Edward Park, columnist and instructor at a Smithsonian Workshop. "Don't spend your life writing query letters," he advised. "Get a column going and you have time to write, not peddle your work." Fine. I sent twelve short pieces to my hometown paper—the Pueblo, Colo. *Chieftain*

"Shorter," they said. "Why not?" I said. That was more than six years ago and I haven't missed a week yet, although I'll admit I write four or five columns at a time. These consist of 400 words about a variety of subjects but always from the viewpoint of my own age—sixty-five.

The column runs in about a dozen small papers now. I get paid by some, but not much. In seven (or so) suburban newspapers, the column runs weekly and I do not get paid at all. Think about this before you say the woman is nutty: What would it cost me every week to put an ad in that paper saying "Frances Weaver is a writer"? Yet those readers see Frances Weaver books in their bookstores and recognize the name and the face. The price paid for two or three books is more than the paper would pay for the column, anyway.

I have found it profitable to give other things away, too. After my first year, I began publishing collections of the columns and thoroughly enjoyed the promotion as well as the rest of self-publishing. More about that in the next paragraph. I hired a friend of my own age, paying a 15 percent commission, to help with the business of book peddling. She and I contacted every library group, women's club, church group, retirees' organization, civic club, or sewing circle we could find, offering a program with a bit of humor and a cut on any books we might sell at the meeting. We fattened the scholarship funds and treasuries of all sorts of organizations, making genuine friendships and spreading my books wherever we went. The group's cut was (and still is in many cases) $2 for each $6-book sold at the meeting. That's a smaller bite than the percentage dealers or distributors get, and certainly more appreciated.

Earning profits, not money

After a couple years of this, invitations to larger, more affluent organizations started coming our way. We were filling a calendar, launching a nationwide audience through principally word of mouth promotion. I have not made a lot of money from this scheme, but the profits are enormous.

But how do I self-publish? I hear that question a lot. I approached a printer I knew to be okay in Saratoga Springs, asking his advice about putting a book together. He was not a book manufacturer, but I wanted only 2,000 books to start, so dared not approach the big guys. Looking for an agent or a publisher for this little book would have been useless, incidentally. I chose good paper, added my own stick drawings to dress up the pages, and put an unretouched photograph of myself on the cover. I had spent enough time in politics in earlier years to know the value of being easily recognizable. Nobody could miss my book. I also chose a picture for the image I wanted, a thoughtful older woman, not glamorous or trying to look young. Judy Madison, who works for me now, took the picture.

My pattern of self-publishing has not changed with the three additional books I've done myself. The control of my own material and the satisfaction of seeing the projects through on my own are gratifying, to say the least. The bookkeeping had to be handed over to my CPA daughter-in-law since we have grown, but the books are mine. I now need an employee for keeping up with the calendar of speeches scheduled all over the country, along with TV appearances and radio guest spots and the mail order business. It can be overwhelming at times.

Early on I wasted a lot of money on newspaper advertising, which was dumb. Nobody with any sense advertises one or two books.

TV and radio shots vary enormously in how much good you get from them as a guest or for an interview. I rely on Bradley Communications entirely for those dates, and have discovered this basic fact: Your effectiveness can be measured in direct proportion to the way the host gets along with his audience.

One or two hosts around the country have such a loyal following, your books will sell like hotcakes just because Jim Bosley said so in Portland, or Dick Woolfsie gave you the big plug in Indianapolis. Don't sell yourself short when not many orders come in, your host didn't have the confidence of his listeners to begin with. Besides, what does it cost you to talk on your phone for an interview, and you never know who might be out there to open even bigger doors for you.

Example: I stopped in Cleveland on my way east to appear on a morning TV show. Book sales poured in, but even more important, I was invited by one of the viewers to appear at a meeting of the American Business Women's Association for a local event in Cleveland. This led to bigger and better meetings until I finally addressed the national convention of 5,000 women and now regularly speak at ABWA spring conferences. One TV show, at my own expense, has paid off a hundred-fold, ...plus. I've met many dandy new friends along the way.

About TV, I enjoy being on camera, although I had little or no experience. I paid some guys in upstate New York to make a tape of me to send ahead for possible TV dates: sitting in a big chair, talking about the positive side of aging, walking around at Lake George—that sort of thing. I showed it only once, to the manager of the PBS station in Pueblo, Colo., who asked me to do a weekly series of short subjects to be broadcast three times a week—commentary-sort of features like my columns. The series has been on the air for almost three years now. We tape six or eight at one time because I spend so much time traveling to make speeches. (Have I mentioned I traveled more than 100,000 miles in 1989?) Response has been really warming. I run into people all the time who have nice comments about the PBS spots. Now the series is on national PBS, available for viewing across the country. Imagine that.

It's beyond me to fathom how all this has happened, except for two factors, both connected with my age:

1)   I am writing and talking about the one subject of absolutely

universal concern—aging—with an upbeat approach appreciated by any audience. Hundreds of fan letters and calls tell me that.

2) I started in this business at a time of my life when I can devote all of my time and attention to my writing and its "fallout." This is my turn to do this. All of the earlier years of my life have contributed to this phase of living. The same can be true for all of us.

Progress continues. Right now I am in negotiation with a major publishing house that wants only distribution rights for my four self-published books. They came to me without me having to work with an agent or any of that stuff. These people don't want to buy my rights, mess up my work, change my format or interfere with my writing. This might be a Real Biggie, it might not. But the original satisfaction of being my kind of a writer remains: I might not get rich, but the profits are enormous.

Midlife Musings, Publisher
c/o Frances Weaver
P.O. Box 970
Saratoga Springs, NY 12866

To:

WHY NOT?
not HOW-TO
for today's most
interesting and
important new breed
of women:
the "girls" over 55.

**THE GIRLS
WITH THE
GRANDMOTHER
FACES**
by
Frances Weaver

Opportunities,
Options,
Attitudes,
Lifestyles,
Quality of life
explained and explored
by the columnist/author
of *Midlife Musings* and
Speaking of the Girls

$5.95

Midlife Musings Pub.
P.O. Box 970
Saratoga Springs, NY 12866
1-800-842-7229

314

Jane Williams

The best advice I would give others is to know your talents, your strengths and weaknesses, and to do those jobs you are good at and find someone else to do those jobs you do badly or inefficiently.

chapter **39**

Women Can Do It All and From the Same Place

by Jane Williams

Nine years ago I began my research, through letter-writing to locate books with a particular philosophical focus for my family's home library. My efforts involved writing many letters to individuals who were specialists in certain subject areas and asking for their recommendations of materials appropriate for ages three to seventeen and older. During this process, I had the great pleasure of striking up an ongoing correspondence with a gentleman who liked many of the ideas I related about learning and children. This gentleman was a published author himself, and at one time during our correspondence, he suggested that we not only collaborate on a book, but that we publish it ourselves and market it through direct mail. He had always been published by large publishing houses, but some of his fellow authors were using this alternative approach quite successfully.

The idea of writing a book was challenging enough for me, but the idea of self-publishing and promoting it through direct marketing was close to overwhelming. As my mind raced (trying to figure out how to purchase a printing press and fit it into my garage, how to bind a book, how to get a cover designed), it became clear I needed some help to learn more about this new venture. A trip to the library placed my mind in the competent hands of experienced small press publishers Tom and Marilyn Ross through their book "The Complete Guide to Self-Publishing." This book was the beginning, and I have read most books on small press and self-publishing and marketing since then. I quickly learned that the printing press in the garage was unnecessary; ditto the binder. But the concern over the cover design was a legitimate one.

When I first began reading self-publishing books, I remember one of the authors stating that when a manuscript was finished ten percent of the work necessary to produce and sell a book was completed. I was astounded! This small manuscript that I had agonized over and which I had finally finished, comprised just ten percent of the publishing process! This author must be wrong. Well, I'm here to tell you that the author was absolutely right! When the manuscript is finished you simply change hats and become publisher (as well as possibly, editor, typesetter, indexer, copyreader, secretary, book-keeper, order fulfillment personage, inventory keeper, and media personality). So, it's extremely important that if you are an aspiring self or small press publisher you take a mental survey of your own strengths, weaknesses, and talents. Discover what you can do well, what you enjoy doing, and what, due to lack of ability or interest, you should subcontract to specialists.

Another item mentioned in the publishing books that was a bit discouraging to me was that little, if any, profits are usually made from the first print run of a book. It's the subsequent printings that show profit. So figure you might be working a year or two before you can count on profit from a single book project. I've also learned that a book needs to circulate for about a year in order to accrue the important review comments necessary to get a good promotion off the ground and keep the book in circulation for many years to come.

Having concluded my initial research on the subject of self-publishing, and having completed my first manuscript, I established my publishing company—Bluestocking Press—in January 1987. My first self-published title, "How to Stock a Quality Home Library Inexpensively" is now in it's second edition with over 5,000 copies sold. The premier edition was photocopied and saddle-stitched at our local copy store. The cover was designed by me and printed at the local town printer. I printed 200 copies. (I didn't want to get into this business with too much financial commitment until I discovered whether anyone else had a desire to buy what I was attempting to sell.)

By following the advice in John Kremer's "1,001 Ways to Market Your Books," the Ross' book, and Dan Poynter's "Self-Publishing Manual," I learned about marketing and about book reviews. By reading "Marketing Without Advertising" I learned the philosophy behind marketing without spending a dime for classified advertising. After sending "How to Stock a Quality Home Library Inexpensively" for review I ended up with reviews in publications like *Changing Times* and *Library Journal*. The *Changing Times'* reviews resulted in several hundred copies sold, a second printing, and more importantly, gave me the confidence I needed to convince myself that I could be successful at this venture.

To date, I have self-published three books through Bluestocking Press: "How to Stock a Quality Home Library Inexpensively", "Who Reads What When," and a special report, "Selling to the Other Educational Markets," which explains to educational product developers how to sell their products to the home schooling and alternative education markets. I have two books in progress: "The Young Thinker's Bookshelf," (an accumulation of the research which resulted from those letters I began writing nine years ago seeking appropriate books for my family's home library); and a book on "Educational Options: A Consumer's Guide to Choices in Education For Parents, Students and Teachers." My books have been reviewed in *Library Journal, School Library Journal, Booklist,* major literacy publications, magazines, and many other places.

In 1989, I made the transition from self-publisher to small press publisher, publishing "Whatever Happened to Penny Candy" by Richard J. Maybury (an introductory level economics primer for young people, as well as adults who consider themselves economically inept). This book has sold more than 5,000 copies, is being used as a premium by a precious metals firm, and has recently had video rights purchased by an educational firm.

While I was reading about publishing and marketing I also read about the benefits of developing a catalog of other books and resources that complement titles I publish at Bluestocking Press. By developing a catalog which includes other publisher's titles, my operation appears much larger, I service my customers better by bringing complementary titles to their attention, and my revenues increase due to the additional sales. So I started Bluestocking Press' "Educational Spectrums" catalog to further extend the focus and philosophy of Bluestocking Press. "Educational Spectrums" sells books, rubber stamps, audiocassettes and other items that focus on three general areas: 1) educational options for children; 2) work options— emphasizing home-based business titles for adults and entrepreneurship titles for kids; 3) resources that promote reading, writing and reasoning. Initially this "catalog" was a recommended book list comprising one, eight and a half by eleven-inch sheet of paper with about six other titles. Then it grew to an eight and a half by fourteen-inch page; then an eight and a half by eleven-inch, four-page brochure. In 1990, it expanded to a twenty-four-page catalog with more than 140 items offered for sale. This year should see even more growth.

By developing a philosophy around Bluestocking Press and its "Educational Spectrums" catalog, it's been much easier for me to pursue media coverage on a number of divergent, but philosophically compatible topics. This also gives me the opportunity to promote an entire catalog of resources sold by Bluestocking Press through it's "Educational Spectrums Catalog," rather than a handful of titles. Contrary to most authors, I seldom make media contact to promote a book I've written. My book promotion is done through reviewers. Rather, I approach the media on topics that encompass the focus of my press and it's consumer catalog, "Educational Spectrums." For example, I'm interested in educating parents about the importance of choosing an educational environment that's consistent with the needs of their children. This has led to several radio interviews on the subject of home schooling, learning styles, and options in education. I'm interested in informing parents about home-based work options for parents and entrepreneurship for kids and the positive aspects of kids being allowed to work. This has led to several radio shows in which I have spoken as a proponent of kids being permitted to work. I'm interested in informing parents and kids about exceptional resources that promote reading, writing, and reasoning skills in young people. This gives me a tie-in with the literacy markets and the current critical thinking skills movement. Also, I'm a free market advocate, which ties my promotional campaign into the hard money enthusiasts, free marketers and entrepreneurship channels for both kids and adults. As a specialist, I have information that can be helpful to the listeners of many radio and television stations. It's my job to contact the producers and let them know I have knowledge that can benefit their listeners or readers. It's my responsibility to deliver an interesting and informative interview. As a final note, as a woman entrepreneur and a "baby boom" mother, I can pursue much of the media attention that's been drawn to this subject over the past few years.

I am a writer, publisher, reviewer, cataloger. I am also a mother, a wife, and a homemaker. So it is possible to live the baby boom life depicted by Diane Keaton in the movie. Women can do it all, home career and family—and all in the same geographical location—the home—with all family members interacting in each other's lives throughout the day.

Self- and small press publishing provides many opportunities for part-time to full-time work by women who wish to have career and family at the same time—and work at home. According to Tom and Marilyn Ross in their "The Complete Guide to Self-Publishing," "some 5,000 new small presses are founded annually." Women can choose to become one of these small press publishers or begin a subcontracting business that can service the small press publisher. Such a business can grow in direct proportion to the amount of time a mother has available as her children grow towards autonomy. For example, book publicists can determine their workload based on the number of titles they wish to promote. One title requires fewer hours than five titles. Order fulfillment can be done on a per-book basis. Find a small publisher and do his/her order fulfillment. The small press industry is exploding with growth. Find a niche and fill it.

ANSWERS TO SPECIFIC INTERVIEW QUESTIONS:

Q: Did you contract with a major publisher or agent? What are the pros and cons from your perspective?

A: I have not attempted to work with a major publisher yet. Everything that I read indicates this can be a very big financial mistake for someone like myself. Unless I am likely to have a best-selling title, or am already a highly notable personage, my book is going to receive a few weeks' effort at promotion, and will then sink or swim on its own merits. More than likely it will sink. My book sits and I have no control over its fate. If it sells even 25,000 copies, my payment from royalties is going to be minimal. The added frustration would be the loss of editorial control over my copy. In spite of all this, if the opportunity should ever present itself I would definitely consider signing with a large publisher. It would be very interesting to observe their methods and compare them to my own. And the prestige gained by being published by a major publisher, as perceived through the media, could be very beneficial in securing future media coverage for any additional writing projects I'd pursue through Bluestocking Press.

Q: Comments on the media?

A: I have made guest appearances on several talk radio shows throughout the United States and have done a cable TV show. I prefer print media because it seems to stay around longer. It's also easier to get order information included in articles than it is to have that same information given on the radio. I still receive occasional orders from readers of *Changing Times* for a review that appeared in 1987! Plus, talk radio can be done from the convenience of your own home.

Q: Tell us your experiences with reviewers.

A: My experience with reviewers has been largely positive. These are professional people so I don't want to take a lot of their time. When making follow-up calls, I restrict my conversation to asking if the review copy was received and if the reviewer has any questions I can answer. I thank the reviewer for her/his time and end the conversation. Follow-up is extremely crucial. One Bluestocking Press title had to be sent three times to the same reviewer, the last copy finally being sent to the reviewer's home address because it kept getting lost somewhere between my office and the reviewer's office.   I've never used sales aids or gimmicks to get a reviewer's attention. This is due in large part to my belief that if I'm working with professionals they should be actively seeking those materials that will best serve their readers.

Q: Tell us your distribution to bookstores.

A: Bluestocking's books, to date, seem to attract certain niche markets. Selling to the alternative education market has been so successful for Bluestocking that I wrote a special report, "Selling to the Other Educational

Markets," updated annually, that explains how other educational product developers can sell their products to the homeschooling and alternative education market. To date, I've had no distribution to bookstores.

Q: Have you done speaking engagements? Were they profitable?

A: I have spoken at homeschooling conferences, writers' workshops, and before education classes. Subject areas include education, publishing, or work-at-home business. Speaking on a variety of subjects to divergent groups gives me more options to market all the products in my "Educational Spectrums" catalog rather than just the titles published by Bluestocking Press. Speaking engagements had been within the local area since I didn't want to travel with my young children. They are now at an age where they can come with me or remain home based on the circumstances of the trip, so I am free to accept speaking engagements that take me out of the state. These speaking engagements have not necessarily been monetarily profitable, but they haven't cost me anything either. Whereas the experience is excellent, the information gleaned from customers is essential to the growth of "Educational Spectrums" and the networking with colleagues is invaluable.

Q: Any suggestions for saving money?

A: The best suggestion I have for saving money is to read "Marketing Without Advertising" by Michael Phillips & Salli Rasberry. It has saved me hundreds, perhaps thousands of dollars, in advertising dollars. Then follow the advice of Dan Poynter and John Kremer who advise the pursuit of reviews rather than paid advertising. Reviews cost nothing except the cost of the book, postage and time to draft a letter to the reviewer. Reviews are perceived as an objective evaluation of a book so are better believed by the buying consumer than a display or classified advertisement.

The best advice I would give others is....

The best advice I would give others is to know your talents, your strengths and weaknesses, and to do those jobs you are good at and find someone else to do those jobs you do badly or inefficiently. It won't do you any good if you're the best writer in the world if you are such a poor marketer that you're unable to announce effectively to the people of the world that this terrific book is available to solve their problems, inform them or entertain them.

If I had to do it over again, I would....

If I had it to do over again, I'd probably do the same things. Realistically, I couldn't move any faster than I'm moving now and still maintain home, family, and business. However, if I were able to start the business over and begin with the knowledge I've managed to accrue to date, I'd probably make some wiser decisions regarding pricing. Initially, I charged too little for shipping books. And, I also have underpriced a couple of titles. Not harmfully underpriced. Usually a range of acceptable prices can be determined for a book based on its size, number of pages, artwork, etc. For example, a seventy-two-page book (five and a half by eight straight text) could range in price from $4.95 to $7.95. I have usually priced my trade titles at the low end of the scale.

Q: Was your family supportive of your efforts? How important is this?

A: My family is very supportive of my efforts. My husband is my sidekick and companion at book fairs. My children help by answering phones, with order fulfillment, and catalog distribution. The children (ages seven and ten) probably have a better understanding of business than most teenagers today and because of this knowledge are pretty understanding when Mom has deadlines to meet and radio phone interviews to conduct.

Q: Anything else?

A: Small press or self-publishing can be a reality for anyone who has the energy and determination to make it work. The wealth of information that is currently available on the subject explains exactly how to do it and makes a self-taught course possible. All it takes is ability, capital and determination.

by Jane A. Williams

Who Reads What When

Literature Selections for Children Ages Three through Thirteen

Who Reads What When is a time-saving reference guide for anyone who wants to select good literature for children, but hasn't the time to do their own research. *Who Reads What When* lists over 500 excellent literature selections for children ages three through thirteen, indexed by age, author and title. No longer do grandparents, aunts, uncles or parents need to guess about book selections for children.

Who Reads What When gives tips on how to identify a child's reading and listening comprehension level, how to encourage a child's interest in reading, and discusses the importance of read-aloud and the home library.

Extensive reading guide.   - **School Library Journal**, February, 1988

Parents interested in read-aloud sessions will find this a perfect guide to age brackets as well as specific books.   - *Bookwatch*, **Midwest Book Review**, June, 1988

A concise and easy-to-use guide to good literature. - **Small Press Review**, February, 1988

This easy-to-use guide is for anyone who wants help identifying some of the best children's books and authors.   - **Gifted Children Monthly**, April, 1988

Spans the literary spectrum from Homer's Iliad......to Ray Bradbury's Something Wicked This Way Comes.   - **Changing Times**, February, 1988

As a guide to your children's reading, or as a record of your home library, Who Reads What When is a valuable reference book.   - **Home Education Magazine**, Jan-Feb. 1988

When I first saw this book, I thought -"At last! A guide to help home schoolers in book selection for their kids!" And it's even better than that because it lists books by age, which lets parents know about what maturity level the kids will need to be before they comprehend some of the material in the books. Reading levels vary, of course, but maturity levels also have an effect on when a child is ready for a certain book. I think this book is a must for homeschoolers!   - **Home Education Resource Guide by Donn Hubbs**

Ordering Information

Who Reads What When $3.95
     ISBN: 0-942617-01-0   LCCN# 87-27854 (CIP)   59 pages (5 1/2 x 8 1/2) Perfectbound
Shipping/Handling: One book, $1.50. Additional books, $0.50 each.
     For orders shipped to California, add appropriate sales tax.
Publication date: February 1988
Send check or money order to: Bluestocking Press, P.O. Box 1014, Dept. WRF,
     Placerville, CA 95667 (916)-621-1123

Jane A. Williams is an educational researcher who has investigated educational options for the past fifteen years. She has taught in the traditional public school classroom, tested innovative educational outreach programs in Bush Alaska, advised home schooling families, and is the founder and president of Educational Spectrums - a book distribution center specializing in educational options and resources, as well as work options for children and adults. Mrs. Williams is a free lance writer and a columnist for *Home Education Magazine*. Her articles have appeared in several publications and books including *Alternatives in Education* , *The Home School Reader* and *Growing a Business/Raising a Family*.

Bluestocking Press • P.O. Box 1014 • Dept. WRF • Placerville • CA • 95667 • 916-621-1123 • SAN 667-2981

James Lee Young

Writers need contact with other writers. I need contact with other writers. For one, it keeps me from feeling alone, from taking myself too seriously, to be aware that the problems I face as a writer and human being are not just mine.

chapter **40**

Advantages and How-tos of Forming a Local Writers' Group

by James Lee Young
Director of the National Writers Club

Networking! Without it writers lose sight of their industry, their perspective, and sometimes their sanity. Writers need contact with other writers. I need contact with other writers. For one, it keeps me from feeling alone, from taking myself too seriously, to be aware that the problems I face as a writer and human being are not just mine.

The answer—for me and thousands of other writers around the world—is the local writers' group or chapter.

Since I am the Director of the National Writers Club, people who don't know me well assume that I have my act together all the time as a writer, that I never suffer from editors' rejections, that I keep a perfect balance in my goals as a writer, and that I always know what markets are open and right at any given time. Those close to me know better.

Sure, my job affords me access to information collectively that most writers don't always see as soon as I might. And, sure, I'm in constant contact with other writers, free-lance organizations, editors, and literary agents. Most of that contact, however, is by telephone, mail, or fax.

In a way, my local chapter—I belong to a group in Denver, Colorado—is like a church fellowship. Several of the members are my close friends, some colleagues in whom I confide, share ideas and dreams, and even engage in writing-related projects. Often, they have information on markets and editors that I haven't run across in my daily information gathering for my national association's members. Some of the information helps the association overall; some of it is for me, personally.

Whether the local group is affiliated with an association or not, most of the organizing steps are the same, except that an independent local group won't report to a larger body of course.

My fellow chapter members and I see several advantages to belonging to a local group, especially one affiliated with a national organization of which several have chapters scattered about the country. The primary reasons for forming a local group are outlined in "The Chapter Development Guide," published by National Writers Club.

Writers join such groups because they want to improve their own writing skills, increase the odds of getting published, join the writing community, and lessen feelings of isolation. And, they join to be motivated and to have fun.

The local chapter provides for such motivation and more:

1) It provides a framework and forum for writers to get in touch with other writers in their immediate geographic area. By doing so, it reinforces the "you are not alone" concept.

   A sense of community exists among the members and an opportunity to obtain feedback and information about the vocation of writing.

2) It serves as a focal point for resources for local publishers and editors.

3) It provides a collective forum for members to put forth ideas and recommendations for new programs that they would like to see implemented on a national or international basis.

   Chapters have central themes such as writing and publishing, but, for the most part, each one defines its overall program based on local needs and interests. Some chapters are large. Some meet often, some meet less frequently.

4) It provides a social outlet for area writers—a chance to meet with people of similar interests and intellectual stimulation.

5) It provides an educational outlet. Trends and new ideas, also the accepted methods and standards in the industry are reinforced for veteran writers and provided to orient newer people to the field.

6) It provides a means for writers to meet editors, literary agents, publishers, and writers "who have made it," for marketing information and inspiration.

7) Even with the fun, inspiration, information, and education provided during the monthly meetings, one aspect of the local group I have always enjoyed is a by-product of sorts.

The local chapter to which I belong always has a group that heads for a local restaurant after the meeting. Members talk over coffee. Solid friendships and even mentor relationships are formed from such intimate gatherings and make them worth the effort.

As one who works full-time for a national organization of free-lance writers, you can bet I am in favor of local groups affiliating with associations, for several reasons.

Advantages of affiliating with associations

1) You normally receive all services and benefits available to the members-at-large, such as one-on-one consultation, manuscript criticism, help in dealing with editors and publishers, publications and bulletins, marketing help and special reports, contest information, bulletin board access, agent referral, insurance programs, conferences and workshops.

2) You obtain the prestige and advantages of affiliation with a national/international group that is a vital force in improving the standards, payment rates, and status of the free-lance writer.

3) These associations are information brokers and clearing houses for the individual writer and for the chapter, providing lists and reports, for example, how to improve attendance at meetings, philosophy of a chapter, how to sponsor workshops, how to effectively network among the members, what markets are hot, current scams, industry changes, etc.

4) For national associations, the chapter as the local entity and its

members as individuals have the advantage of constant contact with other writers and of practicing the adage that in unity there is strength. You receive stimulation and encouragement, and constructive criticism of your books, stories, and articles by networking with other writers, usually both from the national's body staff and the members and from the local writers.

5) You receive official publications and often other key industry publications at discounted rates, to keep you up-to-date on what's happening in the business.

6) It provides an opportunity for networking with other groups and individuals across the country, not only to get information on markets in specific areas but members sometimes attend local chapter functions in communities where they are away from home on business and vacation.

Among the more notable groups with regional and/or local affiliates or centers are: American Pen Women, American Society of Journalists and Authors, Mystery Writers of America, National Writers' Club, National Writers' Union (a labor union), Romance Writers of America, and Western Writers of America.

There are others, of course, and beyond the national/international organization affiliates, there are thousands of regional and local groups formed by volunteers who have a need to interact with other writers. The steps and processes outlined below for organizing a local writers' group include what generally will be required if the local members apply for affiliation with a national association. However, the same steps apply overall when a local group is being formed without national or international affiliation: except when it relates to an association's requirements of reporting to that association.

General requirements for a local group

1) To obtain a local charter with a national/international writers' association, the group will be required to abide by the larger group's bylaws. Regardless, the local group will be required to meet and observe certain standards and rules set forth by the particular state and/or the Internal Revenue Service.

2) To qualify for a local charter, the local club usually will be required to have either a minimum number of members, of which some or all local membership must belong to the larger group.

3) Each chapter generally regulates its dues in keeping with policies stated by the association. All chapter memberships usually are verified by the local chapter officials to the association. Some chapters forward all dues—local and national/international to the association—and these are rebated to the local group. Others collect local dues and the members send the association dues separately to the larger organization.

4) Local chapters usually designate members in associate and/or professional classifications if they desire, but such distinctions generally are not a requirement by the association for voting or holding office on the local level.

5) Usually, you will write to the executive director, president, or chief executive officer of the particular association stating your desire and intent to begin a local chapter.

6) Enlist the number of members required (new or existing members) to form the chapter nucleus. Often, the association will contact members in the local areas to let them know a group may be formed. Most groups will not allow their mailing list to be accessed, however.

7) Publicize your intent to start the local group and publicize it in the area media, to local public and college libraries, to other writers' groups, to creative writing classes, to English, journalism, communications teachers/professors at all levels of learning, and to college and adult education classes. Announce an informational meeting and sign up as many interested people as possible at that meeting. Form a coordinating committee and announce the first formal meeting of the group.

8) Draft a constitution, adopt it, and have all the charter members, at least six, sign it.

9) Nominate and elect officers. In most cases, the coordinating committee chairperson, usually the person who spearheads the organizing of the chapter, is elected president, but that is not always true.

Name the appropriate committee, per the bylaws. Appropriate officers may include: the president, vice-president or president-elect, program coordinator, publicity and newsletter coordinator, treasurer, recording clerk or secretary, refreshments or social chairman, and whatever other positions are designated by the association or the chapter such as critique group or other special coordinators.

10) Choose a regular time and place to meet; outline the programs for the rest of the chapter years.

11) Draft a letter (from the chapter president) to the association's executive director, president, or CEO, noting that the minimum requirements have been met and that all dues are paid both nationally and locally. In the letter, you should include:

✍ A copy of the constitution that has been drafted and adopted and signed by all charter members of the chapter, if required. (I keep an original in our national files, and the other original is kept by the chapter.)

✍ A membership roster, noting who are officers and charter members. Give roster date, member names, addresses, telephone numbers, and provide a regular update, depending on the association's needs.

✍ Specifics on meeting place and time/date and intended regularity of chapter meetings.

✍ A copy of the program calendar for the rest of the current year, and into the new year if you have that information.

12) When the letter of request for the charter arrives at national/international headquarters stating that the newly proposed chapter has complied with requirements for chapter status, the association will usually verify that information and respond with a letter, of which an original will be keep in the association's files.

13) The chapter treasurer-recording clerk (whoever is assigned the responsibility) will normally send the treasurer's and election of officers reports annually, usually toward the end of the year, to association headquarters.

14) The outgoing president may be asked to furnish the headquarters

office with his/her annual report, in the form of a brief summary letter hitting highlights of the chapter year, giving any suggestions to improve the chapter program/structure and support, and attaching any useful documents, historical information, newsletters, minutes, and so on.

15)   The publicity-newsletter editor will send copies of the chapter newsletter and other promotional information concerning the chapter to association headquarters.

16)   Most chapters find it advantageous and necessary to rent a post office box, establish non-profit status (usually approved by the secretary-of-state in the state in which the chapter is located), and set up a checking account in the chapter's name, normally in that order. Some will elect to apply with the Internal Revenue Service for tax-exempt status, which is not the same thing as applying for and/or being granted non-profit status by the state.

Of course, the requirements and needs of each association and local group will differ, and you will have to adapt, adjust, and allow for the differences. Generally, however, I know from my own experience in dealing with and organizing local groups, that what I have outlined here is what you can expect.

Chapters have their own personalities; they can be helpful to their members, community-oriented, informative and enjoyable so that the members want to be involved—to not miss a meeting, to be together even when nothing formal is planned.

They also can be political, fraught with power plays, ego-feeders for the misled and arrogant, and hurtful to sensitive writers.

The success depends on the local leadership, their attitude toward the group, toward the association (if affiliated), and their views in writing. Do they enjoy writing as a vocation or avocation; or is it a drudgery that they endure? Do they enjoy volunteer work—as with the chapter?

Do they enjoy working with people, especially other writers—with all of our eccentricities? Are they program-oriented, and are they sold on the need and worth of the chapter and the association?

I have seen chapters destroyed by one or two key people with negative attitudes or overblown ideas of their own importance.

Others I have seen prosper because the president and her/his officers cared about each other, the members, the association, and the profession of writing. It was their passion, and they passed the commitment and caring on to each chapter member.

Every community should have such a group. Mine does; I'm fortunate, and I know it.

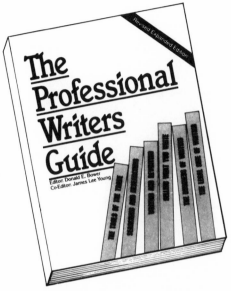

ISBN 0-88100-065-5. Paper $16.95. 152 pages, 6"× 9".

- *The Professional Writers Guide* has been developed by the National Writers School under the direction of The National Writers Club.
- ✓ Learn the techniques used by successful professional writers.
- ✓ Learn how to achieve your goals as a freelancer.
- ✓ Learn how to sell what you write.

MAIN SELECTION WRITER'S DIGEST BOOK CLUB

Contact: National Writers Club
1450 S. Havana, Ste. 620
Aurora, CO 80012
303-751-7844
FAX 303-751-8593 (call first)

SUMMARY OF CONTENTS:

THE WRITER'S CORNER
The Importance of Being a Writer

THE TOOLS OF THE TRADE
The Tools and a Test
Office Equipment
Supplies
A Writer's Library

SEARCHING AND RESEARCHING
Sources of Research Material

THE WRITER'S CORNER
Alibis for Writers

WRITING AND REWRITING
How to Criticize Your Own
Manuscript

Professional Way to Prepare Your
Manuscript
Proofreader Marks

SELLING WHAT YOU WRITE
How and Where to Sell What You
Write
Writing for the Book Market
The Juvenile and Young Adult
Market
The Fantasy/Science Fiction
Markets
The Mystery and Detective Market
Men's Magazines
Women's Magazines
The Confession Market
The Inspirational Market
The Educational Theatre
The Youth Theatre

Fillers and Short Articles
What Syndication is All About
Market Directories
How to Write a Query Letter

THE BUSINESS OF WRITING
Pay Schedule for Writers
The Freelancer's Bookkeeping
System
Income Tax and the Writer

THE LEGAL SIDE OF WRITING
Highlights of the Copyright Law
Literary Rights
Analyzing Your Book Contract
Plagiarism and Piracy
Libel and the Writer
Using a Pen Name

ALTERNATE BOOK PUBLISHING

WHAT USERS SAY ABOUT THIS BOOK

"I would never have believed that so much of value could be packed into a volume of this size . . . I only wish I had been in possession of this fine book when I taught creative writing for nine years in Wisconsin."
—Arthur Wichern
Fairfield Bay, Arkansas

"I wish you and your co-editors to know how valuable this book is. I do not find anything missing—in fact, it covers all of the points a writer, beginning or professional, should have at his or her fingertips."
—Frank Murrell
Campione d'Italia, Switzerland

"And now the National Writers Club has revised its classic guide, not only updating it but adding considerable material. The result: a book that is even more useful in outlining and elucidating the basics in every area of writing and selling your work. The beginner will want it for an overview and for its solid, proven advice on becoming a pro; the experienced writer will be pulling it off the shelf to consult its newly updated tax and legal information, as well as to look into new fields or genres."
—Writer's Digest Book Club Bulletin

Patricia C. Gallagher

chapter **41**

No Thanks, I'll Publish It Myself

by Patricia Gallagher

Many people ask me questions about self-publishing. The following is a hands-on resource guide addressing the most frequent concerns and issues that are raised in my book publishing consulting practice and in the seminars that I offer.

1. Why did you write this anthology, "For All the Write Reasons?"

There are so many step-by-step how-to books available for authors, but I wanted to compile something that would inspire and also guide novice and experienced writers using real life examples. The authors that contributed to this book certainly tell you about their pearls of wisdom and the pitfalls of publishing. I wish I had found a book like this before I made a lot of costly mistakes.

2. How do I obtain a copyright for my book?

To obtain a copyright for your book, call 1-202-707-9100 or 202-479-0700 and request a TX form for each book you plan to publish. You could also write and make your request: Office of the Copyright, Information and Publication Section, Library of Congress, Washington, D.C. 20559. Simply fill out the form and send the current fee of $20 and two "best editions" of your book to the address listed on the TX form. You may call the above hotline number and ask any questions that you may have about registering a copyright. Also request that they send you any booklets or brochures that explain the meaning of copyright. You will notice that most books have a copyright in the front of the book along with some words to the effect of "Copyright, 1991, by Patricia Gallagher. All rights reserved..." (For an example, see the front of my book, "For All the Write Reasons.")

3. What else do I need to do to make my book look professional?

You should have an International Standard Book Number, which is known as an ISBN. Take a look at books in the bookstore and library. Note that most have an ISBN number on the back cover and also on one of the first few pages of the book. An ISBN number is obtained by contacting R.R. Bowker, ISBN Agency, 121 Chanlon Road, New Providence, NJ, 07974, or call 1-800-521-8110 or 1-908-665-6770.

The International Standard Book Number is the means that book stores, wholesalers, libraries etc. identify your book. Contact the ISBN agency and ask them to send you an application. There is currently a fee of $100 for them to give you a list of numbers. Hold on to the computerized list and use the assigned numbers to identify each of your books. For example, you would assign one number to the softcover edition, a different number to the hardcover edition, a third number to the second edition of the same book if you have given it a new price, title, or if it is a revision of an earlier work.

This number is important so that prospective customers can find your book. If they go to the library, the librarian can find your title in one of her reference books and can give people the address where people can contact you about ordering the book.

4. Is it important to have a foreword in your book?

If a famous person, celebrity or expert in your field contributes a few kind words or is amenable to write the foreword in your book, you will find editors respond. A foreword by a celebrity will enhance the marketability of the book. Terry Griffin, author of "Letters of Hope, Living After the Loss of your Child," sent her book to First Lady Barbara Bush, who wrote some beautiful thoughts as she, too, had experienced the loss of her child. She related to Terry's book and felt honored that she was asked.

5. What is a Bookland EAN code or bar code and why do I need one?

You have probably noticed supermarket scanners that "read" the prices from the products. The bar code is the same thing for the book industry, it is a book identification code. On the back cover of the book, you will want to have the bar code printed. You would contact a company such as GGX Associates, 11 Middle Neck Road, Great Neck, New York, 11021, phone: 1-516-487-6370 (ask for customer service), who would take your ISBN number and convert that into a symbol (film master) which your printer will print when the covers are made. By contacting the above company, you can receive a booklet that explains the coding guidelines for the book publishing industry. This company currently charges $20 for the bar code. There are many companies that provide this service. When you contact such a firm, ask for help in selecting the correct code and symbol, advice on color and location, and ask about their turn-around time.

6. I've noticed that many books have a Library of Congress catalog card number (LCCN) on the copyright page of the book. How do I get information about this?

If you want to sell to libraries, you should have this number. Request a form for PREASSIGNMENT OF LIBRARY OF CONGRESS CATALOG NUMBER by writing to Cataloging in Publication Division, Library of Congress, Washington, D.C., 20540. They will send you an explanation of this service. At the same time, call 1-202-707-6372 and ask for their Cataloging in Publication: Information for Participating Publishers.

7. How can I learn more about self-publishing?

I teach one-evening seminars on self-publishing at adult evening schools in the non-credit divisions. Many people think that they can come to one class and then be all set to publish a book. Unfortunately, it is not that easy. You must check out every book in the library about self-publishing and publishing in general and read as much as you can. Most authors give you the same basic information but present it differently. You sometimes have to read about the technicalities of publishing in many different ways before you begin to absorb the material. I would also advise you to read writing and publishing magazines such as *Publisher's Weekly* and *Writer's Digest*—which are in most public libraries. Attend writers conferences and seminars. Join a writers group or start one of your own. The best way to learn about self-publishing is to network with others who are involved in the same business.

8. Who should self-publish?

Someone with lots of time, energy, and enthusiasm is the answer that pops into my mind immediately. Writing the book, believe it or not, is the easiest part, but the real work begins when you begin to design, produce, market, and publicize the book. The person who is most likely to sell books without a lot of publicity would be someone who is a president of an organization, who has a ready made market of members who need or want a book of this type. For most self-publishers, a great deal of time, money, and effort is required to move the books from your storage area into the hands of the people who want to buy the book.

9. What have you found to be most important in self-publishing?

If you are going to publish yourself, do your best to make your book look like one found on the shelves in a bookstore. Don't let it appear home-made. Spiral bindings may be okay for a book that you are going to sell in a seminar, but if you want "respect," follow the example of the major publishers in regard to size of book, paper, cover design, bar code, ISBN number, laminated cover, name of book and author on the spine. See what competing books look like and follow their pattern for success.

You must include a coupon so that people can order directly from you. Look at other books and see how they have designed an order form. I sold about 1,000 books to libraries in 1987. Now, several years later, I still get requests for that book from people who saw it in the library and decided that they wanted their own copy.

It helps to say "satisfaction guaranteed" or "money back" when you are selling by mail. The order coupon is included within my books both in the front and in the back.

10. *How can self-publishers get people to order their book if they are not in bookstores?*

If you have a nice looking book and you are going to promote it on radio and television shows, you could call Faye DeWitt at New Canaan Bookstore's BOOKCALL. Their number is easy to remember if you give it out over the air. Call her and give her information about your publication, send her your book and press materials and if she is interested in fulfilling orders for your book, she will give you permission to use the number of 1-800-ALL-BOOK over the air during an interview.

The 800-number was really a godsend to me when I was doing a segment on "Sally Jessy Raphael" and my books were not in bookstores. If the viewers wanted my book, they would not have been able to purchase it in the major chains or the independent bookstores because I did not have that kind of distribution. Fortunately, the show flashed the above phone number on the screen and they received several hundred requests for my book. They ordered the books from me at a discount, and I packed the books in my kitchen and sent them along with an invoice to their office in Connecticut.

Upper Access Book Publishers, P.O. Box 457, Hinesburg, VT 05461, also offers a service that enables authors to use their 800 number when doing interviews. Lisa Carlson says, "We'll stock your title and give same-day service to your U.S. and Canadian customers." They do not charge any up-front money or warehousing fee. Call one of the very nice folks at (800) 356-9315 for information about fulfillment and book publishing. They publish a mail order catalog that has an annual circulation of 70,000 to 120,000.

11. *What do you think about public relations firms or people who specialize in letting the media know about your book.?*

Before signing any agreements or paying any money upfront, call other authors who have used the service to get their opinion of the value. I know a person who just paid a publicity firm $750 in advance. The company said that they would send her materials to the New York media. She was disappointed to find that she only had two interviews on very small town radio shows that didn't even begin to cover the $750 fee.

12. What does a publicist do in a publishing house?

About six months before my book's publication date, I met with the publicist. She asked me questions about my background, the story behind my writing the book and some personal information about my interests and family. She made up a press kit which was sent out to the media prior to the book's publication.

13. Can I do my own publicity and how do I go about finding out the contact names for radio, television, newspapers, and magazines?

There are many directories in the reference section of your library that list names, addresses, phone numbers, editors, producers, etc. You can use these at the library or purchase them directly from the publishers. Since some of them are rather expensive, you may want to share the cost with another author/friend, or purchase as a desk copy for your writing organization. See the Appendix of this book for sample listings from these sources.

The following materials are ones that I have found very helpful when doing my own publicity:

"The Publicity Manual" by Kate Kelly, 11 Rockwood Drive, Larchmont, NY 10538. It was well worth the $29.95 (1991 price). Some of the subjects include: what free publicity can do for you, how to contact the press and get results, how to get on radio and TV talk shows and how to write sample press releases.

"Publicity for Books and Authors," by Peggy Glenn, Aames-Allen Publishing Co., 1106 Main St., Huntingdon Beach, CA 92648 ($14.95, 1991 price). This book is filled with state of the art promotion ideas and great fun to read.

14. What other techniques are useful in promoting a book even when it's not available in bookstores?

When I recently appeared on CNN talking about how to start a child care program, I was concerned that since my book was published by Doubleday two years ago, that there would no longer be books in the bookstores. Usually with books such as mine, the shelf life in a store is short, although they can be special-ordered by the bookstore personnel. I made up a booklet titled "Common Day Care Problems," which offered tips for people interested in starting their own day care program. It was available free to the viewers of CNN if they would send a self-addressed, stamped envelope. It was a nice little booklet with lots of helpful information but it was also an advertising piece for me because it included order coupons and a description of my books. I received about 300 requests for the booklet, which in turn only converted to fifty orders for my books. That really surprised me because I thought that I would receive thousands of requests. Many people requested the booklet but did not send a SASE, creating unplanned postage expenses as well as printing costs. My "tip sheet" could really have been an eight and a half by eleven-inch paper printed on both sides rather than a booklet that cost me twenty-five cents to print.

Another mistake was not specifying that viewers must send a long envelope with 45 cents postage. Many sent small envelopes and my material did not fit into it. I had to address envelopes and apply postage. I have some articles that were in the newspapers so I usually send a copy of an article along with the booklet. People like to know more about your business, book or product and an article usually gives a human interest side to your story.

15.   *How did you get on your first television show?*

Shortly after I began my home child care business in September 1984, I began writing a booklet, "How to Start a Day Care Business." The book went through several stages as I added information and changed the title and cover design many times. About a year and a half later, I was watching a national show, "Hour Magazine," with a host named Gary Collins. I called my local network and asked for the address of the California-based show. The amazing thing is that I just sent a half-page, typed letter addressed only to "Producer" and as beginners luck would have it, a segment producer called and did a pre-interview over the phone. She asked me to send the book by Federal Express that evening. I remember trying to find a depot to send the book by overnight mail when I passed a Federal Express truck on a nearby street. I flagged him down as if it was some sort of emergency and I asked him if he could possibly take care of this critically important package. (my spiral bound home-made book!) The next day, I was confirmed as a guest on the show. All of my expenses and travel arrangements were arranged by their staff.

Frequently people ask if I get paid as a guest on shows and the answer is "no." The value to appearing as an "expert author" is invaluable in terms of exposure and is also a great experience. The first time that I was invited on "AM Philadelphia" came about as a result of going to sit in the audience as a guest. After the show, I walked up on the stage and introduced myself to the two hosts. I followed up by sending information in the mail and also called twice to suggest a theme for a show. Nothing happened...but about a year later, out of the blue, they called and extended an invitation to be a guest on the show.

Three years after the first invitation, I was invited back after the producer recognized me on the "Sally Jessy Raphael" show and wanted to do a local version on the same topic. They asked me if I could bring someone else along for the panel. My friend and neighbor, Dianna, filled the bill so off we went. From there, the producer had a friend who produced "People Are Talking" in New Jersey and Dianna and I were invited to do that show together. This time, we hired a babysitter to watch our five children and all eight of us took off for fancy hotel accommodations in suburban New York City. While Dianna and I did the show, our kids and babysitter watched us on television in the Hyatt Regency. Of course the kids weren't too happy about that since they were missing their favorite show, "Sesame Street." Somehow their moms on syndicated television paled in comparison to the excitement of Big Bird and Cookie Monster.

16. Do you always see results from your marketing and promoting efforts?

I have found that there is no best way to get on television. I have mailed hundreds of fancy press kits, sent handwritten notes, made phone calls to producers and made personal contacts at conventions. I think that it is just timing and good luck. A combination of different approaches has worked for me. Many, many times, I have said, "This is too hard. I am getting out of this business," but then something good will happen and my enthusiasm is replenished.

A recent example is a situation just a few weeks ago when Family Circle called to tell me that a press release that I had sent them about a year before would be running in their July issue and they wanted to make sure that I had at least 5,000 up to 10,000 of my product on hand because they said I could expect that sort of response. That was good timing for me because I was at the wavering point, wondering if I wanted to stay in this business. It was just the spark I needed to get my adrenalin flowing to work on a related project.

Two years ago, I traveled around the country with my children to promote my book, "Start Your Own At Home Child Care Business," which was published by Doubleday. I sent my press kit to a public relations firm in New York. I was selected to be a product spokesperson for a Fortune 500 company. I will be paid a very nice daily rate to promote a new product that has special appeal to parents with small children. My credentials for this opportunity were as a result of being a published author which to them indicated being an authority on a subject, being a mother of four and on the basis of the video tapes that I sent them. Now you and I know, I am not the most knowledgeable person on the subject, but to the company, I fit the bill of what they were looking for...again an example of delayed reaction for the groundwork laid twenty-four months earlier.

17.   In what directories, listings, and reference books in the library should I be referenced?

If you are going to self-publish a book, you want to make it easy for people to find your company or your book. One of the ways is to get your book title listed in the "Books In Print" series, which is published by R.R. Bowker. To start the ball rolling, write to the Advance Book Information Office, ISBN Agency, R.R. Bowker, 121 Chanlon Rd., New Providence, New Jersey, 07974, or call 1-800-521-8110 and request five copies of the Advance Book Information form. Ask for any additional brochures that describe their services. (There is no charge for the forms). When you receive the "ABI" form fill it out completely and return your book information to their office. They will take your book information and use it to list your book in their series which includes: "Books in Print," "Subject Guide to Books In Print," "Forthcoming Books," paperbound "Books in Print" and several other reference books. You might want to visit a library and take a look at these books so you can visualize them.

There are many times when people are looking for books about starting a child care program but don't know what is available. When they check the "Books in Print" series, my name as the author and my book titles are listed along with my address and the price of the book. During the past few years, I have had a steady stream of orders from people who located my company through these directories. You should contact the ABI office much in advance of the publication date so they can list your book in the "Forthcoming Books" directory.

"Cumulative Book Index" is another place that you want to be listed. Request a CBI Information Slip by sending a note to Cumulative Book Index, H.W. Wilson Company, 950 University Ave., Bronx, New York, 10452 (212-588-8400). They will ask you to send a copy of your book along with the completed CBI form. This listing is free but there are a few qualifiers in order to be listed. Make sure that you tell them that your book is more than 100 pages and that you are going to print at least 500 copies of your book.

18. Are there national associations I can join to network with other small publishers?

I know that you can't join every one, but a few associations which offer seminars, newsletters and a wealth of information to its members are: Publishers Marketing Association, 2401 Pacific Coast Highway #102, Hermosa Beach, CA, 90254; COSMEP, P.O. Box 42073, San Francisco, CA, 94142; and National Association of Independent Publishers, P.O. Box 850, Moore Haven, FL, 33471.

COSMEP is the International Association of Independent Publishers and can be reached at 415-922-9490. It is the nation's oldest and largest association for small publishers. Many of their members are self-publishers and their services are more geared to author-publishers as well as to smaller publishing companies. Their newsletter, which is an excellent source of on-going information, comes out monthly. They'll send you a sample copy along with information on membership if you just request it.

19. How do I get my book distributed or out to the bookstores?

There are many ways, although it is not an easy process. However, beginning self-publishers should do all of the publicity you can and make it easy for people to find your book. If you have only published one book, the major chains will probably not want to deal with you directly because of the time and expense of setting up a business account with you. So what you need to do is to sell to a distributor or wholesaler and they in turn sell to the stores.

20. What are wholesalers and how are they different from distributors?

Wholesalers do not have a sales force and they primarily receive their orders directly from libraries and catalogs. Two of the largest wholesalers are Baker and Taylor, P.O. Box 6920, 652 E. Main St., Bridgewater, N.J., 08807-0920 (908-218-0400) and Ingram Book Co., 1125 Heil Quaker Blvd., La Vergne, TN 37086 (615-793-5000). You can contact them and ask them to send you information about how you can work with them to get your book stocked or ordered as needed.

21. Who are some of the distributors?

Publishers Group West, 4065 Hollis Street, P.O. Box 8843, Emeryville, CA, 94608 (1-415-658-3453). PGW sells to bookstore chains and independent bookstores. They charge you a commission to sell your books.

Quality Books, 918 Sherwood Drive, Lake Bluff, Illinois, 60044 (1-708-295-2010). They sell your books to libraries and charge you a commission. Their specialty is non-fiction and they like to review your book/product before its publication date. At one point, I sent them my book "So You Want to Open a Profitable Day Care Center," and they were initially interested in distributing it for me because they thought it was a timely topic and would sell at least 500 copies, but they declined because the copyright date was 1987 and I submitted it in 1988. Give them a call and they will send you information about how to submit your product for consideration.

22. What books have you found helpful and where did you get them?

The books I am going to discuss here are books I have found in my library. Unfortunately, many are reference books so I could not check them out. In a few cases, although they were quite expensive, I did purchase them because I was doing publicity for my own books as well as for others in my book publicity consulting practice. If your local branch library does not have them, try a college library or your county library. You could also request that the acquisitions librarian order these books for you from the publisher.

"**1991 Writers Market**," annual publication, (Writers Digest Books, 1507 Dana Ave., Cincinnati, OH 45207). Lists over 4,000 places where you can sell your work (articles, books, fillers, greeting cards, novels, plays, scripts, and short stores. To order: 1-800-289-0963. This book includes complete current information on contact names, addresses, editorial needs, pay rates and submission requirements. You can also find "Writer's Market" in most bookstores.

"**Catholic Press Directory**," published annually by the Catholic Press Association, 119 North Park Ave., Rockville Centre, New York, NY, 11570 (1-516-766-3400). The directory lists of Catholic newspapers, magazines, newsletters, book clubs, and associations.

"**Greater Philadelphia Publicity Guide**," Balset Co., Box 365, Ambler, PA 19002-0365, (215) 628-8729. The guide is an annual publication offering a broad listing of primarily local interest media in the eight-county greater Philadelphia area. It includes newspapers, magazines, cable television, and broadcasters.

"**Websters New Work Dictionary of Media and Communications**," by Richard Weiner, published by Prentice Hall Trade ($29.95). This dictionary includes 30,000 up-to-date definitions of today's slang and technical definitions from the media industry. Each definition is written so that the user can understand it even if he or she is not a professional working in the field. Includes twenty-seven fields such as advertising, broadcasting, computer graphics, printing, and public relations, etc.

"**Syndicated Columnist Contacts**," and "**News Bureau Contacts**" are published by BPI Communications, Inc. The book, "Syndicated Columnist

Contacts," is a comprehensive book that lists approximately eighty syndicates, as well as more than 200 self-syndicators.

"News Bureau Contacts," the second volume, includes daily newspapers, news services, magazines, trade publications and television stations, which have bureau systems. Published by BPI Media Services, 210 Canal Square, Schenectady, NY, 12305 (1-800-753-6675).

"Working Press of the Nation - The Media Encyclopedia." Published by National Research Bureau, 225 W. Wacker Drive, Suite 2275, Chicago, IL 60606-1229, (1-312-346-9097). This book is an in-depth comprehensive, five-volume set. The directories are designed for people who need information for contacting media personnel or mailing list compilation, media selection, or market analysis.

"Volume 1, Newspaper Directory" contains more than 8,000 management and editorial personnel of daily and weekly U.S. newspapers.

"Volume 2, Magazine Directory" lists more than 5,400 magazines including consumer, farm and agricultural service, trade, professional, and industry publications.

"Volume 3, TV and Radio Directory" lists more than 10,400 radio and TV stations, plus more than 25,900 local programs by subject.

"Volume 4, Feature Writer and Photographer Directory" lists more than 2,100 feature writers and photographers, their home addresses, subject areas of interest and publications accepting their work.

"Volume 5, Internal Publications Directory" offers detailed information about internal and external publications of more than 2,800 U.S. companies, government agencies, clubs, and other groups.

"Standard Directory of Advertisers," Volume 1 and Volume 2 (known as the Red Book)—Guide to more than 62,000 trade names and 26,000 companies, it includes Trade Name Index, Standard Industrial Classification Index, Who's Where in Corporate Advertising. Published by National Register Publishing Company, Macmillan Directory Division, 3004 Glenview Rd., Wilmette, IL 60091. To order, call 1-800-323-6772. I have used this book extensively to find corporate sponsors for my projects.

"Literary Market Place," considered "the directory of the American book publishing industry." Published annually. List of book publishers, editorial services and agents, book manufacturers, associations, courses, awards and events, Publisher Toll Free Directory. R. R. Bowker, 245 W. 17th St., New York, NY 10011. (Price $124.95, 1990 Edition) To order, call 1-800-521-8110.

"**Bacon's Publicity Checker**," published in two volumes, the 1991 edition includes more than 17,000 publication listings and more than 110,000 editorial contacts for the United States and Canada. Volume 1 lists all magazines organized by industry classifications. Volume II lists all daily and weekly newspapers and all multiple publisher groups. Coil-bound to lay flat while using, these books are conveniently sized at six by nine inches. Published annually in October, the Checker includes quarterly updates in January, April, and July. A one-year subscription is $190, plus $5 shipping and handling. To order call 1-800-621-0561. In Illinois 312-922-2400.

"**Writing Related Audio Tapes**," by Nightingale–Conant Corporation, 7300 North Lehigh Avenue, Chicago, IL 60648. 1-800-323-5552.

"**Yes! You Can Write**," by Elizabeth Cowan Neeld, set of six tapes (Twelve sides that include topics such as: rediscovering yourself as a writer, the creating stage, variations on a theme, editors, bosses and rejections slips, and much more.)

"**Write to the Point: Business Communications from Memos to Meetings**," by Dianna Booker, set of six tapes. (Twelve sides includes topics such as: thirty-seven ways to reduce paperwork, proposals that sell, communicating face to face, five steps to effective writing and much more.) The complete set costs $59.95.

23. Are there any books for writers who want to write for TV?

"**Write and Sell Your TV Drama**," by Ann Loring and Evelyn Kaye helps writers who have always wanted to write for TV but didn't know how to begin. This book tells you everything you need to know to prime your script for prime time. You can order the book by writing to: ALEC Publishing Company, 147 Sylvan Ave., Leonia, NJ 07605.

24. To whom at the publishing house do I send my manuscript, query letter or proposal?

The major publishers have acquisition editors who specialize in particular types of books. It is best to direct your correspondence to an appropriate acquisitions editor. Call the publisher and inquire as to who handles psychology, fiction, popular business, or how-to books. You can find the address and telephone number of publishers in the "Literary Market Place" or the "Writer's Market." You should include a self-addressed, stamped envelope as a courtesy, making it easier for the editor to respond.

You should be aware that although you direct your letter to a specific person, it doesn't mean that person will see it. Editors move around often, within the company and externally. Your book idea may be read by an assistant or intern who may make an editorial decision on it. The "slush pile" is the term used to describe the pile of unsolicited manuscripts that arrive and just sit waiting for someone to go through it. "Unsolicited" means that a writer sent it in without being asked to send it.

25. What does an editor do for your book?

In my case the editor was the person who initially liked my book and who in turn sold her boss on it. A lot of time went into competitive analysis to make sure that it had good sales potential and that the book would make money. She also considered how much reworking would need to be done on my manuscript. She read the manuscript with a fine tooth comb and gave me suggestions on a page by page basis to improve what the publishers call "the work." She added and changed sentences that would improve the readability or clarify my ideas. When the manuscript was complete, a copyeditor went through and found every spelling error, typo, grammatical flaw or anything that just didn't make sense. She was an expert in detecting errors of any kind and for her expertise I was extremely grateful.

26. Do editors prefer to receive manuscripts from agents?

There is no hard and fast rule about this, but editors feel that if a reputable agent has presented it, the book has already been screened and they have to at least read it. Editors like to see the works of people who have already been published because it demonstrates a good track record. If you do not have a book published to your credit, anything that you have that has been published will make a nervous editor more secure about offering you a contract. Have you written articles for magazines, newsletters or a newspaper? If so be sure to include your credentials for writing the book in your cover letter.

27.   What is a literary agent and how do I find one?

A literary agent is a person who has connections to editors and publishers. An agent acts as an intermediate person between the author and the publisher. If he feels your manuscript or proposal is marketable, he will approach publishers on your behalf and negotiate a contract. The agent charges a commission for his services and usually all monies will be paid to him. After taking out his portion, he will forward your money to you. Agents usually get a percentage of the author's advance as well as continued payments on the royalties earned and other subsidiary sales. Agents usually charge ten to fifteen percent commission, although I have heard some get twenty-percent commissions.

Agents are beneficial in some cases because they know the market and know the appropriate contact person at the publishing house. However, agents aren't always necessary. I know many writers who have queried editors and negotiated their own deals, usually with the guidance of a lawyer who reads the contract and modifies it to the author's benefit.

Agents do not usually take on the work of "unknowns" or people who do not have a publishing track record. However, an agent will consider great ideas by anyone, even if a first-time writer. Remember that they work on a commission basis so they cannot afford to spin their wheels peddling work that won't make it.

If sending your manuscript to an agent, be sure to inquire if there is a reading fee before you send it. I recently sent a finished book to an agent who said she would be happy to take a look at it. A few weeks later, I received her decision that she did not feel that this book was for her, along with an invoice for $25.

The best way to find the name of an agent is by word of mouth. Attend writer's conferences, ask your local librarian for help, take a course in writing, or just tell your fellow friends you are looking for an agent. You could also look in the acknowledgments section of other books to see who is credited as being the agent. I stumbled on the name of an agent through a fellow who attended an authors' tea at my house. In addition to providing the agent's name, he filled me in on the agent's rate, personality, and how he was to work with. It is important that you have a good working relationship with the person who is going to represent you.

You can find a list of agents in the "Literary Market Place." The listing will tell you the name, address, phone number, and their speciality such as fiction, non-fiction, horror, science fiction, TV, young adult, juvenile, etc. You will also see information as to how to approach an agent such as, "No unsolicited manuscripts, query first with self-addressed, stamped envelope (SASE) or submit outline and sample chapters.

One agent who looked at my book turned it down, saying she couldn't generate any excitement for it in publishing circles. The book she turned down was "Start Your Own At Home Child Care Business," which I sold to Doubleday on my own about two weeks later.

28. *How did you get Doubleday to publish your first book?*

I had self-published a book on starting an at home child care business and had sold several thousand copies through seminars, reviews and mail order. In May 1987, I went to the American Booksellers Convention and showed my book to a senior editor. After showing her a folder filled with newspaper articles about my book, she said it looked interesting and asked me to send her a copy of the manuscript. Within a week, I received a letter from her saying that she was moving on to another position but that another editor would be contacting me.

During that summer, the editor and I talked several times and the following September she made a verbal offer to me for the book. It was much lower than I expected, so I declined until later when the offer multiplied about four times.

However, after the first offer, I called three other authors who recently had published with major publishers and they coached me. One had negotiated a fifty-fifty split with her publisher, which had been arranged by her certified public accountant and a lawyer. This meant that she and the publisher would share equally in the profits.

My other "counsel" told me that her book was sold by "auction" and her payment was a straight upfront $50,000 and she would not receive any further monies as royalties. She had a Ph.D and wanted to have a book published to give her credibility as a speaker on the lecture circuit. After the initial publisher's thrust for publicity and a grueling author tour, her book was out of print. (I feel that she carved an excellent deal for herself.)

My other friend received a $2,500-advance for a very timely topic, but the book was never printed because the publisher reconsidered the title and decided it was a "no go." In her particular case, she did not have to return the money and was free to submit the book to another publisher.

29. Where can you find the names and related information about publishers?

"Writer's Market" is a great source for finding names and information. This annual book lists more than 4,000 contact names, addresses, editorial needs, pay rates, and submission requirements. Since about eighty-five percent of the information changes from year to year, it is best to use a current edition. In this business, it is very common for editors' and publishers' names, addresses and phone numbers to change constantly. This book will keep you on top of the latest information to accurately target your market and sell what you write. Also included is a wealth of information tips for approaching various markets, sample magazine query letters and articles about copyrighting your writing, manuscript mechanics, mailing submissions, etc.

30. What are some of the important things to know about contracts if an editor accepts your book?

When the editor made me an offer that we both agreed to, I asked if she would send me the offer in writing. She said that our verbal agreement on the phone was the agreed upon advance and that there would be no further changes allowed. Since I verbally agreed, the deal was complete. The contract, which arrived a few days later, was a formality.

When I mentioned to the editor I would have a lawyer review it, she basically told me the contract was very straightforward and that she could see no reason why I should need a lawyer. She was careful to tell me that I had sold "all rights" to them, but I really did not understand what that meant. With that, I did not consult with a lawyer before signing the contract. There were many areas where the guidance of a lawyer or agent would have been helpful to me.

31. What were some of the points that were covered in your contract?

The agreement was signed in mid-September and the contract stated I was required to deliver a manuscript of 90,000 words by the following February. The editor said I would receive her suggested revisions immediately. I did not actually receive the revisions until the following September, a year later than planned.

It seemed there was always an excuse as to why the revisions were not forthcoming. Finally, the editor said some senior editors were considering to drop my book but she assured me that she had smoothed things out and to continue with the additions to the book. I worked on the suggestions and mailed them back to her section by section.

I received half of my advance when the contract was signed and I received the balance after the manuscript was completed. I also had to provide them with two black and white photos. One picture was used for the back cover of the hardcover edition and for the press kit that was sent out to the media. The contract also stated that I could no longer engage in any promotional appearances or marketing campaigns without prior permission from the publisher.

32. What are subsidiary rights?

Subsidiary rights are those that mean selling the book in another way such as serial, movie, TV, foreign rights, or book club. In your contract, the profit for publisher and author are negotiated. I remember how excited my editor was when the Better Homes and Garden Book Club bought a large quantity of my hardcover book, "Start Your Own At Home Child Care Business." This purchase validated her selection of my book.

33. If I want to find a listing of United States book publishers, where can I look?

The "Literary Market Place" has an alphabetical listing of U.S. publishers that have produced an average of three or more books annually. The listing includes name, address, phone number, and key contact people. In some listings, you will find the types of books that they publish such as journals in behavioral sciences, parapsychology, Christian family life, travel classics, etc. Be very careful when looking for publishers to determine which are vanity presses or author-subsidized publishers. Publishers of this type may require that an author pay a significant sum of money to the publisher. Authors should be very suspicious with such an arrangement and try to determine what the value of that publishers imprint is in the field. There have been many very disgruntled authors who have seen advertisements stating that they can publish your book. Let the author beware!

34. Where can I find a listing of editorial services?

The "Literary Market Place" has a section devoted to information on editorial services such as copy and line editing, fact checking, manuscript analysis, proofreading, indexing, and ghost writing.

Once again, it is your responsibility to investigate the credentials and the suitability of the services company to your project. You will also find information about lecture agents, advertising agencies, public relations services.

35. Where can I find the names of columnists and commentators who might be interested in mentioning my book?

You can find information on syndicated columnists in *Editor and Publisher*, Annual Directory of Syndicated Service, 11 W 19th St., New York, NY 10011. In the LMP you will also find lists of columnists and commentators listed by their special interest such as automotive, fashion, health, nutrition, politics, etc.

An important part of your marketing campaign is contacting the appropriate contact names for radio and TV programs that feature books and authors as well as magazines and book review syndicates. These names are also listed in the "LMP." Spend a few hours studying this directory to learn about the publishing industry.

36. Where can I find a book manufacturer, someone that specializes in printing and binding books?

In the book manufacturing section of "LMP," you will find pertinent information about companies that print hard- and soft cover books, journals, directories, and manuals. It is important to send a "request for quote" to at least ten companies who have manufactured your kind of book.

When I solicited quotes for this book, there was an $11,500 difference between the highest and lowest quote. You don't necessarily want to go with the lowest, but you want to make a choice based on many factors. Even though the printer may be low for your particular job, someone else might find that book manufacturer on the high end. Different manufacturers have specialties and you must investigate the specialists for print run size, type of press used, services offered, reliability to meet deadlines and quality of completed book. One manufacturer told me that he was usually at the high end of quotes but in my case, he was in the lowest third. He explained business was slow and he would rather have my business at any cost since he still had employees and overhead to pay.

37.   What is meant by an "advance?"

An advance is the amount negotiated upfront between an author and publisher. It is usually paid in parts, such as half upon contract signing and the balance after the completed manuscript is approved. Royalties are usually paid to the author after they have earned back the advance. After the publisher recoups his costs, the author starts to receive royalties.

Many times, an author never sees a penny of royalties because the advance was not earned back. An agent may be able to protect your interests so that you do not have to pay back the advance if the book is not successful. There are many details of a contract that should be scrutinized by an expert in order to avoid first-time authors from losing money earned.

38.   What is meant by an "auction" in the publishing vocabulary?

A friend, who was a first time author, had a great idea for a book which was definitely an "Oprah Winfrey" topic. She wrote a book proposal and sample chapters of this "how-to guide" and submitted it to an agent. She was a doctor and so was a marketable expert to write this book. The agent felt it had "best seller" potential and sent the idea out to major publishing houses who were told to mail in their best confidential bid for the book. The highest bidder was the one who ultimately published the book.

39. How many copies does an author usually receive from the publisher?

My contract stated I would receive ten copies, but I was fortunate to receive about 100 during the past few years. The publisher knew that I was putting them to good use by doing my own publicity. The next time, I would try to negotiate more than the usual ten copies.

You can usually buy your own book at a fifty-percent discount on a non-returnable basis and they pay the freight costs to ship books.

I have probably purchased 750 copies of the paperback to sell at my workshops at community colleges. Some authors have received discounts as high as seventy percent, depending on the quantity purchased. Your contract might prohibit you from selling books out of fear of competition between you and the bookstores. For example, if you were to appear on a national show and give your address for ordering purposes then people would not be inclined to purchase from retailers.

40. What are advance orders?

Several months before a book's publication date, sales representatives from the publishing house call on their accounts to order new titles. The reps learn about the selling points of the new line at sales meetings. Armed with dust jackets and promotional information, they take advance orders. If they are excited about your title becoming a potential commission for them, they will push your book. If not, advance orders may be low and the publisher will not spend a great deal of money for publicity.

Conversely, if the book shows great sales potential, they may adjust their publicity budget upward to keep the momentum going.

41. Do most authors go on an authors tour arranged by the publisher?

No, in my experience I've known very few authors sent on publicity tours unless they were celebrities, best-selling authors or had a hot topic. Many authors arrange media interviews at their own expense. They usually tie radio, television, and newspaper interviews into business travel plans, vacation or visiting relatives.

I received some very nice publicity in Des Moines because I tied into the fact that we were visiting my uncle who owned a printing shop there. They mentioned my uncle and his business in the Des Moines Register as well as in the introduction of a top-rated radio show. Always try to think of the local angle. Did you grow up there, attend college there, or have a business there?

42.   If a book is a backlist title, does that mean it is doomed?

A new book has a shelf life of just a few months. Editors and publicists work on books by seasons. My Doubleday book, "Start Your Own at Home Child Care Business" was released in June 1989. Almost immediately after the publication date, it was yesterday's news as far as the publisher was concerned. (Mainly because the publisher devotes time and energy to the book during the prepublication period.) After June, the publisher was concentrating on books to be released in the fall.

A backlist title means that it is not current, but could still be selling well through catalogs and special orders from the bookstores. It may no longer be on the shelves, but the book can be obtained from the publisher. Backlist is not synonymous with "out of print." In my contract, it stated that if Doubleday wanted to discontinue selling my book and decides not to reprint it, I will have the opportunity to purchase the remainder stock. If I am not interested, they can sell the books to a remainder dealer at any price that they see fit.

43.   How did you sell 3,500 hardcover copies of your book to the Better Homes and Garden Book Club?

The subsidiary rights department of Doubleday sold an initial 1,000 copies of the hardcover edition pre-publication. The publisher and I split the royalties on that sale fifty-fifty as stated in my contract. The book club bought this quantity at a great discount and the book was advertised or sold through the book club. A few months later, post publication, they ordered another 2,500 copies. The royalties that I earned on this sale were charged against my advance.

Having my book listed with the book club was really great exposure for the book. In their catalog, they featured a picture of the book and a descriptive blurb. In the future, I plan to make book clubs a priority to my marketing strategy before publication date. They demand a very high discount because they in turn sell the books at a discount to their book club members. The price that Better Homes and Garden Book Club paid for my book was much lower than I would have to pay for my own book if I wanted to purchase the hardcover edition.

44. How do I get my book from my house into the houses of people who desperately want my information? (Or, so I hope.)

If your book is self-published, you must do it all. In the "Literary Market Place" you will find lists of distributors, wholesalers, and by networking with publishing organizations and other self-publishers, you can find the names of independent sales reps. If your book is handled by a major publisher, you must depend on the sales force hired by the publisher. I asked my publisher who the local rep was that handled my area and met him for lunch. I hoped that by making personal contact and perhaps offering him a little background on the book would help in getting him to promote the book to his customers.

45. What are book reviews?

Before a book is published, it is helpful to have it reviewed in industry magazines, newsletters and newspapers. Some of the major ones are *Booklist, Publishers Weekly, Library Journal, Kirkus Reviews,* but there are many others listed in the "Literary Market Place." Before spending a great deal of time and money mailing the book without careful consideration, contact the appropriate reviewing source and ask for their submission guidelines. Join publishing groups where other authors can share insider secrets and contact names with you.

46. What is a galley?

In my case it was an uncorrected proof of my book which was bound with a very dull blue cover. The final cover was absolutely beautiful but the galley is prepared in advance of the finished book and is used by the publisher to send out in advance of publication to key reviewers and to magazines to see if they would be interested in buying excerpts or selected sections of the book.

47. *Do favorable quotes on a book cover help to sell books?*

People seem to read the cover before they read the table of contents when browsing in a bookstore, so if you know any celebrities, or experts who might say a few sentences about the merits of your book, it wouldn't hurt to ask them for a comment. Be sure to obtain their written permission to use their favorable quotes. One fellow author sent his book to a well known radio personality who had high praises for the book and told him so in a letter. The author used the celebrity's comments on an advertising piece and found himself in a heap of legal trouble to say nothing of dealing with an irate voice on the other end of the phone. The radio personality told him that he had written his comments in a personal letter and he had no business using them for promotional purposes.

48. *Any other tips for first-time authors?*

Don't ever send your "only copy" of a manuscript or document. If you only have one, make several copies of it before sending it out to an agent, editor, or television show.

Try to think like an editor. If the editor received a letter or manuscript from you, would it look professional and neat, with your subject clearly presented? Try to be a mindreader when trying to impress an editor about the merits of publishing your book.

Keep your eyes and ears open for the latest statistics about your subject. Editors like to see statistics. In my case, I researched the number of working mothers, the anticipated increase in the 1990's. I had to prove that there was a need for information on how to start quality day care programs.

Librarians like to have books with an index in order to quickly look up subject matter. The index is an alphabetical listing of the names, subjects, and events, along with the page number where it is found in the book. It is also beneficial to have a list of related books, article, films, and associations in the appendix of your book. Sometimes if a trade publisher is publishing your book, they will ask you to provide an index or will hire someone to do it and charge the expense to you.

49. *What else have you done to publicize books?*

I purchased a great book, "Top 200 Television Shows," ($30) and "Top

Radio Shows," ($30) both can be ordered by calling: Marie Kieffer, Ad-Lib Publications, (800) 669-0773.

I used this information to make contact with producers and researchers for the major shows. I recommend these directories if you are serious about being on the major shows.

If you have self-published, you may want to call Upper Access Book Publishers, (800) 356-9315, and inquire about being listed in their catalog. They will want to see a brochure or other descriptive material from you so they can evaluate the the appeal of your book to their particular audience.

50) *Once you get going and business is booming, how can you manage your computer for keeping track of accounts dues, customer statements, sales by title, etc.?*

This probably won't happen overnight. In the beginning, you may be handwriting or typing your records. Perhaps your basic computer software package will be enough.

Independent publishers have used a software package, "PIIGS", Publishers' Invoice and Information Generating System. If you are in the market to purchase an invoicing/accounts receivable package, you might want to call (800) 356-9315 and ask them to send you information or a demo disk ($15). They offer a manual plus toll-free telephone support and versions are available for IBM and Macintosh. Upper Access, Inc., One Upper Access Road, P.O. Box 457, Hinesburg, VT 05461.

51) *I often see bookmarks, buttons, gadgets, etc. used at trade shows or included in press kits. Where do people buy advertising items?*

I think it is a good idea to use low cost ways to keep your book's name in front of your customers.

I have used the following suppliers to promote my new titles by purchasing a quantity of their products imprinted with the name of my book or business:

   1)   Rainbow Magnets, 3031 S. Harbor Road, Santa Ana, CA 92704, (800) 248-6200 and (714) 540-4777. Custom magnets, noteholders in a variety of shapes and sizes for use in promoting products from

books to cereals. Has imprinting facilities to print your information; used by corporations, hospitals, newspapers, etc.

2) Lite-R-Line, 1819 Main Street, Sarasota, FL 34236-4703, (813) 365-1600. Leading advertising specialty supplier. Wendy LaMacchia, Product Manager, suggests you consider low cost, highly visible specialties for self-promotion. Giveaways such as emery boards, magnets, and keychains enable you to reach a large volume of prospective customers at a relatively low cost. She does not sell directly and suggests that you contact your local specialty advertising distributor for information on Lite-R-Line's accessories for promotion. Check the Yellow Pages.

3) D & J Manufacturing Co., 4758 Angola Road, Toledo, OH 43615; (800) 634-5982 and (419) 382-1327. The company manufactures keyrings for advertising promotions for use in a variety of industries. I had keyrings made that said: "Unlock the Key to Getting Your Book Published! Read For All The Write Reasons by Patricia Gallagher. (215) 364-1945"

52) *Where can you get an author's photo taken?*

Originally for my Doubleday book jacket, I just looked in the Yellow Pages for a portrait studio and asked them to take a picture. Unfortunately, at that point, I did not know about proper make-up and lighting. The picture really wasn't very good.

I would recommend that you call a photographer who photographs models. Gale Photographers in Philadelphia did mine. Their phone number is (215) 629-0506. They guided me as to the best look, did my make-up professionally, and gave me a contact sheet to select from. I am very happy with all aspects of their service. The cost was about $200.

Other authors have told me about sources for black and white glossy photos. Mention you heard about them in this book.

1) ABC Pictures, 1867 E. Florida Street, Springfield MO 65803; (417) 869-9433. Approximate costs: 4 x 5 B&W, minimum order 2,000 — $80.00 and 8 x 10 B&W, minimum order 500 — $65.00

2) Ornaal Glossies, 24 W. 25th Street, New York, NY 10010; (800) 826-6312. Very reasonable prices for 4 x 5 glossies

3) Midwest Photo Company, P.O. Box 686, Omaha, NB 68101-0686; (800) 228-7208 and (402) 734-7200. They offer complete services for black and white, transparencies, and enlargements. Perhaps the cover of your book could be enlarged for trade shows or speaking engagements. They could also photograph the cover of your book and make prints in quantity to be included in press kits.

4) Kirk Kleinschmidt, 746 East Street, Box 1987, New Britain, CT 06050; (203) 827-9077. Kirk Kleinschmidt produces a really nice full-color postcard of your book cover and on the back side prints ordering information, author bio, your distributor's information, or whatever you request. Evelyn Clark Mott, who is the author of Steam Train Ride, had about 2,000 printed for about $139.95. They were really a nice promotional handout and an easy way to announce your book. You could write and request the Postcard Packet and info about any of his other services for authors.

53) Do you have any ideas that will increase the chances of being invited as a guest on a television show? Any advice on what to do once you're invited?

Rick Frishman of Planned Television Arts, a New York City publicity firm, offers the following tips:

1) Producers look for a guest who is articulate, takes control of the interview, and, most importantly, talks about a subject that is interesting and useful to their audience. They always consider a guest by asking, "Will my audience care about this subject?"

2) You must have a great subject, deliver a super press kit, and, if you can afford it, it would help to hire a good publicist who knows the producers well.

3) If you give the audience good information and are also entertaining, then there is no problem "plugging" your book.

4) Ask the producer to get the host to mention and show your book. It is better if they talk about the book. That way, you don't appear to be a "pushy" author.

5) Follow-up is the most important part of getting the booking. Producers receive hundreds of books a week. Your follow-up call

will make it... or break it. Remember they are interviewing an author—a person— not a book!

6) Guests are not paid to be on shows. They are on for the value of publicity. No money changes hands.

7) Men — business suit and tie. Women — nice dress, solid, red, purple, ... These days the cameras are so good, almost any color will come out fine.

8) Take control of the interview—know your subject inside out—have statistics and anecdotes—be entertaining.

54) *Is there a toll free 800 phone number to order the book,* **For All the Write Reasons?**

Yes, all of Patricia Gallagher's books are available by calling (800) ALL-BOOK. You may use your credit card. If you have any difficulty finding my books, please call me at (215) 364-1945. All of my books are available for fundraisers at quantity discounts. I love to speak for writers' groups and conferences. Please call for fees and schedules.

Tips From Successful People

I asked famous people if they had any words of inspration or helpful advice that they could offer the readers of *For All The Write Reasons*. Here are some of their responses....

William Parkhurst
Author of the Foreword and *True Detectives*

WPVI|TV

6

Maybe one reason I have a hard time recog-
nizing the enviable extent of my accomplishments in TV is that I am still "putting on a
show in my mother's livingroom." Literally. And
half-a-million other livingrooms too, certainly. But, having built my entire broadcasting
career in my hometown of Philadelphia—where all
the people who ever taught and helped me live—I
just put all my focus on an honest day's work
for an honest day's pay. The talent was a gift
to me. The effort is just the pipeline for
distribution. So far—for a woman who is no
"Barbie doll"—it has rewarded me with 14 years
in daily broadcasting and seven full years of
high-profile success. I don't know any
shortcuts except one: winning the lottery. (And
I play every week.)

Trisha, I am so excited for your success. I
can still picture myself at your day care
center near King of Prussia [PA] holding
strangers' kids and praying I could handle it
calmly for a couple of "takes". Now *I'm* a happy
mom who plays with toy trucks all weekend long.
Go figure!

Lizabeth Starr
Co-Host of AM Philadelphia

I was leaving as managing editor of my little newspaper in Mid-Missouri, going to what I thought was the big league of journalism, The Courier-Journal in Louisville, KY, and wondering if I would be good enough. An Associated Press bureau chief who had been my unofficial mentor took me to lunch one day, and I was amazed to discover that he had no doubts at all that I was good enough. He seemed to take my success as something that was predestined, and he suggested that I do the same. Moral of story: listen to the people who believe in you and believe what they say.

DARRELL SIFFORD

Courier Times
July 24, 1991

Trish:

This is more than a couple of sentences. If too long, let me know.
I can try a different approach.

Good luck with the book. I wish I had your ambition and time. Maybe
when I retire I will do something with a book. Old columns to be
reprinted, if nothing else.

Thanks for the opportunity to be included.

Sincerely,

Joe Halberstein
Associate Editor

I am a believer in the adage that many times it is important to be
in the right place at the right time and to do the right thing.

I was a junior majoring in journalism at Ohio State University in the
spring of 1943. J-students one Saturday were permitted to publish the
Columbus, Ohio, Citizen, a Scripps-Howard newspaper. I was to be the
sports editor.

My task was to cover the Columbus Redbirds baseball team's game. That
night, Joe Garagiola, one of the anchors on the Today television show,
was catching his first game as a 16-year-old. I wrote a lead combining
his debut, my debut and the veteran pitcher, Preacher Roe, that Garagiola
caught, and my mentor, sports editor Lew Byrer.

I was offered a full-time job the next day. Forty-eight years later,
I'm still writing.

Los Angeles Features Syndicate

• Midwest Office •
650 Winnetka Mews, Suite 110 • Winnetka, Illinois 60093

Alice O'Neill, Senior Editor

Aug. 1, 1991

Dear Patricia,

I folled the oldest advice ever given in the field of writing: write what you know intimately. I was a film extra and like a fly on the wall, saw and heard what went on behind the scenes in Hollywood. My "Live from Hollywood" column was the result.

In 1985 I sold the column to my hometown newspaper, then gradually sold to more dailies, weeklies and monthlies. Today, "Live from Hollywood" appears in 100 publications and is syndicated by Los Angeles Features Syndicate.

Two years ago I married a businessman from Chicago, so I moved my business operations to the Midwest, where I manage much of the company's business and write my column. Regular trips to Hollywood and a hot phone line keep me abreast of what's happening back on my old beat.

Good luck with the book. Sounds like a good idea.

Yours truly,

Having made and lost three fortunes in my
lifetime... I learned that the only thing that
could bring me down was a negative attitude.
Call me an eternal optimist, but my positive,
persevering attitude helped me net my fourth
fortune of $8 million when I sold my plastics
company in 1969.

I'm now a full-time philanthropist and live
by my motto: "He who gives while he lives, also
knows where it goes!"

— Percy Ross

NATIONAL REVIEW·150 East 35th Street, New York, New York 10016
Tel. 679-7330

WILLIAM F. BUCKLEY, JR.

July 29, 1991

Dear Miss Gallagher:

I'm afraid I can't be much help to you, because success,
measured by the finding of a publisher, came very easily to me: I
sent my book on Yale to Henry Regnery and he accepted it within a
week. I have never since then had any problem in finding a
publisher so please forgive me. In the event these words are
useful to you for whatever reason, feel free to use them. If you
want a picture of me, ring Frances Bronson in my office. With all
good wishes,

                    Yours cordially,

                    Wm. F. Buckley Jr.

Miss Patricia C. Gallagher
Gallagher, Jordan & Assoc.
P.O. Box 555
Worcester, PA 19490

JAMES JACKSON KILPATRICK
POST OFFICE BOX 957
CHARLESTON, SOUTH CAROLINA 29402-0957
(803) 577-4123

1 August 1991

Dear Patricia Gallagher--

      The best way that I know of for a writer
to get her book published is to establish a
reputation that will cause a publisher to come calling.
Otherwise, it's a matter of talent, perseverance,
and luck.

      Best wishes,

James J. Kilpatrick

P.C. Gallagher,
Gallagher, Jordan & Associates,
P.O. Box 555,
Worcester, PA   19490

JJK:eqr

Contributors

For author presentations, catalogs, book orders, or information about specific projects, you may write to the contributors of *For All the Write Reasons*.

Name	Address
Lou Alpert	P.O. Box 2159 Dept. PG Halesite, NY 11743-2159
Joan Wester Anderson	P.O. Box 1694 Dept. PG Arlington Heights, IL 60006
Becky Barker	P.O. Box 72666 Dept. PG Corpus Christi, TX 78472
Jean Horton Berg	207 Walnut St. Dept. PG Wayne, PA 19087
Jane Bluestein	160 Washington S.E. Suite 64 Dept. PG Albuquerque, NM 87108
Barbara Brabec	P.O. Box 2137 Dept. PG Naperville, IL 60567
Julie Adams Church	33 East Circle Dept. PG Oakland, CA 94611
Gloria T. Delamar	7303 Sharpless Rd. Dept. PG Melrose Park, PA 19126-1810
Paula DuPont-Kidd - Editor PDK Communications	P.O. Box 52202 Dept. PG Philadelphia, PA 19111
Mary Flower	600 West End Ave. Suite 10D Dept. PG New York, NY 10024
Patricia C. Gallagher Gallagher, Jordan & Assoc.	P.O. Box 555 Dept. PG Worcester, PA 19490

Peggy Glenn

1106 Main St. Dept. PG
Huntington Beach, CA 92648

Michelle S. Gluckow
Book-mart Press

2001 Forty Second Street, PG
North Bergen, NJ 07047

Teresa Griffin

P.O. Box 2 Dept. PG
Richboro, PA 18954

Jane Dewey Heald

420 Rutgers Ave. Dept. PG
Swarthmore, PA 19081

Jeff Herman

500 Greenwich St.
Suite 501 C Dept. PG
New York, NY 10013

April Hubbard

12 Amaranth Dr. Dept. PG
Newark, DE 19791

Michael Hoehne

201 N. Broad Street Dept. PG
Doylestown, PA 18901

Priscilla Huff

111 Almont Rd. Dept. PG
Sellersville, PA 18960

Evelyn Kaye

147 Sylvan Ave. Dept. PG
Leonia, NJ 07605

Kate Kelly

11 Rockwood Dr. Dept. PG
Larchmont, NY 10538

John Kremer

51 N. 5th St. Dept. PG
P.O. Box 1102
Fairfield, IA 52556-1102

Vicki Lansky

18326 Minnetonka Blvd. PG
Deephaven, MN 55391

Jeffrey Lant

50 Follen St.
Suite 507 Dept. PG
Cambridge, MA 02138

Judy Lawrence

P.O. Box 13167 Dept. PG
Albuquerque, NM 87192

Dorie Lenz - WPHL-TV

5001 Wynnefield Ave. Dept. PG
Philadelphia, PA 19131

Carol J. Manna

P.O. Box 3301 Dept. PG
Skokie, IL 60076

Claire Jordan Mohan

P.O. Box 265 Dept. PG
Worcester, PA 19490

Evelyn Clarke Mott

45 West Afton Ave. Dept. PG
Yardley, PA 19067

William Parkhurst

311 W. 75th Street
New York, NY 10023
(212) 580-9390

Doris Patterson

152 Grandview Rd. Dept. PG
Ardmore, PA 19003

Jean Ross Peterson

1259 El Camino Real
Suite 221 Dept. PG
Menlo Park, CA 94025

Diane Pfeifer

P.O. Box 52404 Dept. PG
Atlanta, GA 30355-0404

Dan Poynter

P.O. Box 4232-823 Dept. PG
Santa Barbara, CA 93140-4232

Tom & Marilyn Ross

P.O. Box 1500 Dept. PG
425 Cedar St.
Buena Vista, CO 81211

Marcia Routburg

P.O. Box 59730 Dept. PG
Chicago, IL 60645

Catherine Thomas Skwara

651 Rising Sun Ave. Dept. PG
Holland, PA 18966

Rita Tarmin

P.O. Box 260 Dept. PG
Eagleville, PA 19408

Charlotte E. Thompson, M.D.

2000 Van Ness Ave.
Suite 307 Dept. PG
San Francisco, CA 94109

Frances Weaver

P.O. Box 970 Dept. PG
Saratoga Springs, NY 12866

Jane Williams   P.O. Box 1014 Dept. PG
                                 Placerville, CA 95667-1014

James Lee Young   1450 S. Havana
                                 Suite 620 Dept. PG
                                 Aurora, CO 80012

About the Cover Designer

Ted Slampyak is a freelance designer and illustrator who lives in Warminster, Pa. His credits include album covers and posters for Chrysalis and Warner Bros. Records, an ad campaign for Philadelphia Advertising Committee, and posters for Electronics Boutique.

Currently, Ted works in the field of comic books. His series Jazz Age Chronicles is available in comic book specialty shops nationwide, and he's also working on other projects.

Ted Slampyak is available on a freelance basis for book cover design and book illustration, and he can be reached at (215) 672-0324.

About the Editor

Only in a book like *For All the Write Reasons* can one find the common denominator among mothers, doctors, scholars, lawyers, illustrators, parachutists, entrepreneurs, historians, chefs, teachers, and TV personalities. Writing is the common denominator, empowering people of all walks of life to express themselves.

Paula DuPont-Kidd

Like the other contributors in this book, I, too, share those ingrained writer qualities that compel me to scribble notes in the middle of the night, to defend the First Amendment when the occasion arises, and to yearn to learn as much about writing as possible. Like you, I'm a writer who hates to turn my precious copy over to an editor. For this reason, as an editor, I approach editing like a peace activist in an inevitable war: keeping casualties down to the least amount to get the job done.

Working with Trisha Gallagher was more than a typical writer-editor relationship. With her heavy-hitter ideas and boundless energy, she has pushed out the walls of conventional approaches to writing and publishing and created a new architecture for the industry. When she first approached me with twenty diverse authors' chapters and asked me to "not really change the authors' voices, but somehow make them cohesive," I knew it would be a challenge. What I didn't count on was learning as much as I did from a single source about the writing-marketing-publishing industry. The fact that Trisha was so adamant about each author telling his or her story themselves instead of drawing from them and writing it herself, was a great call.

Rich in diversity and readability, each chapter's author offers wisdom from the most competent perspective: their's. Who better to tell how a literary agent works than a literary agent? Who knows the ropes better to publishing a children's book than a published children's author?

More than informing, educating, and entertaining, *For All the Write Reasons* goes beyond by inspiring the reader to put the book down and run to the typewriter.

Through PDK Communications, I have helped authors like Trisha who want to publish their marketable messages in a unique voice. With more than ten years of journalism and media experience, I have written everything from features and news stories to press releases, brochures, and book chapters.

Paula DuPont-Kidd lives with her husband, Michael, and two "archangels," Michael-Paul and Gabrielle in Philadelphia, Pa. Currently, she is writing and editing for a major corporation and individual clients as well as working on her own book.

About the Author

Need a Speaker? Author, Child Care Expert, Publishing Consultant?

After leaving her corporate position at AT&T to care for her children at home, Patricia Gallagher decided to combine her business savvy with her love for children. She began a child care center out of her home and has turned the years of experience into six books, numerous journal articles, pamphlets, and publications.

Patricia C. Gallagher

Start Your Own At-Home Child Care Business, So You Want to Open a Profitable Day Care Center, Nature and More... Let's Go Explore, Get Up and Go with Your Kids, and How to Entertain Children at Home or in Preschool, have served as guidelines for those interested in starting a day care center and keeping children entertained and educated through learning, leisure, and recreational activities.

This mother of four was selected as the product spokesperson for "OFF! Skintastic" insect repellent which was recently introduced by S. C. Johnson Wax, offers seminars and workshops for parents, teachers, and administrators on a variety of topics related to child care and early childhood development activities, and frequently presents publishing workshops for new and experienced writers.

After earning a BA in Early Childhood and Elementary Education and an MBA in Finance and Management, Trisha enjoyed many professions which include being an Elementary School Teacher, College Instructor, Preschool Director, and Day Care Mother.

Regarded as one of the country's top child care consultants, Mrs. Gallagher has been a featured guest on the Oprah Winfrey Show, Sally Jessy Raphael, People Are Talking, Hour Magazine, FNN, and CNN. Articles about Trisha Gallagher's expertise have also been featured in over 100 national and local magazines and newspapers.

Trisha Gallagher and her husband, John, currently reside in Richboro, Pennsylvania, with their four children, Kristen, Katelyn, Robin, and Ryan.

She is a member of several writers' associations, including COSMEP, Publishers' Marketing Association, National Writers Group, and is president of Bucks-Mont Writers Network. She has also been a speaker for the Spring Conference of the American Society of Journalists and Authors and Book Pub World, sponsored by Publishers Weekly. Phone (215) 364-1945.

Appendix

This Appendix lists a sampling of various types of resources for authors, taken from the directories and other sources listed throughout this book. Reprinted with permission from R. R. Bowker. For additional detailed listings in each of these categories, please see the current year Literary Marketplace in your library.

MAGAZINES FOR THE TRADE

ABA Newswire
American Booksellers
Association
11th Floor
137 W 25th St.
New York, NY 10001-7201
(212) 463-8450

American Bookseller
American Booksellers
Association
137 W. 25th St.
New York, NY 10001
(212) 463-8450

Authorship
National Writers Club
Suite 620
1450 S. Havana
Aurora, CO 80012
(303) 751-7844

Publishers Weekly
249 W. 17th St.
New York, NY 10011
(212) 463-6758

The Small Press Book Review
Box 176
Southport, CT 06490
(203) 268-4878

Small Press Review
Dustbooks
Box 100
Paradise, CA 95967
(916) 877-6110

Small Press: The Magazine and Book Review of Independent Publishing
Meckler Publishing
11 Ferry Lane West
Westport, CT 06880
(203) 226-6967

Library Journal
Cahners Publishing Company
249 W. 17th St.
New York, NY 10011
(212) 463-6822

COSMEP Newsletter
COSMEP Inc.
Box 42073
San Francisco, CA 94142
(415) 922-9490

Horn Book Magazine
Horn Book Inc.
14 Beacon St.
Boston, MA 02108
(617) 227-1555

Huenefeld Report
Huenefeld Company, Inc.
Box 665
Bedford, MA 01730
(617) 861-9650

The Writer
The Writer Inc.
120 Boyleston St.
Boston, MA 02116
(617) 423-3157

Writer's Digest
F & W Publications
1507 Dana Ave.
Cincinnati, OH 45207
(513) 531-2222

Writer's Journal
Minnesota Ink Inc.
Box 9148
North St. Paul, MN 55109
(612) 433-3626

WRITERS CONFERENCES & WORKSHOPS

American Society of Journalists & Authors Annual Writers' Conference
Suite 1907
1501 Broadway
New York, NY 10036
(212) 997-0947

American Women in Radio & TV
Suite 700
1101 Connecticut Ave.
Washington, DC 20036
(202) 429-5102

Christian Writers' Conference & Workshop
Christian Writers Institute
388 E. Gunderson Dr.
Wheaton, IL 60188
(708) 653-4200

NWC Annual Conference
The National Writers Club
Suite 620
1450 S. Havana
Aurora, CO 80012
(303) 751-7844

Professional Development Seminar
Canadian Book Publishers'
  Council
Suite 203
250 Merton St.
Toronto, ON M4S 1B1
Canada
(416) 322-7011

St. David's Christian Writers' Conference
St. David's Christian Writers'
  Associations
1775 Eden Rd.
Lancaster, PA 17601
(215) 341-5800

Women in Communications National Professional Conference
Box 17460
Arlington, VA 22216
(703) 528-4200

Writers Conference
Writers Digest School
1507 Dana Ave.
Cincinnati, OH 45207
(800) 759-0963

Writers Workshop in Children's Literature
Society of Children's Book
  Writers, Florida Chapter
Apt. 103
2000 Springdale Blvd.
Palm Springs, FL 33461
(407) 433-1727

Writing for the Computer Industry
Massachusetts Institute of
Technology
The Writing Program
14E 310
Cambridge, MA 02139
(617) 253-2101

WHOLESALERS

Baker & Taylor Books
Division of W. R. Grace & Co.
Box 6920
652 E. Main St.
Bridgewater, NJ 08807-0920
(201) 218-0400
Southern Division
Mount Olive Road
Commerce, GA 30599-9988
(404) 335-5000
Midwestern Division
501 S. Gladiolas St.
Momence, IL 60954-1799
(815) 472-2444
Eastern Division
50 Kirby Ave.
Sommerville, NJ 08876-0734
(201) 722-8000
Western Division
380 Edison Way
Reno, NV 89564-0099
(702) 786-6700

Ballen Booksellers International Inc.
125 Ricefield Lane
Hauppauge, NY 11788
(516) 543-5600

Blackwell North America, Inc.
Bldg. G
6024 SW Jean Rd.
Lake Oswego, OR 97035
(503) 684-1140

The Book House Inc.
208 W. Chicago St.
Jonesville, MI 49250
(800) 248-1146

Bookazine Co. Inc.
303 W. Tenth St.
New York, NY 10014
(800) 221-8112

Publishers Distribution Service
121 E. Front St. Suite 203
Travers City, MI 49684
(616) 929-3410

Brodart Co.
500 Arch St.
Williamsport, PA 17705
(800) 233-8467

The Distributors
702 S. Michigan
South Bend, In 46618
(800) 348-5200

Emery-Pratt Co.
1966 W. Main St.
Owosso, MI 48867
(800) 248-3887

Ingram Book Co.
1125 Heil Quaker Blvd.
LaVergne, TN 37086
(800) 759-5000

LITERARY & WRITERS ASSOCIATIONS

American Society of Journalists & Authors
Suite 1907
1501 Broadway
New York, NY 10036
(212) 997-0947

Associated Writing Programs
Old Dominion University
Norfolk, VA 23529
(804) 683-3839

Authors Guild
234 W. 44th St.
New York, NY 10036
(212) 398-0838

382 Appendix — Resources

Canadian Authors Association
Suite 104
121 Avenue Rd.
Toronto, ON M5R 2G3
Canada
(416) 926-8084

Christian Writers Guild
260 Fern Lane
Hume, CA 93628
(209) 335-2333

Council of Writers Organizations
17000 Executive Plaza Drive
Dearborn, MI 48126
(213) 301-8546

Mystery Writers of America Inc.
Suite 600
236 W. 27th St.
New York, NY 10001
(212) 255-7005

National League of American Pen Women
Pen Arts Building
1300 17th St. NW
Washington, DC 20036
(202) 785-1997

The National Writers Club Inc.
Suite 620
1450 S. Havana
Aurora, CO 80012
(303) 751-7844

PEN American Center
568 Broadway
New York, NY 10012
(212) 334-1660

SELECTED TELEVISION STATIONS WITH NEWS BUREAUS

The following listings were reprinted with permission from 1990 News Bureau Contacts and 1990 Syndicated Columnists Contacts. For additional detailed listings, please see these annual directories which are published by BPI Communications, Inc. These directories are designed to assist publicists, journalists, editors, librarians, authors, and others.

ABC Channel 7
7 West 66th St.
New York, NY 10023
(212) 456-7777

KABC (ABC) Channel 7
4151 Prospect Ave.
Los Angeles, CA 90027
(213) 668-2800

KCBS (CBS) Channel 2
6121 Sunset Boulevard
Los Angeles, CA 90028
(213) 460-3000

KPNX (NBC) Channel 12
KPNX Building
P.O. Box 711
1101 North Central Avenue
Phoenix, AZ 85001
(602) 257-1212

KTVB (NBC) Channel 7
P.O. Box 7
Boise, ID 83707
(208) 375-7277

WFSB (CBS) Channel 3
3 Constitution Plaza
Hartford, CT 06103
(203) 728-3333

WGRZ (NBC/CNN)
259 Delaware Ave.
Buffalo, NY 14202
(716) 856-1414

WPLG (ABC) Channel 10
3900 Biscayne Blvd.
Miami, FL 33137
(305) 576-1010

WSVN (NBC) Channel 7
Sunbeam Television Corp.
1401 79th Causeway
Miami, FL 33141
(305) 751-6692

WTNH (ABC) Channel 8
8 Elm Street
New Haven, CT 06510
(203) 784-8888

WXIA (NBC) Channel 11
1611 W. Peachtree St. NE
Atlanta, GA 30309
(404) 892-1611

SELECTED NEWS SERVICES

The Associated Press
50 Rockefeller Plaza
New York, NY 10020
(212) 621-1500

The Associated Press
P.O. Box 2553
Birmingham, AL 35202
(205) 251-4221

The Associated Press
Suite 102
750 W. Second Ave.
Anchorage, AK 99501
(907) 272-7549

Gannett News Service
Gannett Company, Inc.
P.O. Box 7858
Washington, DC 20044
(703) 276-5800

Gannett News Service
Press Room Capitol
Harrisburg, PA 17120
(717) 783-3763

Gannett News Service
Room 205
336 East College Avenue
Tallahassee, FL 32301
(904) 222-8384

The Hearst Corporation
959 Eighth Avenue
New York, NY 10019
(212) 649-2000

Knight-Ridder Newspapers
One Herald Plaza
Miami, FL 33132-1693
(305) 376-3800

McGraw-Hill News
1211 Avenue of the Americas
New York, NY 10020
(212) 512-4005

Morris News Service
Suite 550
1 CNN Center, South Tower
Atlanta, GA 30303
(404) 589-8424

SELECTED SELF-SYNDICATORS

Do You Agree?
Anita Sumner
619 Oakwood Court
Westbury, NY 11590
(516) 333-4822

Nine To Five Woman
Mary Margaret Carberry
1349 Douglas Ave.
Flossmoor, IL 60422
(312) 799-6360

Review of Books
J. J. Edwards
International Businessman News
    Bureau
5595 Rockefeller Center Station
New York, NY 10185
(212) 503-0802

Video News and Notes/Technology
Sid Holt, Editor
c/o Rolling Stone
745 Fifth Avenue
New York, NY 10151
(212) 758-3800

Entertainment News
  Lee Caanan, Editor
  310 East 44th Street
  New York, NY 10017
  (800) 553-1338

VIP Medical Grapevine
  Ruth Nathan Anderson
  161 Nasa Circle
  Round Lake, IL 60073
  (312) 546-6557

What's New in Medicine
  L. A. Chotkowski, M.D., FACP
  1143 Chamberlain Highway
  Kensington, CT 06037

Managing Your Money
  Merle E. Dowd
  7438 SE 40th Street
  Mercer Island, WA 98040
  (206) 232-2171

Mort Olshan's Sports Features
  Mort Olshan
  Suite 200
  9255 Sunset Blvd.
  Los Angeles, CA 90069
  (213) 274-0848

SYNDICATOR PACKAGES

NEW CARS SPECIAL PACKAGE

United Press International
  1400 Eye Street NW
  Washington, DC 20005
  (202) 898-8200

FAMILY PACKAGE

Copley News Service
  P.O. Box 190
  San Diego, CA 92112
  (800) 445-4555

EDUCATION PACKAGE

Copley News Service
  P.O. Box 190
  San Diego, CA 92112
  (800) 445-4555

United Press International
  1400 Eye Street NW
  Washington, DC 20005
  (202) 898-8200

DECORATING PACKAGE

United Press International
  1400 Eye Street NW
  Washington, DC 20005
  (202) 898-8200

BUSINESS PACKAGE

Copley News Service
  P.O. Box 190
  San Diego, CA 92112
  (800) 445-4555

BOOKS PACKAGE

United Features Syndicate
  200 Park Avenue
  New York, NY 10166
  (212) 692-3700

AUTOMOTIVE PACKAGE

Copley News Service
  P.O. Box 190
  San Diego, CA 92112
  (800) 445-4555

HOBBIES PACKAGE

Copley News Service
  P.O. Box 190
  San Diego, CA 92112
  (800) 445-4555

RETIREMENT PACKAGE

Copley News Service
P.O. Box 190
San Diego, CA 92112
(800) 445-4555

DAILY NEWSPAPERS

Edwardsville Intelligencer
117 North 2nd Street
Edwardsville, IL 62025
(618) 656-4700

The Journal Gazette
P.O. Box 88
Fort Wayne, IN 46801
(219) 461-8333

The Wichita Eagle-Beacon
c/o Knight-Ridder
700 National Press Building
529 14th Street NW
Washington, DC 20045
(202) 383-6000

The Kentucky Post
421 Madison Ave.
Covington, KY 41011
(606) 292-2600

Boston Globe
South Weekly Edition
Lincoln Trust Bldg.
Route 53, 1165 Washington
Hanover, MA 02339
(617) 826-1000

Boston Globe
10 Rockefeller Plaza
New York, NY 10020
(212) 333-2493

Boston Herald
1 Herald Square
Boston, MA 02106
(617) 426-3000

New York Post
210 South Street
New York, NY 10002
(212) 815-8000

Philadelphia Inquirer
400 North Broad Street
Philadelphia, PA 19130
(215) 854-2000

The Dallas Morning News
P.O. Box 655237
Dallas, TX 75265
(214) 977-8222

CATHOLIC MEDIA

Reprinted with permission from the Catholic Press Directory, 1990. For additional detailed listings in each of these categories, please see current year Catholic Press Directory, published annually by Catholic Press Association, 119 North Park Avenue, Rockville Center, NY 11570.

NEWSLETTERS

The Angel Guardian Herald
6301 12th Avenue
Brooklyn, NY 11219
(718) 232-1500

Archdiocesan Bulletin
827 N. Franklin St.
Philadelphia, PA 19123
(215) 627-0143

Benedictine Orient
2400 Maple Avenue
Lisle, IL 60532
(312) 968-4264

Bringing Religion Home
205 W. Monroe St.
Chicago, IL 60606
(312) 236-7782

Catholic League Newsletter
1100 W. Wells St.
Milwaukee, WI 53233
(414) 289-0170

Catholic Trends
3211 Fourth St. NE
Washington, DC 20017
(202) 541-3250

Catholic Update
1615 Republic St.
Cincinnati, OH 45210
(513) 241-5615

Christian Foundation for Children
& Aging
I3001 Wornall Road
Kansas City, MO 64145
(816) 941-9100

Communications Update
P.O. Box 24000
Jacksonville, FL 32241
(904) 262-3200

Crux of the News
75 Champlain St.
Albany, NY 12204
(518) 465-4591

MAGAZINES

Catholic Digest
P.O. Box 64090
St. Paul, MN 55164
(612) 647-5296

Catholic Forester Magazine
425 W. Shuman Blvd.
Naperville, IL 60566
(312) 983-4920

The Catholic Pharmacist
1012 Surrey Hills Dr.
St. Louis, MO 63117
(314) 645-0085

Catholic Press Directory
119 North Park Avenue
Rockville Center, NY 11570
(516) 766-3400

Catholic Singles Magazine
8408 S. Muskegon
Chicago, IL 60617
(312) 731-8769

Catholic Teen Magazine
P.O. Box 1463
Havertown, PA 19083
(215) 564-6576

Catholic Workman
111 West Main
P.O. Box 47
New Prague, MN 56071
(612) 758-2229

The Catholic World
997 Macarthur Blvd.
Mahwah, NJ 07430
(201) 825-7300

The Jesuit Bulletin
4511 W. Pine Blvd.
St. Louis, MO 63108
(314) 361-3388

Liguorian
1 Liguori
Liguori, MO 63057
(314) 464-2500

CATHOLIC BOOK CLUBS

Catholic Book Club
106 W. 56th St.
New York, NY 10019
(212) 581-4640

Catholic Digest Book Club
Suite 1268
475 Riverside Drive
New York, NY 10115
(212) 870-2552

Clergy Book Service
12855 Silver Spring Drive
Butler, WI 53007
(414) 781-1234

Orbis Book Club
Walsh Building
Maryknoll, NY 10545
(914) 941-7590

Thomas More Book Club
205 W. Monroe
Chicago, IL 60606
(312) 951-2100

Spiritual Book Associates
Notre Dame, IN 46556
(219) 287-2838

RELIGIOUS PRESS ASSOCIATIONS

Associated Church Press
P.O. Box 306
Geneva, IL 60134
(312) 232-1055

Canadian Church Press
The Link and Visitor
Unit 12
35 Waterman Ave.
London, ON N6C 5T2
Canada

Evangelical Press Association
P.O. Box 4550
Overland Park, KS 66204

American Jewish Press Association
11313 Old Club Road
Rockville, MD 20852
(301) 881-4113

Catholic Press Association
119 North Road Avenue
Rockville Center, NY 11570

GENERAL PUBLISHERS

Abbey Press
Saint Meinrad, IN 47577
(812) 357-8011

American Catholic Press
16160 South Seton Drive
South Holland, IL 60473
(312) 331-5485

BROWN Publishing – ROA Media
P.O. Box 539
Dubuque, IA 52004
(319) 588-1451

Catholic Book Publishing Corp.
257 West 17th Street
New York, NY 10011
(212) 243-4515

Catholic News Service
3211 4th Street NE
Washington, DC 20017
(202) 541-3250

Charisma Press
459 River Rd.
Andover, MA 01810
(508) 851-7910

Clarity Publishing Inc.
75 Champlain St.
Albany, NY 12204
(518) 465-4591

Daughters of Saint Paul
50 St. Pauls Ave.
Boston, MA 02130
(617) 522-8911

Doubleday Division, Bantam Doubleday, Dell Publishing Corp.
666 Fifth Avenue
New York, NY 10103
(212) 984-7238

Franciscan Mission Associates
P.O. Box 598
Mount Vernon, NY 10551
(914) 664-5604

SELECTED MEDIA INFORMATION

The following listings are reprinted with permission from 1991 Working Press of the Nation. For additional detailed listings which include name and address, publishing company, circulation, frequency of publication, wire services, publicity materials requirements, and editors names, please see the current year Working Press of the Nation directories (Volumes 1 through 5) which may be located in the reference section of a library.

Jacksonville Daily News
116 W. Hickory
Jacksonville, AR 72076
(501) 982-6506

Daily Ledger
1650 Cavallo Road
Antioch, CA 94509
(415) 757-2525

Colorado Springs Gazette Telegraph
30 S. Prospect
Colorado Springs, CO 80903
(719) 632-5511

Clearwater Sun
P.O. Box 2078
Clearwater, FL 34617
(813) 462-2000

The Florida Times–Union
1 Riverside Avenue
Jacksonville, FL 32202
(904) 359-4111

Peoria Journal Star
1 News Plaza
Peoria, IL 61643
(309) 686-3000

The State Journal Register
One Copely Plaza
Springfield, IL 62705
(217) 788-1300

Des Moines Register
715 Locust
Des Moines, IA 50309
(515) 284-8000

Carson City Nevada Appeal
200 Bath St.
Carson City, NV 89703
(702) 882-2111

Las Vegas Review–Journal
1111 W. Bonanza
Las Vegas, NV 89125
(702) 383-0211

WEEKLY NEWSPAPERS

Bay City Valley Farmer
905 S. Henry
Bay City, MI 48706
(517) 893-6507

Japan Detroit Press
47900 W. Huron River Dr.
Belleville, MI 48111
(313) 697-4999

Pleasantville Mainland Journal
69-73 East West Jersey Avenue
Pleasantville, NJ 08232
(609) 641-3100

Waconia Patriot
124 West Main St.
Waconia, MN 55387
(612) 442-4414

Minnetonka Sailor
464 Second Street
Excelsior, MN 55331
(612) 474-0285

Mansfield Enterprise–Journal
202 Adams St.
Mansfield, LA 71052
(318) 872-0317

Stone Mountain – DeKalb Neighbor
827B North Hairston Road
Stone Mountain, GA 30083
(404) 292-5572

The Burlington News
120 Cambridge St.
Burlington, MA 01803
(617) 272-2369

Chicopee Herald
Depot Street Delta Park
Chicopee, MA 01013
(413) 592-9441

Fort Dix Post
HQS, USATC & Fort Dix
ATZD - PAC - 1
Trenton, NJ 08640
(609) 562-5890

RELIGIOUS NEWSPAPERS

BAPTIST

Southern Cross
700 Marion Way
San Diego, CA 92110
(619) 574-6393

L'Union
1 Social Street
Woonsocket, RI 02895
(401) 769-0520

CATHOLIC

Arlington Catholic Herald
Suite 614
200 N. Glebe Rd.
Arlington, VA 22203
(703) 841-2590

JEWISH / JUDAICA

The Jewish Floridan
2808 Horatio Street
Tampa, Fl 33609
(813) 872-4470

Baltimore Jewish Times
2104 N. Charles Street
Baltimore, MD 21218
(301) 752-3504

New York Jewish Daily Forward
45 E. 33rd Street
New York, NY 10016
(212) 889-8200

The Way – Ukranian Catholic Bi-
Weekly
827 N. Franklin St.
Philadelphia, PA 19123
(215) 922-5231

Pittsburgh Jewish Chronicle
5600 Baum Blvd.
Pittsburgh, PA 15206
(412) 687-1000

MENNONITE

Mennonite Weekly Review
129 W. 6th St.
Newton, KS 67114
(316) 283-3670

The Messenger
720 Madison Avenue
Covington, KY 41011
(606) 581-2271

NATIONAL NEWSPAPERS

The Christian Science Monitor
One Norway Street
Boston, MA 02115
(617) 450-2000

Journal of Commerce
110 Wall Street
New York, NY 10005
(212) 425-1616

The Wall Street Journal
New York Bureau
200 Liberty Street
New York, NY 10281

Chicago Bureau
21st Floor
One South Wacker Drive
Chicago, IL 60606
Philadelphia Bureau
121 South Broad Street
Philadelphia, PA 19107

Barron's National Business and Financial Weekly
200 Liberty
New York, NY 10281
(212) 416-2000

USA Today
1000 Wilson Blvd.
Arlington, VA 22209
(703) 276-3400
Atlanta Bureau
P.O. Box 77053
Atlanta, GA 30357
(404) 892-1611
Los Angeles Bureau
924 Westwood Blvd.
Los Angeles, CA 90024
(213) 208-6425
New York Bureau
6th Floor
535 Madison Avenue
New York, NY 10022
(212) 715-5410
San Francisco Bureau
Suite 908
1390 Market Street
San Francisco, CA 94102
(415) 861-3975

NEWSPAPER-DISTRIBUTED MAGAZINES

Dawn
628 N. Eutaw Street
Baltimore, MD 21201
(301) 728-8200
Editorial statement: A supplement to
45 Black newspapers across the country.

National Black Monitor
Penthouse C
410 Central park West
New York, NY 10025
(212) 222-3555

Parade Magazine
750 Third Avenue
New York, NY 10017
(212) 573-7000
Editorial statement: A Sunday
newspaper supplement, PARADE publishes feature articles that are oriented to
news, issues, and personalities. Areas of
interest include health, consumer issues,
the family, and communities that have
national application.

Pennywhistle Press
1000 Wilson Blvd.
Arlington, VA 22209
(703) 276-3796

USA Weekend
1000 Wilson Blvd.
Arlington, VA 22209
(703) 276-3400

SELECTED BOOK MANUFACTURERS

There are many additional book
manufacturers listed in Literary
Market Place. The book manufacturers listed below are a sampling of
the ones that authors in this book
have received quotes from. Please be
aware that there are many variables
to consider when selecting the best
printer for your particular project.
My personal experience has been
that the price range varied by as
much as $4.00 per book from the
lowest to the highest for exactly the
same project.

Book-mart Press
2001 Forty Second Street
North Bergen, NJ 07047
(201) 864-1887

Columbus Bookbinders & Printers, Inc.
P.O. Box 8193
1326 Tenth Avenue
Columbus, GA 31908
(800) 553-7314

Cushing-Malloy, Inc.
Box 8632, 1350 N. Main Street
Ann Arbor, MI 48107
(313) 663-8554

Delta Lithograph Co.
28210 North Avenue Stanford
Valencia, CA 91355

Edwards Brothers, Inc.
Box 1007
2500 S. State Street
Ann Arbor, MI 48106-1007

Griffin Printing and Lithograph Co., Inc.
544 W. Colorado Street
Glendale, CA 91204-1102

Horowitz-Rae Book Manufacturers, Inc.
Box 1308
300 Fairfield Road
Fairfield, NJ 07004

BookCrafters
P.O. Box 370
Chelsea, MI 48118

Adams Press
25 E. Washington Street
Chicago, IL 60602

Walsworth Publishing Co.
306 N. Kansas Ave.
Marceline, MO 64658

Malloy Lithographing Co.
5411 Jackson Road
P.O. Box 1124
Ann Arbor, MI 48106

Patterson Printing
1550 Territorial Road
Benton Harbor, MI 49022

Princeton University Press
3175 Princeton Pike
Lawrenceville, NJ 08648

R. R. Donnelley & Sons Co.
Suite 102
127 E. Main Street
Crawfordsville, IN 47933

Thomson-Shore, Inc.
7300 West Joy Road
P.O. Box 305
Dexter, MI 48130-0305

Arcata
Suite 311, GSB Bldg.
Bala Cynwyd, PA 19004

Other Resources and Sources

You may want to shop around your local area for some of these products and services. The people in this book have mentioned the following companies in their discussions with me so you may want to contact them for prices and see how they compare. Call and request prices and samples. Mention that you read about their company in this book—it may help you.

Color Impressions (800) 626-1333 (Bob): four color sell sheets, catalogs, postcards, etc.

Econocolor (800) 877-7405: specialize in full color direct mail pieces, response vehicles, coupons, and catalogs

Tu-vets Corporation (213) 723-4569: full color 8½ x 11 advertising flyers

Synergistic Data Systems, Inc. (California) (818) 351-7717 (Dale Schroeder): This company can produce camera ready pages from computer disks from your IBM and compatible files. Their equipment can read typeset, typed, xeroxed, or Fax documents

Publishers' Photographic Services (301) 750-6225 (John): photographs books for advertising, brochures, and catalogs. Ask for free catalog (does not print actual photos in quantity but takes a picture of your book which you have reproduced elsewhere)

Separacolor International, Inc. (800) 779-1158: color separation at low prices

Direct Press (800) 645-5302: full color flyers and sell sheets

Antioch Publishing (800) 543-2397: bookmarks

Quality Artwork (800) 523-2306: bookmarks

Ago Plastics (800) 344-4712 (Bill): business card cases that can be imprinted

Usher Candy Company (800) 531-7690 (Mr. Castillo): mint candy like you find in a hotel room imprinted, for giving out at trade shows, special events

Miller Bag Company (612) 378-3200 (Mike): imprinted canvas book bags

Amko Plastic Book Bags (800) 543-7030 (Mary)

Dove Enterprises (800) 233-DOVE: very reasonable for audio tape duplication

The Dub Center (800) 382-0080 (Nate Cohen): reasonable cost for video duplication

Evatone (800) EVA-TONE: duplication service

World in Color (607) 732-0715 (Patrick): reasonable for audio duplication

Planned Television Arts (212) 921-5111 (Rick Frishman): Public Relations Firm

Metro Creative Graphics (212) 947-5100 (Pat): supplier of promotional material for newspaper themed sections

The Cat's Pajamas (800) 462-8799: computer systems for publishers

Deborah Durham and Company 316 West 81st Street, New York, NY 10024: Product Spokesperson Network

Michael Hoehne, 201 N. Broad St., Doylestown, PA 18901, (215) 340-0993 comprehensive, computerized book design from your word processor files

Kirk Kleinschmidt, (203) 827-9077: photo business cards on card stock, 500 for $69.95 (request sample kit)

Paula Dupont Kidd (215) 289-5615: free lance writer, editor, ghost writer

Beverly Payton P.O. Box 2402, Warminster, PA 18974, (215) 364-1692: free lance writer, press releases.

Barbara Crawford, 171 Hillcroft Way, Newtown, PA 18940 (215) 968-6829: typesetting, design services, scanning of text. She has done brochures, flyers, and books for Claire Mohan, Teresa Griffin, and Patricia Gallagher who are all contributors in this book.

Susannah Thomer, (215) 279-9516: 29 Church Road Norristown, PA 19401: free lance illustrator, very easy to work with. Has done work for three people in this book: Claire Mohan, Teresa Griffin, and Patricia Gallagher

Publishers Distribution Service, 121 E. Front St, Travers City, MI 49684, (616) 929-3410: (Tim Schaub): Kickoff Kit, $99, with money-back guarantee, a comprehensive book marketing system for independent publishers which contains a complete how-to guide combined with specific promotion and distribution lead lists.

Yearbook of Experts, Authorities, and Spokespersons, 2233 Wisconsin Ave. NW #540, Washington, DC 20007, (202) 333-4904

KSB LINKS, 55 Honey Creek NE, Ada, MN 48130, (616) 676-0758: Publicity service for all types of authors and budgets. Call Karen or Doug for brochure. One of their special services is mailings to a list of reviewers, editors and producers.

Huenefeld Publicity Consultants, Box U, Bedford, MA 01730   Publishes a newsletter for publishers: THE HUENEFELD REPORT

Tools of the Trade, Box 12093, Seminary Post Office, Alexandria, VA 22304, (703) 823-1919: catalog of books for communicators, including a large selection of books for graphic designers,desktop publishing, journalism design

TOWERS CLUB NEWSLETTER, PO Box 2038, Vancouver, WA 98668 newsletter of interest to publishers and authors

Selected Reviewing Sources for Books

It is important to call the telephone numbers listed below before sending your galleys for review. Be sure to find out the contact name and ask for their current submission policies for your particular kind of book. Some review general interest titles while others only review children's books, college texts or particular specialties. This is just a sampling of review sources.

BOOKLIST (312) 944-6780   LIBRARY JOURNAL (212) 463-6819
HORN BOOK (617) 227-1555   CHOICE (203) 347-6933
PUBLISHERS WEEKLY (212) 463-6758
SCHOOL LIBRARY JOURNAL (212) 463-6759

ALSO AVAILABLE FROM
PATRICIA GALLAGHER

Would you like to hear audio taped interviews with some of the authors in this book as well as with other experts in the field?

Each audio tape is priced at $15. Titles available are:

EVERYTHING YOU WANT TO KNOW ABOUT SELF-PUBLISHING A BOOK BUT DIDN'T KNOW WHO TO ASK (60 minutes of information that will save you countless hours which means savings in time and money. Listen to this honest discussion of why authors selected a particular book manufacturer, would they do it again and what would they recommend to you in regards to pricing, publicity and promotion.)

INSIDERS SECRETS TO GETTING ON TELEVISION SHOWS AND WHAT REALLY GOES ON BEHIND THE SCENES (60 minutes of friendly conversation with authors who have been on national shows who tell you exactly how they interested a producer and the results of national media exposure. Also the inside scoop on how successful authors managed to get mentions in USA TODAY, GUIDEPOSTS, FAMILY CIRCLE and other major publications.)

HOW TO FIND A MAJOR PUBLISHER AND WIN! (60 minutes of solid advice for authors who want to be published by the major publishers. Before you sign on the dotted line and lose all of your publishing rights, listen to the experiences of authors who have been published. Don't make mistakes. Profit from their mistakes and get the best deal for yourself.

SPECIAL REPORTS FOR WRITERS — The advice in these invaluable reports are from the experts- people who have done it successfully.

- ✍ ADVICE ABOUT GETTING A CHILDREN'S BOOK PUBLISHED ($5.00)
- ✍ SHOULD I SELF-PUBLISH OR TRY FOR A MAJOR PUBLISHER? ($5.00)
- ✍ PITFALLS OF SELF-PUBLISHING ($5.00)
- ✍ MOST COMMON COMPLAINTS FROM PEOPLE WHO HAVE BEEN PUBLISHED BY THE MAJOR PUBLISHERS ($5.00)
- ✍ HOW TO GET YOUR PRESS RELEASES NOTICED AND PRINTED! ($5.00)
- ✍ HOW TO GET A COLUMN GOING IN MAGAZINES AND NEWSPAPERS ($5.00)
- ✍ BEING A RADIO TALK SHOW GUEST FROM YOUR OWN HOME ($5.00)
- ✍ HOW TO GET A FEATURE STORY WRITTEN ABOUT YOU IN THE NEWSPAPER ($5.00)

✍ DISCUSSION ABOUT HOW TO GET ARTICLES PUBLISHED IN MAGAZINES ($5.00)
✍ IF I HAD IT TO DO OVER AGAIN I WOULD... PUBLISHED AUTHORS TELL YOU THEIR TRUE FEELINGS ABOUT THEIR PUBLISHING EXPERIENCES ($5.00)

Make checks payable to Gallagher, Jordan and Associates, Box 555, Worcester, PA 19490
Special reports are $5.00 each, or all ten reports for $45.00.
Audio tapes are $15. each or all three for $40.
Special Offer: ORDER THE ABOVE SET OF THREE TAPES AND ALL SPECIAL REPORTS AND RECEIVE A FREE COPY OF THIS BOOK, *FOR ALL THE WRITE REASONS!* Simply send $45 plus $40 = $85.00 and you will receive three audio tapes, ten special reports, and a free copy of this book.

This book, *For All the Write Reasons*, is available at special quantity discounts for bulk purchases, sales promotions, fund-raising, premiums, school textbooks, and for seminars and conferences. For information on discounts, contact:
SPECIAL SALES DEPARTMENT
Young Sparrow Press
Box 265 PG
Worcester, PA 19490
(215) 364-1945

This book
is set in
Adobe Times Roman, Adobe Futura Book, and Adobe Courier
and was composed and designed on
Apple Macintosh computer equipment.
Masters were printed on
an Apple LaserWriter IINTX.
Software involved was
Microsoft Word and QuarkXPress.

Have You Called Our "Ask Trish Hotline"?
Individual Telephone Assistance

If you would like individual assistance via a "telephone consultation", Trish Gallagher is available to offer suggestions and advice in regard to self-publishing or finding a major publisher. If you are a novice or experienced author and would like to discuss your problems or ideas regarding printing, marketing, promotion, distribution, etc., she will effectively assist you in reaching your goals and will help you avoid costly mistakes.

The fee is $100   per hour
$50   per half hour
$25   per quarter hour
(may be billed to MasterCard or VISA)

Feel free to "ask Trish" about...
- ✍ finding an interested publisher, agent, or editor
- ✍ negotiating a favorable contract
- ✍ getting your book mentioned in newspapers and magazines
- ✍ obtaining favorable book reviews
- ✍ appearing on local and national TV shows
- ✍ self-publishing a book
- ✍ and so much more...

Call (215) 364-1945 NOW!

Patricia Gallagher and several of the contributors in this book, *For All the Write Reasons,* are available to speak to writers' groups and publishing associations and would look forward to being interviewed by the media in regard to "Getting Published".

For All the _Write_ Reasons
Forty Successful Authors, Publishers, Agents, and Writers
Tell You How to Get Your Book Published

Order Form

(Did you borrow this book? Why not order your own so you can highlight, underline? Special discounts for quantity purchases. Why not sell these books through your organization as a fundraiser?)

Telephone orders: (215) 364-1945   (VISA or MasterCard accepted)
Postal orders: Patricia Gallagher
                    Box 555 PG
                    Worcester, PA 19490

Make checks payable in U.S. funds to Patricia C. Gallagher.

Qty.	Name of book	Price Each	in PA 6% tax	Shipping	Total
____	For All the _Write_ Reasons	$24.95	____	3.00	____

Please expedite my order for Patricia Gallagher's book:

☐   I have enclosed a check or money order for $_____
☐   Charge the total amount to: ☐ VISA   ☐ MasterCard

Card number: _ _ _ _   _ _ _ _   _ _ _ _   _ _ _ _

Expiration date: ____/____

Phone number: (_____) _____-_____

Name on card: _____

Please print your complete mailing address below:

Name: _____

Organization or Company: _____

Address: _____

_____

City, ST, Zip: _____

Phone number: (_____) _____-_____